THE ART OF THE
CHOCOLATIER

THE ART OF THE
CHOCOLATIER

FROM CLASSIC CONFECTIONS TO SENSATIONAL SHOWPIECES

EWALD NOTTER

PHOTOGRAPHY BY JOE BROOKS AND LUCY SCHAEFFER

WILEY

JOHN WILEY & SONS, INC.

Published by John Wiley & Sons, Inc., Hoboken, New Jersey

Published simultaneously in Canada

For general information on our other products and services or for technical support, please contact our Customer Care Department within the United States at (800) 762–2974, outside the United States at (317) 572–3993 or fax (317) 572–4002.

Wiley also publishes its books in a variety of electronic formats. Some content that appears in print may not be available in electronic books. For more information about Wiley products, visit our web site at www.wiley.com.

Library of Congress Cataloging-in-Publication Data:

Notter, Ewald, 1955-
    The art of chocolatier : from classic confections to sensational showpieces / Ewald Notter ; photography by Joe Brooks and Lucy Schaeffer.
        p. cm.
    Includes index.
    ISBN 978-0-470-39884-5 (cloth); ISBN 978-0-470-40265-8 (ebk)
    1. Chocolate candy. 2. Chocolate. 3. Confectionery. I. Title.
    TX791.N62 2011
    641.3'374--dc22
                                2010001901

Printed in The United States of America

SKY10030690_102021

Designed by Memo Productions, NY

Acknowledgments

I would like to take this opportunity to thank the following people for their support and assistance on this book:

Rachel Livsey, who first suggested that I write this book, and Christine McKnight, who saw the project through.

Kathryn Gordon, Abigail Lowe, Miguel Rosales, Jody Hyunmi Lee, and Alison Hodges, for reviewing the chapters in their earliest stage.

Philipp Braun, President and CEO of Albert Uster Imports, for the company's invaluable research on the history of chocolate.

Gilles Renusson and Ciril Hitz for being so generous with their time, knowledge, and friendship.

Jackie Lopez, Candy Waterfield, Susan Kolman, and Laurie Merz, whose hard work and dedication were immeasurable.

The students at the Notter School of Pastry Arts, who helped with research, preparation, and recipe testing.

Photographers Lucy Schaeffer and Joe Brooks, for their creativity and artistry.

And my business partner, Beverly Karshner, for her continued support.

Contents

Preface

This book was developed to share the knowledge I have gained from more than thirty-five years in our profession and more than twenty-five years of teaching in hotels, schools, and kitchens. To achieve success in the pastry kitchen, it is essential to gain exposure to a wide range of chocolate-working techniques with practical applications for making candies and showpieces. This book will guide you in learning all the skills you need to make beautiful, delicious chocolate creations in a professional hospitality environment or even in your own home.

Part One provides a basic overview of chocolate, including the equipment, ingredients, and basic techniques needed to work with this much-loved substance. Part Two covers all types of small chocolate candies, and Part Three outlines the techniques needed to create large-scale chocolate showpieces. It is very important to focus on both types of chocolate work, as they complement each other. Mastering the techniques and recipes for basic candies in Part Two first will give you a strong foundation in working with chocolate, which will help you immensely as you move on to creating showpieces for competition or display.

While techniques and hand skills are very important for success as a chocolatier, I believe taste is the most important element of all. To provide something that looks exquisite is one thing, but once the consumer tastes your work, nothing else matters. The recipes in this book provide a solid foundation for understanding the way different ingredients can be combined and can work together to create wonderful flavors. Flavors and smells bring memories to life, and it is this power that can help you build a connection with those who will relish your delicacies.

Of course, your chocolate candies and showpieces should also look as wonderful as they taste. As I learned early in my career, if you create something that is pleasing to the eye, your customers will be inspired to try your products and come back for more. It is a wonderful thing to be able to use your creativity to provide joy to people of all ages and from all walks of life. Through diligent practice and use of this book as a permanent reference, you will soon develop the artistry and technical skills needed to delight and amaze your customers, and you will be on your way to a most satisfying career.

Part 1: Introduction to Chocolate

1

Chocolate and Other Ingredients

Chocolate has long been made from the cocoa bean, and now more than ever, there are a wide range of different varieties of chocolate available for the chocolatier. However, a number of other distinctive ingredients play an important role in working with chocolate as well.

The History of Chocolate

The history of chocolate has been written about many times, but for anyone who works with chocolate, it is essential to have an understanding of this all-important product's journey into prominence. Chocolate has a long and storied history, from aristocratic to bourgeois imbibers, from chocolate as a medicine to chocolate as an indulgence, and from bitter chocolate drinks to sweet chocolate drinks to bitter chocolate drinks again.

The Origins of Chocolate

Historians maintain that the origins of chocolate are rooted in the history of the Olmecs, who occupied a tropical area on the Gulf of Mexico, and not in the Aztec culture as is commonly believed. Conditions in this region of Mexico were ideal for the cacao tree; the earliest known cacao plantations were cultivated there in the years between 1500 and 400 BC. Initially cacao trees were grown for the white fruit of the cacao pod, but ultimately the Maya of Mesoamerica discovered that grinding and mixing the (cocoa) beans with water could produce a bitter drink, which they called *cacahuatl*.

In the years between AD 1000 and 1200, cocoa beans were so highly valued by the peoples of Central and South America that they were actually used as a form of currency. When the Aztecs moved southward into Mesoamerica from northern Mexico in the twelfth century, the beans were traded for goods. The ritual beverage made from the beans was reserved for the nobility, priests, and high officials, as it was believed to have restorative and aphrodisiac powers. The word "chocolate" comes from the Aztec word for this beverage, *xocolatl*, from *xocolli* (bitter) and *atl* (water).

Chocolate Travels to Europe

Although Christopher Columbus landed in Nicaragua as early as 1502, he was not interested in the cocoa beans and chocolate drinks he found in the New World. It was not until Hernán Cortéz reached South America in 1519 that the potential of the cocoa bean was recognized by Europeans. When Cortéz failed to unearth the Aztec gold for which he was searching, he turned to cocoa beans instead.

Cortez took the first cocoa beans to Europe in 1528, along with the tools to create chocolate. The Spanish welcomed these innovations and experimented with chocolate beverages, sweetening the chocolate with honey and cane sugar, adding orange blossom water, anise seeds, almonds, hazelnuts, cloves, and egg yolks, and using boiling water instead of cold water to create the first hot chocolate drinks.

Spain managed to keep the discovery of chocolate a secret for more than a century, but in 1606 the Italian merchant Antonio Carletti brought the drink to Italy, breaking the Spanish monopoly of the chocolate trade.

The Spanish princess Anne of Austria helped to spread chocolate's popularity further throughout Europe when she married Louis XIII and introduced the drink to the French court. In Paris, chocolate became a status symbol and was drunk only by the aristocracy and upper echelons of society.

London's first chocolate shop, which opened in 1657, made it possible for chocolate to be enjoyed by all levels of society, and in the late 1600s, Heinrich Escher, the mayor of Zürich, helped spread chocolate's popularity to Switzerland. By the turn of the eighteenth century, cocoa beans and the cocoa trade finally made their way to North America, and the chocolate trade continued to blossom. Venezuela became the world's leading producer of cocoa beans during this time period, producing half of the world's cacao.

The Industrial Chocolate Revolution

Chocolate factories began to appear in Europe as early as 1728, but they used age-old labor-intensive methods to grind and churn their products. It was not until 1819 that the first sophisticated chocolate factory was established in Corsier, Switzerland, by François-Louis Cailler. Cailler had learned the art of chocolate making in Italy, and his Swiss chocolate is the oldest brand still in existence today. Swiss chocolate factories continued to proliferate throughout the 1800s, and in 1875, Swiss chocolate maker Daniel Peter—who was married to Cailler's eldest daughter, Fanny Cailler—changed the world of chocolate forever when he added milk to chocolate and created the first milk chocolate.

The 1800s also saw the introduction of the first boxed individual chocolates from the Cadbury chocolate company, and in 1879, Rodolphe Lindt developed the process known as conching, which produced the first creamy, smooth-textured chocolate that melted on the tongue.

Milton S. Hershey, who sold his first Hershey Bar in Pennsylvania in 1900, used mass-production techniques to make chocolate less expensive, which provided new opportunities for mass consumption in the commercial market. A huge variety of chocolate products were developed during this time period, beginning with the first filled chocolates created by Séchaud Fils in Montreux, Switzerland, in 1913. The 1930s brought about the production of the first white chocolate by Henri Nestlé, and soon a huge range of chocolate products including truffles, bonbons with fillings, ganaches, chocolate bars, chocolate-covered fruits and coffee beans, and molded and sculpted chocolates were available throughout the world.

Chocolate—It's Good for You

Today, chocolate is more popular than ever, and serious studies have suggested that eating chocolate has positive health effects. Scientists claim that chocolate may be capable of alleviating depression, preventing heart attacks, lowering blood pressure, promoting happiness, and easing pain. Dark chocolate in particular has a high concentration of flavonoids, a type of antioxidant. However, as is always the case with food, let's not forget that "moderation is good in all things."

Harvesting and Manufacturing Chocolate

Over 3,000 different plants and trees have been identified as cacao. Of those varieties only one cocoa bean is commercially produced, the *Theobroma*. The four main varieties of *Theobroma* cacao are: Criollo, Forastero, Trinitario, and Arriba Nacional. Each variety has its own unique flavor that is influenced by the growing area and soil.

Growing and Harvesting the Cocoa Bean

The cacao tree is a delicate tree that thrives in tropical regions between 20 degrees south and 20 degrees north of the equator. West Africa, South America, and Southeast Asia are the largest producers of cocoa beans in the world. The tree requires high humidity, temperatures of 64° to 90°F/17.8° to 32.2°C, and 40 to 100 inches of rain a year. It grows to 40 to 50 feet/12.20 to 15.24 m in height. Most trees are planted among larger trees to protect them from wind and excessive sun. A neutral to slightly acidic soil is important to the quality of cacao.

During its second or third year, the cacao tree will start to bear fruit. Blossoms appear on the trunk and thicker branches of the tree and are pollinated by insects. Once pollinated, each blossom develops into a cacao pod, which takes six months to fully develop and can weigh as much as 2½ pounds/1.13 kg. The tree will bear approximately twenty-five to fifty pods at a time and

THE BEANS	FLAVOR	POD AND TREE	ORIGIN	% OF WORLD'S CROP
CRIOLLO	Rich and intense; has the widest range of flavors	Soft skinned, reddish color, smaller variety, delicate and highly prized beans	South America	1%
FORASTERO	Soft; beans have a pungent aroma; is usually a "base" bean and not complex	Pod is thick-skinned with a red-yellow color; trees are hearty and produce a large number of beans	West Africa	80%
TRINITARIO	Fine-flavored; exhibits Criollo and Forastero characteristics	Hearty and withstand infestation well; small yellow pods; a hybrid of the Criollo and Forastero beans	Trinidad	15%
ARRIBA/NACIONAL	Full, smooth cocoa flavor with additional floral, nutty notes	Large, green, wrinkled pods; beans are large and purple	Ecuador	4%

ABOVE: From left to right: a cacao pod, cocoa beans, and finished couverture coins. *Courtesy of Albert Uster Imports*
BELOW: Cocoa Bean Varieties. *Courtesy of Albert Uster Imports*

can bear for twenty-five to thirty years. Pods are oblong and football shaped, and their colors and textures vary according to the variety of cacao. As pods ripen, they change from green to yellow or red.

The pods are harvested twice a year. It takes several months to harvest a tree, since pods ripen at different times. Every two to four weeks, the fruit is cut from the tree with a machete or sickle-shaped knife. The pods are carefully opened, and the cocoa beans (seeds) and pulp are removed to begin the fermentation process. Each pod contains an average of forty to eighty cocoa seeds. Each seed consists of two cotyledons (the nib), which contain the germ (center), and is surrounded by a protective outer shell.

Fermentation

Fermentation lasts for five to seven days and begins as soon as the pods have been opened. The fresh beans and pulp are placed in piles and covered to help regulate the temperature. Temperatures that are too high will allow the seeds to germinate, but in this case the goal is to have the bean die so that fermentation, which initiates the development of flavor, will begin. During fermentation, natural bacteria and yeast begin to multiply and break down the sugar in the pulp surrounding the beans. This breakdown results in the creation of alcohol that kills the bean. Lactic acid bacteria feed on the alcohol and other organic acids and convert them into lactic acid. At this point, acetic acid bacteria take over and convert the lactic acid into acetic acid. It is very important to monitor the beans so that the correct length of fermentation occurs. Too short a fermentation period will result in no flavor, while too long a period will destroy the bean. (The fermented pulp is not used in chocolate making.)

Drying and Shipping

It is important to dry cocoa beans and stop fermentation before the high water content of the beans causes them to rot. Exposing the beans to air and sunlight allows the water to evaporate and reduces the acetic acid content. This causes the bean to turn brown and reduces the humidity within the bean, which allows for better preservation by preventing mold growth during storage. Once the drying process is complete, the beans are bagged and shipped to manufacturers.

Cleaning and Roasting

Once the beans arrive at the manufacturer from the plantation, they are cleansed of impurities such as metal, sand, and plant matter. They are then roasted at 230° to 428°F/110.0° to 220.0°C (depending on the type of bean) to develop the chocolate flavor of the nib. During this time, the moisture content is reduced to about 2 percent, and the starch in the beans is transformed into dextrin.

Shelling and Winnowing

After the beans have been roasted, the thin, lightweight husks (or shells) must be removed, leaving the cocoa nibs to be further processed. Beans can be pretreated with infrared radiation to soften the husks, making them easier to remove. There are two ways to remove the husks: drop the beans into a series of rotating blades, or pass the beans through a series of low-velocity impact crushers. The broken pieces are passed through a series of screens to sort them by size. As the similar-sized cocoa nibs and husks pass into the chamber, air is blown through the pieces. The nibs continue to fall to the next chamber and the husks are blown off into a separate chamber. The husks are recycled as mulch. The cocoa nibs pass to the next processing stage.

Blending, Grinding, and Mixing

Different varieties of cocoa beans are custom blended according to the recipes of the chocolate manufacturer. The blends then are sent to be ground. At this stage, the sugar, milk powder (for white and milk couverture; see Chocolate Products, page 11), and vanillin are added to the cocoa bean blend and ground into a chocolate mass. The chocolate mass is sent on to be rolled into finer particles in a process called refining.

Refining

The refining of the chocolate mass takes place between two steel rollers on repeated passes. The distance between the rollers decreases and the mass is sheared into smaller particles each time it passes through the rollers. Once the mass particles have reached 120 microns in size, it is sent through a series of five rollers to refine the mass to a particle size of 20 microns. It is important to maintain this size, as too large a grind results in a coarse mouthfeel and too fine a grind results in stickiness on the palate in the finished chocolate.

Conching

After grinding and refining, the chocolate mass will still have a high acidic flavor. The process of conching or milling produces chemical and physical changes that reduce the acidity and allow the other natural flavors to develop. A conching machine continuously kneads and churns the mass for 8 to 72 hours at a temperature of 122° to 212°F/50.0° to

Conching reduces the acidity of the chocolate mass. *Courtesy of Albert Uster Imports*

100.0°C to achieve the desired finish. The length of time and the temperature depend on the type of chocolate and the manufacturer specifications. There are three phases of conching:

DRY CONCHING: The moisture of the mass is reduced under slow-speed rotation.

PLASTICIZING: Cocoa butter is added and the temperature and speed increased. This is when the chocolate flavor begins to emerge.

LIQUID CONCHING: The direction of the blade is reversed, and the mass begins to cool. At this point the remaining cocoa butter, lecithin, and natural vanilla, if used, are added on high speed.

Tempering, Molding, and Packaging

The conched chocolate is cooled down and tempered to induce stability and to give the chocolate the proper snap, sheen, and mouthfeel. The tempered chocolate can then be molded into bars or coins or used in candies as desired. The chocolate must be cooled from 87°F down to 68°F/30.5° to 20.0°C to allow the stable crystals to form. Temperatures are then dropped to between 50° and 55°F/10.0° and 12.7°C to speed up the solidifying process. Finally the temperature must be brought back up to 68°F/20.0°C to prepare the chocolate for warmer storage temperatures. The chocolate is then packaged to protect it from light, heat, odors, and humidity.

Chocolate Products

There are a variety of products made from cocoa beans that result from the processing steps above. These include the products listed below, which are used during the production of confections.

COCOA MASS: Made of cleaned, roasted, broken, and ground cocoa beans.

BLOCK COCOA: Unsweetened, finely ground, conched cocoa mass. Has a cocoa butter content of at least 50%.

COCOA BUTTER: A natural fat that is present in cocoa beans, yielded by the pressing of the cocoa mass.

COCOA POWDER: The finely ground pressed cake that appears as the cocoa butter is pressed out of the cocoa mass. A good quality cocoa powder should have a fat content of 20 to 22% and be dark brown, possibly with reddish tones, depending on the processing used.

SWEETENED COCOA POWDER: A mixture of cocoa powder and sugar. Has a maximum sugar content of 68%.

DARK CHOCOLATE: A homogenous mixture of cocoa mass and sugar. Has a minimum cocoa butter content of 18%.

CHOCOLATE POWDER: Pulverized chocolate. Has a minimum cocoa butter content of 16%.

MILK CHOCOLATE: Normally contains about 35% total fat and is made of 20% milk solids, 30% cocoa beans (15% cocoa mass and 15% cocoa butter), 40% sugar, and 10% additional cocoa butter.

WHITE CHOCOLATE: Consists of at least 20% cocoa butter and 14% milk solids, with 3.5% milk fat and a maximum of 55% sugar.

COUVERTURE. A very high quality chocolate with 32 to 39% cocoa butter. The fat content can vary according to the desired use for the couverture. The total percentage of combined cocoa butter plus cocoa solids must be at least 54%.

CHOCOLATE GLACE: A mass similar to couverture, but with the cocoa butter replaced by another type of fat. This allows for a simpler method of work, as it does not have to be tempered, but it will result in a lower quality product. In countries like Switzerland, chocolate glace cannot be used for truffles, fillings, or covering and molding chocolates.

Premium Couverture

For the recipes and techniques in this book, it is recommended to always use premium couverture. There are many chocolates available worldwide, but only a small number of them are considered premium couvertures. The term "couverture" is protected by Swiss law and good Swiss manufacturing practices and is defined in Switzerland as "chocolate for the pastry shop." Couverture is always of higher quality than chocolate, as it is made under stringent guidelines.

To create a true premium couverture, a manufacturer must control the complete supply chain, carefully selecting the country and the cacao plantation of origin for the beans. Premium couverture is made from only the finest Criollo, Arriba Nacional, Trinitario, and Forastero beans and the best-quality milk products, natural vanilla, and other ingredients. The whole beans must be roasted under the direction of a roast master, and the chocolate mass must be conched for up to 72 hours. A Master Chocolatier may use up to seven different beans per recipe to assemble complex and harmonic flavor profiles for a premium couverture, and the origin and type of cocoa beans, roasting parameters, and recipes must be adjusted constantly to achieve a consistent premium flavor profile in spite of variances in harvests.

Premium couverture includes the highest-quality natural vanilla. *Courtesy of Albert Uster Imports*

Understanding Couverture Percentages

The percentage assigned to a couverture represents the amount of bean in the couverture. The bean is made up of 45% nonfat cocoa solids (the flavor) and 55% cocoa butter (the flavor carrier). Since dark couverture is largely made up of the bean component (fat and nonfat solids) and sugar, the higher the percentage of cocoa, the lower the sugar content.

Even if couvertures from different manufacturers have the same percentage, the quality of the couvertures may vary depending on the origin of the beans, the quality of the ingredients, and the manufacturing process, as well as the split between cocoa butter and nonfat cocoa solids. The same percentage in two different brands of couvertures does not equal the same taste. For example, one 73% couverture may consist of 31% cocoa solids and 42% cocoa butter, while another may consist of 27% cocoa solids and 46% cocoa butter. Even though they have the same total percentage, they are not identical. The first couverture, which consists of 15% more cocoa solids, will have a stronger chocolate flavor and a greater viscosity than the second. As a result, the application possibilities and results will vary greatly. Some manufacturers indicate the percentage of cocoa solids and cocoa butter separately on their packaging, which is helpful in selecting a premium couverture for a particular use. When developing new recipes, the chocolatier should carefully record the type and brand of chocolate or couverture used to ensure production consistency.

Three different couverture recipes labeled 73% may all contain very different percentages of cacao solids, cocoa butter, and sugar. *Courtesy of Albert Uster Imports*

Storing Chocolate and Couverture

Chocolate is sensitive to odors, light, and warmth. It is important that the storage place is dry, free from foreign odors, and at a stable temperature. The ideal temperature for storage of all chocolate products is 60° to 65°F/15.6° to 18.3°C with 50 to 60 percent humidity. When stored properly, dark chocolate has a shelf life of approximately twelve months, and milk and white chocolate have a shelf life of about eight months. Block cocoa has a minimum shelf life of fourteen months. Cocoa mass, cocoa powder, sweetened cocoa powder, and chocolate powder can all be stored for up to twenty-four months, and cocoa butter can have a shelf life of more than three years if stored properly.

Other Distinctive Ingredients

There are certain ingredients that are essential for quality chocolate production. Dairy, if not the most distinctive ingredient, is of course the most important in making chocolate.

Dairy Products

Dairy products such as milk, cream, buttermilk, and yogurt are often used in baked products and candy. Dairy products contribute to texture, flavor, crust color, shelf life, nutritional value, and moisture.

Most dairy products go through a pasteurization process in which they are heated to 161°F/71.7°C for 15 seconds to destroy pathogenic bacteria. Pasteurization destroys enzymes that cause spoilage.

Milk

Milk can be found in many different forms, including fresh whole, low-fat, and skim, and dried.

FRESH WHOLE MILK comes straight from the cow and has 3.5% milk fat.

LOW-FAT MILK is produced by removing part or all of the milk fat from whole milk. Low-fat milk contains between 1 and 2% milk fat.

SKIM MILK is also called fat-free milk and contains up to 0.5% milk fat.

MILK POWDER is made from whole milk by removing all the moisture. It is also made from skim milk (nonfat milk powder).

Milk is primarily used in baking applications and seldom in confectionery work.

Cream

Cream is a rich milk product containing at least 18% milk fat that is pasteurized and homogenized. The milk doesn't separate, and the fat is broken down into small particles that are evenly and permanently distributed in the milk.

HALF-AND-HALF consists of whole milk and cream with a fat content between 10 and 16%.

LIGHT CREAM contains between 16 and 32% milk fat.

HEAVY CREAM must contain at least 36% milk fat. It can be whipped easily, and it holds its texture for a long time. Heavy cream is never homogenized.

Heavy cream is the type of cream most frequently used in confectionery work. It is used for making ganache because of its fat content, which carries flavor and gives the ganache its smooth texture.

Evaporated and Sweetened Condensed Milk

EVAPORATED MILK is whole milk from which 60 percent of the water has been removed, resulting in a slightly darker color than fresh and a cooked flavor. Evaporated milk is canned and may last years without refrigeration.

SWEETENED CONDENSED MILK is evaporated milk with sugar added. It has a distinctive caramel flavor and is ivory in color. It also comes canned and should not be substituted for evaporated milk because of its sugar content.

Evaporated and sweetened condensed milks are rarely used in chocolate confections.

Other Dairy Products

BUTTERMILK originally was the by-product of churning cream into butter. Today buttermilk is a fresh nonfat milk to which bacteria are added, resulting in a sour taste, thick texture, and a very small amount of butterfat (0.5 to 3% fat).

SOUR CREAM is cream that has been cultured by adding lactic acid and bacteria, which give it a thicker consistency and tangy flavor. It should have at least 18% fat.

YOGURT is milk cultured with *Lactobacillus bulgaricus*, resulting in a thick, tart product. The fat content depends on how much fat the milk contains.

BUTTER is a great emulsifier and can form a stable emulsion on its own. American butter contains about 80 to 81% fat, and European butter is generally closer to 85% fat. Good quality butter has pale yellow color and a sweet flavor. Salt acts as a preservative to the butter, and if added, should not exceed 2 percent of total weight.

Butter is used frequently in chocolate confections, especially in ganache. Yogurt is also sometimes used in the making of ganache.

Sugar

Sugar plays an important role in many aspects of creating ganache. As sugar comes in many different forms, it is necessary to have a clear understanding of each variety. The table below outlines how each type of sugar is manufactured, its power of sweetness, and its many different traits and uses.

TYPE OF SUGAR	WHAT IT IS/HOW IT IS MANUFACTURED	SWEETENING POWER VERSUS SUCROSE	TRAITS AND USES
Brown Sugar	A type of sucrose; refined cane sugar containing molasses. The darker the sugar, the higher the percentage of molasses and the more intense the molasses flavor.	97%	Hygroscopic (readily absorbs moisture). Used in sweet and savory foods; used mostly for flavor in confectionery work.
Confectioners' Sugar – Powdered sugar (alternate name)	A type of sucrose; granulated sugar ground to a powder with cornstarch added (3%) to prevent lumping. Available in different grades; the higher the number (10X), the finer the grind.	100%	Dissolves quickly in liquids; produces light and tender cakes. Used in icings and glazes and for decorating baked products. Good for making gianduja or fruit ganache.
Fructose	Simple sugar found in honey, fruits, and vegetables	130%	Hygroscopic; inhibits crystallization without adding sweetness; very temperature sensitive. Products sweetened with fructose tend to be moist because fructose attracts more water.
Glucose (Dextrose) – Corn syrup (most common form)	Syrup extracted from the starches in corn, potatoes, rice, or wheat in a process called acid hydrolysis	50–60%	Hygroscopic; helps prevent moisture loss and increases the shelf life of various products; slows down crystallization. Used in icings, caramel, nougat, marshmallows, and other candies.
Honey	Natural invert sugar (fructose) produced by bees from flower nectar. The lighter the color, the milder the flavor; the darker the color, the stronger the flavor.	125–150% Honey has a high fructose content, 25–50% sweeter than sugar (sucrose)	Hygroscopic. Baked products made with honey are moist and dense. It is also used to add flavor to ganache.

TYPE OF SUGAR	WHAT IT IS/HOW IT IS MANUFACTURED	SWEETENING POWER VERSUS SUCROSE	TRAITS AND USES
Invert Sugar – Trimoline	Produced by heating a combination of sugar syrup and a small amount of acid (cream of tartar or lemon juice). This process inverts the sucrose into glucose and fructose.	125%	Hygroscopic; inhibits crystallization in creams. Provides aroma and color when heated. Because it has a fine crystal structure, it produces a smoother product and is used in making candies, fondant, etc. It is best used in items with high water content that must be kept soft.
Maple Syrup	Made from the sap of maple trees, which is about 80% sugar and 20% water. The sap is boiled to evaporate the water content, leaving the sweet, brown syrup.	60–67% Grading differs among US states and between US and Canada; grades include: Extra Light AA; Light A; Medium B; Amber C; Dark D	Provides distinct flavor to baked goods, frostings, pancakes, and waffles. Amber C is normally used for flavoring and baking because of its strong flavor and thickness and is often used for making ganache, especially for holiday time.
Molasses	A liquid by-product of sugar cane refining. It contains sucrose, invert sugar, acid, moisture, and other substances.	Three grades: First Stage (Unsulfured): light and very sweet, 65% Second Stage (Sulfured): darker and not as sweet, 60% Final Stage (Blackstrap): the least sweet of the three, 50–55%	Provides strong flavor and dark color but is not as sweet as sugar. It has a slightly bitter, robust taste. Molasses is not generally used in chocolate.
Sorbitol	Sugar alcohol produced by reduction of glucose. It also comes in powdered form. Sorbitol can be found in ripe fruits: apples, pears, and berries.	50–75%	Moisture stabilizer; can be used to partially replace sugar. Also an emulsifier.
Sucrose – Cane sugar – Beet sugar – 50% sucrose and 50% glucose	The sugar derived from either sugar cane or sugar beets is 99.5% pure sucrose. Granulated sugar is refined sucrose that has been crystallized. It is composed of equal amounts of glucose and fructose.	100%	Hygroscopic; crystallizes when oversaturated; provides aroma and color when caramelized. It is the most common type of sugar used.

Nuts

Nuts have been an essential ingredient in the kitchen for more than 2,000 years. Nuts go hand in hand with chocolate and confections, and one would not think to create either without thinking about nuts. Nuts provide the distinctive flavor and fat content that gives richness to many chocolates and confections, as well as added crunch.

Almonds – *Fat content 45 to 55%*

Almonds are the young developing fruit of the deciduous *Prunus* genus tree. The fruit, called a drupe, takes approximately seven to eight months to develop and matures in the autumn. It has an outer fleshy membrane or hull that surrounds a hard shell that contains the seed, which is the almond kernel. Almonds can be eaten raw or toasted, ground, and made into flour. Almond flour is popular because the almond contains practically no carbohydrates, making it an excellent choice for those on low-carbohydrate diets, diabetics, and those who require gluten-free flour due to allergies.

Coconut – *Fat content 60 to 70%*

A coconut is the dried nut of the coconut palm tree. Coconut palms are grown in tropical climates. Nearly every part of the tree is usable by humans. The coconut palm has been called the "tree of life" because, in theory, if a person were stranded, the tree could supply everything he or she would need to survive. Coconut palm trees have both male and female flowers that continuously produce seeds. The seed (endosperm) is hollow and contains coconut water. The seed, known as the "meat" of the coconut, is white and fleshy and is protected by a thin brown skin known as the endocarp. The encapsulated seed nestles inside a green shell that is thick, fibrous, and hairy. When the seed is mature, the outer shell turns brown and falls from the tree. Each tree produces up to seventy-five nuts per year. Coconut meat is high in saturated fat and minerals and contains sugar and protein. The meat of the coconut can be eaten fresh or dried.

Hazelnuts – *Fat content 55 to 65%*

Hazelnuts grow on shrubs that can reach up to 45 feet/13.71 m tall. The flowers, which are both male and female catkins, hang from the bush. They are produced in spring and are wind pollinated. The fertilized catkins produce clusters of one to five nuts held in place by a husk. After seven to eight months, in mid autumn, the ripened hazelnuts fall from the husk. The nuts can be used raw, roasted, or ground into paste. Hazelnut butter is fast becoming as popular as peanut butter. Hazelnuts are rich in protein and unsaturated fat and contain significant amounts of vitamins. Hazelnuts are widely used for oils, coffee flavorings, liqueurs, and the ever-popular Nutella spread.

Macadamia – *Fat content 72 to 76%*

Macadamia nuts are highly nutritious. They contain the highest amount of monounsaturated fats of any nut and are rich in protein, carbohydrates, fiber, and multiple vitamins. Macadamia nuts grow on an evergreen tree that can mature up to 40 feet/12.20 m tall. It takes seven to ten years before a tree can produce commercial quantities of nuts, but the tree continues to produce for 100 years. The first commercial orchard of macadamia trees was planted in 1880 in New South Wales, Australia; currently Hawaii, Australia, California, South Africa, and Costa Rica continue to commercially produce the nuts.

Peanuts – *Fat content 45 to 50%*

As the peanut plant matures, the pea-like flowers self-pollinate in clusters. The flowers wither and the stalk bends toward the ground and forces the fertilized fruit into it. The seeds continue to develop and the seed pods turn from white to a reddish brown when mature. The pods are wrinkled and contain seeds, usually two in each pod, that have a paper thin "skin." It takes four to five months and plenty of water for peanuts to ripen. When ready for harvest, the plant is cut just below the soil level and pulled from the ground. The plants are then placed root side up and left to dry for two to three weeks before the peanuts are removed from the plant. Peanuts are a rich source of protein and antioxidants.

Pecans – *Fat content 65 to 70%*

Pecans grow on a deciduous tree from the hickory genus. The flowers are wind pollinated, with male and female catkins on the same tree. Once pollinated, the flowers produce fruit from the endocarp, an oblong nut enveloped in a hard shell formed from the exocarp. The exocarp opens at maturity to release the nut. Pecan trees can continue to thrive and produce nuts for more than 300 years. The United States started commercially producing pecans in the 1880s and now produces 80 to 95 percent or more of the world's pecans. The nuts are rich and buttery and used in cooking and candy making. They are a good source of protein, antioxidants, and unsaturated fat.

Pistachios – *Fat content 50 to 55%*

The trees of pistachios are unisexual, with separate male and female trees. The trees are planted in orchards and bloom biennially, meaning they bear fruit yearly but only produce a good crop every other year. It takes around ten years for a pistachio tree to reach production size, and the trees bear well until around twenty years of age. The fruit has a hard exterior shell that changes from green to yellow when ripe. The shell then splits partially open to expose the green nut with a papery mauve skin. Iran is the main exporter of pistachios, with the United State's production a close second. Pistachios are high in mono-unsaturated fat; in fact, bulk shipping containers of pistachios can be prone to spontaneous combustion due to their low water and high fat content. Pistachios can be eaten and used in cooking and confections either fresh or roasted.

Walnuts – *Fat content 50 to 55%*

Walnuts are grown from deciduous trees of the Juglandaceae family. There are many varieties of walnuts, but the most popular is the Peruvian walnut, which has a large nut and a thin shell. The pollinated fruit develops an outer husk that hardens and protects the nut. Walnuts are rich in oil, which can be used for cooking. Walnuts have been made into syrup, flour, and dye and even pickled in vinegar. Ninety-nine percent of the United States' walnut production comes from a small region in California, where over thirty varieties are grown.

Spices

Spices are derived from the seeds, berries, bark, fruit, branches, and roots of plants and used to add flavor to foods. They are usually dried and ground or grated into powder and sold by weight. Spices provide the characteristic flavors and unique aromas found in many different foods and desserts. In chocolates, spices are used primarily to flavor ganaches through infusion. This is done by bringing the cream and spice to a boil and letting the mixture infuse for ten minutes, then straining and using the spice-infused cream to create the ganache.

Be careful when using spices. Spices should be used to enhance the flavor of a confection, and adding too much of any one spice or too many different spices in combination can ruin the product. Chocolate and spices are expensive, so it is best to test new products in small batches. The flavor and aroma of seed spices, such as poppy and sesame, can be accentuated by toasting in a heavy skillet until lightly browned.

The shelf lives of spices vary according to the spice and even its form. Whole spices such as nutmeg or cloves will last longer than ground spices, as their protective coatings prevent exposure to oxygen and light. Oil-rich seeds can be refrigerated or frozen to prevent them from becoming rancid. Storing spices in an airtight container and avoiding exposure to light, heat, oxygen, and moisture are the keys to maintaining freshness. Date all spice containers, check spices yearly, and discard any that do not give off an aroma when pressed in the palm or that have lost their fresh color.

CLOCKWISE FROM BOTTOM LEFT: Cinnamon, cloves, cumin, red chile, black pepper, cardamom, and star anise can all be used to enhance the flavor of confections.

Vanilla

Vanilla is the most important flavoring used by bakers because of its strong flavor and aroma. It comes in three forms: whole beans (vanilla pods), vanilla extract, and vanilla powder. Vanilla beans are the dried fruits of the tropical vanilla orchid. They are mainly grown in Mexico, Tahiti, China, India, and Madagascar, and they need to be hand pollinated, which makes them one of the most expensive spices. Vanilla beans have different flavors depending on where they are grown. The most popular varieties of vanilla are Tahitian and Madagascar Bourbon. It is generally recommended to use whole beans in the confectionery kitchen.

Saffron

Saffron is the most expensive spice by weight in the world. It comes from the dried inner threads, known as the stigmas, of the purple saffron crocus plant. Each plant produces three stigmas, and it takes 150 flowers to yield 1 g of saffron threads. Since the saffron crocus is sterile, it cannot reproduce except by corms. Corms, which are short vertical underground plant stems that serve as food storage for the plant for survival in cold weather, are hand separated and planted in order to grow more flowers. Saffron threads are golden yellow and used to color and flavor foods in different cuisines such as Spanish and Middle Eastern. It is important to store them in an airtight container to minimize exposure to air, which breaks down the saffron.

Nutmeg

Nutmeg is the seed inside the fruit of the tropical evergreen nutmeg tree. The seed is dried and ground or freshly grated into soups, sauces, cheeses, vegetables, sweet desserts, and other products. The flavor and aroma of nutmeg are strong and sweet. The lacy reddish outer covering of the nutmeg seed is known as mace when it is dried and ground.

Ginger

Ginger is obtained from the rhizome of the tropical ginger plant, which produces fragrant yellow flowers. Ginger has a peppery flavor, is slightly sweet, and has a spicy aroma. It can be pickled, made into syrups, dried, or candied, and it is used in many sweet and savory dishes.

Coffee

The coffee bean is the seed of the coffee bush (sometimes grown as a small tree), which is picked, dried, and roasted. Coffee is grown in tropical and subtropical regions throughout the world, and its flavor differs according to where it is grown. Coffee is one of the most popular beverages worldwide, and it is brewed from ground coffee beans. There are two main types of beans grown, Arabica and Robusta. Arabica is the most popular because it is smooth tasting and the most suitable for drinking purposes. Robusta has a more bitter flavor and contains 40 to 50 percent more caffeine than other beans. Because of this, it is either blended with other coffees or used for espresso. For use in cooking, baking, and candy making, roasted beans or ground coffee may be steeped in milk or cream and then strained out. Brewed coffee may be reduced to a thicker consistency for use as a flavoring, and commercial coffee extracts are also available. The smoky, rich taste of coffee goes well with chocolate.

Clove

This spice originates from the dried unopened flower buds of a tropical evergreen tree called the clove tree. Eighty percent of the world's cloves are produced in Indonesia. The spice's aroma is soothing, and as a result the fragrance is often used for candles and perfumes. Cloves can be used in whole or ground form. Cloves have a very strong flavor, so a small amount goes a long way. Cloves are usually blended with other spices.

Cinnamon

Cinnamon is one of the most popular spices. It comes from the inner bark of an evergreen tree in the same family as laurels. It can be purchased ground or in sticks, which are used in dishes where the cooking time is long enough to extract the flavors from the stick. Cinnamon is grown in tropical regions throughout the world. It is suitable for use in sweets such as cakes, puddings, desserts, and drinks as well as savory dishes, and it is often used in chocolates, especially for holiday ganaches.

Allspice

Allspice, sometimes known as the Jamaican pepper, is derived from a plant grown in tropical regions, with white flowers and reddish round berries. The berries are available whole or ground and have a peppery aroma. Although allspice tastes like a mixture of cinnamon, cloves, and nutmeg, it is not a blend of these three. It is used in pickling spices as well as cakes, jams, and fruit pies, and it can also be used in ganaches.

Anise

Anise is one of the oldest spices grown in India, North Africa, and Southern Europe. It has a white umbrella-shaped flower that blooms and releases seeds. The seeds are small, gray-green oblongs. They have a strong, sweet flavor similar to licorice. Anise is used all over the world to flavor a variety of food and drinks, as well as in liqueurs, aromatherapy scents, and digestive aids.

Cardamom

Cardamom seeds are encased in ¼-inch-long/6-mm-long, light green or brown pods. Cardamom is highly aromatic with a unique cool, fragrant flavor, and it is used in both sweet and savory dishes as well as in beverages and medicines. This is the spice that gives spiced tea (chai) its unique taste. Cardamom is widely used in India, the Middle East, and Europe to flavor drinks, pastries, and breads. The second most expensive spice behind saffron, ground cardamom loses its flavor and aroma rapidly, so it is best to store the pods and grind the seeds as needed or keep only small amounts on hand.

Liquors

Liquor has always been an important ingredient in making chocolate, although it is less popular today than in years past. Liquor is used to bring out the flavor as well as increase the shelf life of ganache. The list below includes those liquors that are most commonly used in confections.

Rum

Rum is one of the oldest liquors in the Americas, dating to the seventeenth century. Rum is an alcohol that is distilled from sugarcane. Plantation slaves found that a by-product of sugarcane, molasses, could be fermented and distilled into liquor. The types of rum available for use in confections include:

LIGHT RUM: Very little flavor, slightly sweet. Light rums are sometimes filtered to remove any color. Used for cocktails.

GOLD RUM: Amber-colored, medium-bodied rum that is aged. Aging in wooden barrels contributes to the dark color.

DARK RUM: Aged longer, dark rum has a stronger flavor than light or gold rums. There are strong molasses and caramel overtones to this rum, as well as a slightly spicy bite. It is the most commonly used rum in cooking.

SPICED RUM: Dark in color, the flavor is derived from the addition of spices and sometimes caramel. Some of the cheaper brands use white rum with artificial color added.

FLAVORED RUM: One of the newest variations on the market, these rums are infused with different fruit flavors and have fruity fragrances. Common flavors include lime, mango, pineapple, coconut, and orange. Rums with flavoring can be used to create interesting variations in candy making.

OVERPROOF RUM: Highly concentrated rum with an alcohol content of 60 to 84.5 percent (120 to 169 proof). Standard rum is usually in the 40 percent (80 proof) range, so overproof rum is very potent by comparison.

PREMIUM RUM: Normally reserved for sipping like a fine Cognac, this rum is aged and carefully cared for in order to reach this quality. This is not rum that you would use in mixed drinks, cooking, or candy making, as these uses would detract from its superb character.

Baileys Irish Cream

This is an Irish whiskey-and-cream-based liqueur that was first introduced in 1974. Its alcohol content is 17 percent. According to the manufacturer, Baileys was the first liqueur to combine alcohol and cream in a manner that was stabilized enough for commercial distribution. In order to prevent separation during storage, the whiskey, cream, emulsifier, and flavors are homogenized. The manufacturer also states that no preservative is necessary due to the alcohol acting as a preserver for the cream. When properly stored, the shelf life can be as long as twenty-four months. This liqueur is normally enjoyed by itself, over ice, or mixed with other beverages such as coffee. Baileys has several flavors on the market, including mint chocolate, caramel, and coffee. These different versions can be used to enhance the flavors of pralines. Caution must be used when working with Baileys in recipes using acid, as it is sensitive to curdling when it comes in contact with acidic ingredients.

Fruit Brandies

Quality fruit is important in the making of fruit brandies. The flavor and aroma depend on the distiller's expertise in the selection of fruit and careful eye over the fermentation process. To make brandy, fruits are placed in tanks to allow the natural sugar to ferment. The majority of the sugar transforms into alcohol in the first ten days, then the fermentation slows down and takes around six weeks to complete. Because of their low sugar content, some berries will not produce much alcohol from fermentation, so they are paired with alcohol to macerate. After fermentation, the liquor is distilled. The alcohol content of brandies should be 40 to 50 percent. There are many types of brandy available, but Kirschwasser and Williams pear brandy are two of the most commonly used in confections.

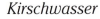

Kirschwasser

Commonly known as Kirsch, Kirschwasser is German for "cherry water." This brandy is clear and colorless, and it is double distilled from cherries. There are over 350 varieties of Kirsch. Any variety of cherries can be used, but the type traditionally used in Kirsch are Morellos, which are fermented with their stones. This brandy is not sweet but has a hint of cherry flavor with a slightly bitter almond taste from the stones. Around 22 pounds/9.98 kg of cherries are needed to produce one 750 ml bottle of Kirsch with an alcohol content of 40 to 50 percent. This brandy is generally sipped as an after-dinner drink, but it is also very popular to use in chocolates and a vast array of desserts.

Williams Pear

A popular and interesting pear brandy that is widely used in chocolates is *eau-de-vie de poire Williams*. It is made by fermenting the crushed, ripened fruit of the Williams pear for up to six weeks, then distilling the brandy and allowing it to age. It has a rich pear flavor that is soft to the palate. Many bottles of Williams pear brandy are sold with a pear inside. To achieve this, growers hang empty bottles on their trees and insert the young fruit buds, which are trained to grow inside the bottles until the fruit becomes fully matured and ripened. The bottle and pear are removed from the tree and carefully cleaned. The brandy is then added and the bottle sealed.

Acids

Acids are both flavor enhancers and preservers of food. Common acids used in cooking and confectionery work include tartaric acid, citric acid, and vinegar.

Tartaric and citric acid are both commonly used in kitchens. The choice between these two acids comes down to individual preferences and availability; citric acid is easier to find. Tartaric acid is 30 percent stronger than citric acid, so care must be taken with its use.

Tartaric Acid

Tartaric acid is a white crystalline organic acid. It occurs naturally in many plants, particularly in bananas and grapes. Tartaric acid is one of the main acids found in wine. It is used as a flavoring agent in foods to create a sour taste.

The potassium salt of tartaric acid is a weak acid and is known as cream of tartar. Tartaric acid is mostly used in jelly to activate the gelling process, and it can also be used to enhance the flavor of fruit used in ganaches.

Citric Acid

Citric acid is a weak colorless organic acid naturally found in citrus fruits such as lemons, limes, oranges, and tangerines. It is a natural preservative with a strong tart taste. It is used as a preservative in food and soft drinks and as a flavoring to give a tart taste to foods and candy. Citric acid comes in a white crystalline powder that easily mixes into liquids. Many sour candies have a fine, white powder coating of a citric acid mix on the exterior to give them an extra punch of sour taste when eaten.

Lemon juice contains about 5 percent citric acid. It can be used to enhance the flavor in fruit ganaches such as raspberry, strawberry, peach, and mango—but if too much is used in ganache, it can develop a bitter taste.

Vinegar

Vinegar can be produced from a range of products, including fruits, berries, potatoes, beets, malt, grains, and even coconuts. Vinegar is created when the natural sugars of the product ferment to form alcohol then continue on to a secondary fermentation that changes them into an acid. Vinegar has been around for more than 10,000 years. It was originally discovered when a cask of wine had gone past its prime, turning into *vin aigre* ("sour wine" in French). Vinegars range in strength from table vinegar (around 5 percent acid) to pickling vinegar (18 percent acid). Balsamic, distilled white, cider, and rice vinegars are common varieties found in most stores that are used for flavoring, cleaning, and preserving. Balsamic vinegar is a good choice for imparting flavor to recipes—even though it has a high acid level, it lends a somewhat mellow flavor because its sweetness balances the tartness. Balsamic vinegar is ideal to use with strawberries or mango. New spice-infused vinegars such as cinnamon, clove, and nutmeg can also lend an interesting flavor to recipes.

2

Essential Equipment

Candy making and sculpting are rewarding and pleasant experiences that are enhanced by having the right equipment. Most candies can be made without a lot of specialized equipment. This chapter will outline the use of basic kitchen tools as well as the commercial equipment that can be used in candy making.

Basic Kitchen Tools

BASIC EQUIPMENT. *Back, from left to right:* Food processor, microwave, compressor. *Front, from left to right:* Chocolate spray gun, immersion blender, torch, heat gun, aerosol propellant can for power airbrushing, airbrush for cocoa butter, airbrush for water colors.

This equipment includes small hand tools and appliances used in candy making that are normally found in the everyday kitchen.

Small Appliances

Immersion Blender
A handheld, stick-shaped blender with a small blade, used to blend and emulsify products at high speed. For the professional kitchen, invest in a heavy-duty model. For everyday kitchen use, there are several good brands on the market that are easily found in kitchen and department stores.

Food Processor
A high-powered machine with various blade attachments used to chop, dice, and liquefy foods. The power is pulsed on and off until the product reaches the desired consistency.

Microwave Oven
Uses microwave radiation to heat and cook. It heats foods quickly without browning like a conventional oven. Only microwave-safe containers may be used in it.

Hand Equipment

Ballpoint Tool

Ballpoint tools are used to soften, flatten, or frill the edges of petals made of modeling paste.

Brushes (2 and 4 inch/50 and 100 mm)

Brushes are used for precise application of a product onto a surface. Small brushes can be used to apply coloring or designs to molds, acetate, or other clean surfaces. Larger brushes can be used to wash the sides of pans when cooking syrups or performing decorative cocoa butter techniques.

Stainless-Steel or Glass Bowls

Assorted sizes of stainless-steel or glass bowls are essential in the kitchen. Find your favorite and keep plenty on hand for mixing and storage.

Cooling Rack/Tray

Cooling racks are made of open-weave metal to allow air to circulate around the product for quick cooling. The tray underneath catches drips.

Cutting Tools

Wheel Cutters

SINGLE WHEEL (PIZZA CUTTER): This tool has a beveled blade that rotates as it cuts. Press down on the handle and push or pull the vertical cutting wheel through the food.

MULTIWHEEL (CARAMEL CUTTER): This tool looks like a metal rolling pin—but instead of a solid center, it has multiple round blades evenly spaced along the length of the shaft. This tool is used in pastry for cutting multiple strips of sponge or dough, and it is useful for marking ganache, caramel, and similar confections. Because these candies are too sticky to allow the blades to cut cleanly, using the cutter allows one to quickly mark surface lines to use as a guide for cutting the caramel or ganache with a knife.

Knives

BAKER'S KNIFE OR SLICER (14 IN/356 MM): This knife has a thick blade for durability but is semiflexible. With a rounded tip and a thin cutting edge, this knife is used for creating chocolate decor such as curls and cigarettes.

FRENCH OR CHEF'S KNIFE: Usually 8 inches/203 mm long, this knife is used for chopping, slicing, and dicing.

EXACTO KNIFE: This craft knife with changeable blades is ideal for cutting pastillage and chocolate for showpieces and for trimming flaws on chocolate.

PARING KNIFE: This knife is used for peeling, coring, and—in chocolate making—trimming and making petals. Usually 3 to 4 inches/76 to 100 mm in length, it is available with both serrated and straight- or smooth-edge blades.

HAND TOOLS. *Counterclockwise from top:* Metal bowls, turntable, parchment paper, piping bag, piping tips, ladle, metal ruler, whisk, timer, thermometer, digital thermometer, tablespoons, paring knives, Exacto knife, slicer, offset spatula, silicone heatproof spatula, plastic spatula, pencils, paintbrushes, eraser, rubber comb, large brush, two small paint rollers, metal comb, small offset spatula, acetate sheet, sponges, Silpat. *Center, left to right:* Scissors, scale, plastic tubes, textured metal and plastic rolling pins, triangle spatula (three different sizes).

Ladle

A ladle with a 4 in/ 8 oz bowl can be used to ladle chocolate into molds.

Paper

GOLD/SILVER LEAF: Add a small piece to the tops of candies for a finishing touch.

NEWSPRINT: Unprinted newspaper is used as a protective barrier when spraying or as an absorbent layer when spreading chocolate for showpieces.

PARCHMENT: This silicone-coated nonstick paper allows for easy removal of a product from pans. It can be cut and shaped into disposable pastry bags known as cornets.

Pastry Bags/Tips

Keep pastry bags and tips on hand in an assortment of sizes. Both reusable and disposable pastry bags are available. Pastry bags offer a cleaner and faster alternative to a spoon when filling molds. Cut the tip off the end of a disposable bag to create a small opening or insert a tip on a reusable bag to fill or pipe decorative finishes on candies.

Piping Bags/Cornets

Piping bags, often called cornets, are hand-shaped bags made of parchment paper cut into triangles and rolled into a cone shape. Pastry chefs often prefer these bags to pastry bags for piping chocolate decorations and smaller amounts of ganache or other ingredients, because they are less expensive and, with a little hand skill, can be made in any size. Of course pastry bags also come in a variety of sizes and can be used instead of piping bags if desired.

Ruler

To make precise measurements, rulers are the tool to keep on hand. Metal rulers are the most desirable.

Scale

Digital scales are excellent for accurately weighing products. Purchase one that can be read out in both ounces and grams. Pocket scales are extremely helpful for scaling in 1 gram increments, which is necessary for spices, acids, and other ingredients used in very small amounts.

Scissors

Scissors are used for cutting acetate, transfer sheets, paper, and more. Kitchen scissors or shears are built for heavy-duty cutting.

Scrapers and Paddles

These are used to clean surfaces, to cut candy, nougat, or dough, and to spread candy in pans. Plastic scrapers are shaped to fit the contours of bowls, while straight metal scrapers made of stainless steel are used for flat surfaces.

Silicone Mat

Silicone mats (Silpats) are pliable, flexible, and reusable mats coated with silicone to create a nonstick surface. They can withstand temperatures up to 482°F/250.0°C and are microwave, freezer, and refrigerator safe. They are widely used in the kitchen and should be washed with soap and water and laid flat to dry.

Spatulas

Spatulas are available in stainless steel, carbon steel, and silicone and in various sizes.

SILICONE: These heatproof spatulas are ideal for stirring chocolate and sugar syrups.

TRIANGLE: Four-inch/100-mm stiff triangle spatulas are used for tempering chocolate on a stone. Six-inch/152-mm flexible triangle spatulas are used for making chocolate decor and for scraping excess chocolate off molds.

STRAIGHT: These are 10 inches/254 mm long and used for spreading and smoothing the surface of chocolate.

OFFSET: An 8-inch/203-mm angled blade is ideal for spreading and smoothing the surface of chocolate.

PALETTE KNIFE: Four inches/100 mm long, these can be used for making chocolate decorations.

Spoons

Keep assorted sizes and shapes on hand, including both teaspoons and tablespoons.

Thermometers

CANDY: Use this thermometer when cooking products in a saucepan. Look for the type that has a clip that attaches it to the pan for hands-free use. Be sure the tip is fully immersed and not touching the bottom of the pan. As the temperature rises, the mercury or other liquid in this type of thermometer moves upward, making it easy to see when the candy is at the correct temperature.

DIGITAL INSTANT-READ: A great tool for all types of cooking, a digital thermometer reads quickly. Some have timers and audible temperature alerts.

INFRARED: This is the best thermometer to use when working with chocolate. This thermometer displays instant readings of the chocolate temperature, allowing accuracy when the correct temperature is absolutely critical. They are also very sanitary, as no probe is in contact with the food. These are available in kitchen and specialty stores and at home improvement stores.

Turntable

A round platform that rotates in place on a base. Useful when decorating or airbrushing larger pieces, it allows the chef to turn items without damaging them. Turntables are extensively used in the pastry field when glazing or icing a cake.

Whisks

Whisks (14 inches/360 mm long) are not as widely used in candy making as in cooking and baking, but they can be used in addition to spatulas and blenders to aid in bringing ingredients together.

Basic Candy Tools

The following list includes specialized equipment used in candy making.

BASIC CANDY TOOLS. *Front, from left to right:* Dipping fork set, circle rubber mat, acrylic frame, metal frame, cooling rack and tray, acetate, caramel cutter, metal bars (various sizes).
Back, from left to right: Candy molds, funnel dispenser, chocolate warmers.

Air Compressor

Compressors provide power to a variety of tools by blowing pressurized air through a hose attached to the tool. Select a compressor with a high CFM (cubic feet per minute) rating, not by its horsepower.

Blow Dryer

Blow dryers are mostly used in competition to blow cold air over chocolates right after dipping to blow off excess chocolate and achieve a thinner coating and faster crystallization of the chocolate.

Capping Trays

A capping tray is a metal sealing tray used to save time and labor when capping truffles.

Chocolate Melter/Warmer

This machine melts chocolate and keeps it in a liquid state. It is necessary to manually adjust the temperature on this machine, increasing the temperature to melt the chocolate and then decreasing it to maintain the chocolate's liquidity. It is necessary to stir the chocolate and periodically check the temperature.

Dipping Forks

Dipping forks can be bought individually or in a set of assorted shapes. The shapes are specific to the candy being dipped, such as round for truffles, two-pronged forks for squares, and so on. A smooth, professional finish can be obtained by using dipping forks.

Filling Trays

Filling trays are metal trays used to save time and labor when filling truffle shells.

Frames

Metal or acrylic frames are used to contain ganaches, nougat, and other confections. Frames can be placed atop each other to build different layers of ganache or candy.

Funnels

Invest in a metal candy funnel with a stand for making candy with hot sugar. Funnels also come in plastic, which will do fine with chocolate but cannot withstand the high temperatures of hot sugar. The funnel is used to dispense precise amounts of liquid into molds in a quick and efficient manner.

Gas

PROPANE TANK/HEAD: Used to heat surfaces and food and to brown toppings. An open flame is emitted from a nozzle that is fed by compressed propane gas.

PROPELLANT FOR SPRAY PAINTING: This is used as the power for airbrushing. Gas is pushed through a regulator into a small hose and then into the airbrush head. This is a good alternative to a large power compressor and is great for small jobs or to take along for touch-ups.

COLD SPRAY: Compressed air that instantly drops the temperature of sugar-based or chocolate products. This cold air is useful for adhering two pieces of chocolate together by quickly crystallizing the cocoa butter.

Guns

HEAT GUN: Used to heat surfaces, a heat gun produces high heat output without an open flame.

SPRAY GUN, AIR GUN, OR AIRBRUSH: Powered by a compressor, this spray nozzle can be used for larger airbrush jobs, particularly airbrushing with chocolate. Finishing a sculpture this way lends another dimension to the look and texture of the showpiece.

AIRBRUSH HEAD: A small handheld tool attached to a compressor for airbrushing items. The air is pushed through a chamber with liquid color in it. The forced air disperses the color into the air in minute droplets. Airbrushes are available in single- and dual-action triggers. Single-action disperses the compressed air and color together. Dual-action allows the user control over how much air and how much color are released. Dual-action airbrushes are more expensive than single-action airbrushes.

GLASS JARS: Liquid color for the air gun is kept in glass jars. Some compressors have an attachment that allows the small jar to screw onto it with a tube that rests inside the jar. The color is sucked into the tube and out through the nozzle of the air gun.

Metal Bars

Metal bars are placed together to form the desired dimensions of a slab of candy. The candy is poured or spread between the bars and left to set up. The bars are then removed and the candy cut.

Molds

Molds are used to form candy or chocolate into decorative shapes or to create shells for filling. There are molds made from polycarbonate, silicone, and other plastics. Inexpensive plastic molds are primarily for the hobbyist and are not used in the professional kitchen. Silicone molds work well for jellies, but for chocolates you should use a high-quality polycarbonate mold. It will withstand the hard tap needed to release the air in the chocolates and will give candy that sought-after high-gloss finish. Be careful not to scratch the molds, as this will show on the candies. Improperly cared-for molds will result in a dull finish on candies. Wash molds by hand with gentle soap and water, then dry with a soft towel. If cared for properly, molds will last for years.

Magnetic molds have magnets and a metal backing sheet. This holds transfer sheets in place to allow the addition of decorative patterns or textures to your molded chocolates.

Natural Stone Slab

A stone slab used to temper small batches of chocolate is a necessary investment. Marble, granite, and onyx are all suitable for tempering. Allot yourself sufficient work space, as the stone needs to be 2 by 3 feet/610 by 914 mm or larger and approximately 1 inch/ 25 mm thick.

Plastics

ACETATE SHEETS: Acetate sheets are clear plastic sheets used to create transfer sheets for decorating chocolates.

ACRYLIC BASE: These are available in various sizes and thicknesses and can be custom cut. Acetate sheets can be adhered to acrylic bases when creating transfer sheets, chocolate discs, and slabs of ganache. Acrylic bases have multiple uses in the kitchen and will last for years with proper care. They are very durable but should be washed by hand and never placed in the dishwasher, as the hot water could deform them.

ACRYLIC TUBES: Chocolate can be pulled into tubes to form solid chocolate tubes for sculptures.

Shell Trays

Shell trays are plastic trays used to hold hollow truffle shells.

Professional Candy Tools

Professional tools are necessary when entering into high production. The tools listed below are usually expensive, but they provide a return on the investment.

Guitar

A guitar is ideal for cutting cakes, pastries, and soft confections into strips, squares, rectangles, or diamond-shaped portions. This tool can be placed on a countertop or attached to a rolling stand for portability. Made from stainless steel, it has a fixed, slotted base frame and a pivoting frame that can be raised and lowered. The cutting frame has evenly spaced stainless-steel "guitar" wires secured to the pivoting frame. To use a guitar, place the candy on the base and lower the top frame to slice through the slab, creating strips. Lift the cutting frame, turn the candy 90 degrees, and slice again into the desired shape and size. The advanced model, a double guitar, has two cutting frames attached: one on top and one on the side. The candy is cut with one frame and then with the second frame without it having to be moved. Using a guitar allows precise, quick, and efficient cutting, and it is a must in larger-scale operations.

Refractometer

A refractometer measures the refractive index of a substance (the rate at which light bends and passes through a liquid or clear solid, indicating the concentration of a substance in that liquid). In cooking, it is mainly used to determine the concentration of sugar, known as the Brix level, of fruit purees, juices, honey, wine, and other ingredients. This allows the chef to determine the sweetness of a product and then make appropriate adjustments to his or her formula. Handheld and digital handheld refractometers are the most commonly used in the kitchen.

Tempering/Enrobing Machine

This is the machine that every chocolatier would love to have. For use in mass production, it is a good investment. The basic tempering machine automatically melts the chocolate, then allows it to reach and maintain the correct temperature. It alternates heating and cooling while constantly moving the chocolate. More advanced models have accessories for enrobing that include a feeding belt, enrobing curtain, vibrating belt, and cooling tunnel.

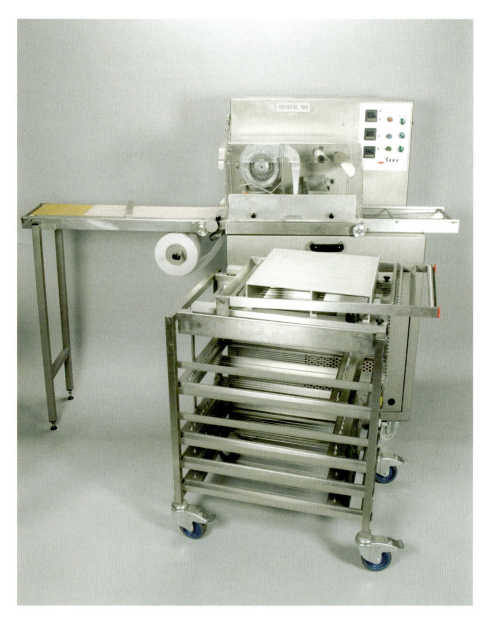

PROFESSIONAL CANDY TOOLS. *From back to front:* Tempering machine, enrober, chocolate guitar.

3

Composition and Basic Techniques

One of the most important steps in working with chocolate is tempering, which results in a glossy sheen and good snap. To achieve this, it is essential to understand the composition of chocolate. All chocolate is composed of the same liquid and dry components. The different ratios of these ingredients result in different varieties of chocolate, such as milk, white, and dark, and determine each variety's tastes and textures. The dry components of chocolate are cocoa, sugar, and sometimes milk powder. Cocoa butter is the only liquid component.

Cocoa Butter

Cocoa butter gives chocolate its shiny appearance, smooth consistency, and workability and fluidity when it is melted and tempered properly. Cocoa butter is a polymorphic fat, which means that when melted, it has the ability to assume the identity of six different stable and unstable crystals with varying melting points. Cocoa buter is the only ingredient in chocolate that melts and forms crystals. Stable crystals in the cocoa butter will allow chocolate to set quickly and to have a silky and lasting sheen, strong contraction, and good mouthfeel. Unstable crystals will inhibit the setting of the chocolate, resulting in dullness, streaks of cocoa butter, and a crumbly texture. Only two of the six crystals are stable, forms V and VI.

CRYSTAL MELTING TEMPERATURES

CRYSTAL FORM	MELTING TEMPERATURE	NOTES
I	63°F/17.2°C	Soft, crumbly, melts too easily
II	70°F/21.1°C	Soft, crumbly, melts too easily
III	78°F/25.6°C	Firm, poor snap, melts too easily
IV	82°F/27.8°C	Firm, good snap, melts too easily
V	94°F/34.4°C	Glossy, firm, best snap, melts near body temperature (98.6°F/37°C)
VI	97°F/36.1°C	Hard, takes weeks to form

Creating Cocoa Butter Crystals

The purpose of tempering is to force the cocoa butter within the chocolate to crystallize in a stable V (or beta) state and form as many of the beta crystals as possible. An example is shown below using pure cocoa butter to achieve this stable crystallization. First, heat the cocoa butter to 110° to 120°F/43.3° to 48.8°C in a heatproof container. In this temperature zone, there are no more crystals, stable or unstable. Remove the cocoa butter from the heat and stir gently to avoid burning or splashing. Stirring or agitating during the cooling process will trigger the beginning of crystallization and assure the spread of the stable crystals evenly through the mass. When stable crystals begin to form, notice that the butter will turn from clear to cloudy, displaying the beginning of proper beta crystal structure. Once crystallization has begun, the stable V crystals will continue to multiply until the cocoa butter is completely set.

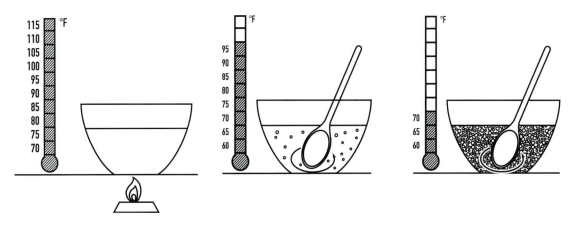

- Heat the cocoa butter to dissolve all the crystals.
- Stir to force crystallization as the cocoa butter cools.
- The crystals will continue to multiply until the cocoa butter is completely set.

Improper Crystallization Forms

Overcrystallization occurs when the cocoa butter in chocolate is overagitated during tempering and too many crystals are produced during the liquid phase. This causes the chocolate to thicken and become hard to work with. To correct this, the amount of crystals must be decreased by removing a portion of the overtempered chocolate and replacing it with untempered melted chocolate to achieve a balanced crystal structure. When mixing, it is important to distribute and blend the crystals evenly throughout the mass to ensure proper temper this time. If this is done poorly, gray streaks will appear on the surface of your chocolate. These streaks are cocoa butter that was not mixed thoroughly enough throughout the mass. (See page 51 for more on fat bloom.)

Another way to correct overcrystallization is to reheat the chocolate gently in a double boiler over simmering water. Some of the crystals will remelt, leaving enough stable crystals in the chocolate to bring it to temper. However, heating the chocolate for too long or to too high a temperature (above 91°F/32.7°C) will melt all the crystals, including the stable ones. This means that temper has been destroyed, and the process must be started all over again.

Undercrystallization occurs when not enough stable crystals have been created during the agitation and tempering process. The chocolate will then take a long time to set, and the cocoa butter will crystallize in an irregular or "wild" form. To correct this, the tempering process must be started all over again.

Wild crystallization occurs when cocoa butter or chocolate is left alone to set without agitation. This results in an unstable crystal form, with parts of the mass remaining in a liquid state for an extended period of time. The resulting mass will contain crystals of all forms and therefore will show signs of bad tempering such as a dull appearance, streaks, gray spots, and a crumbly texture.

- Cocoa butter allowed to cool without stirring, as on the right, will remain clear. If agitated during cooling, as on the left, it will turn opaque.
- When poured into molds to cool, tempered cocoa butter will set properly, while untempered cocoa butter will crystallize irregularly.
- The untempered cocoa butter on the right will remain in a liquid state for a longer time than the properly tempered cocoa butter.

- After two hours, the untempered cocoa butter shows signs of wild crystallization.
- When unmolded, the properly tempered cocoa butter will have the correct appearance and texture.
- Properly tempered cocoa butter and cocoa butter with wild crystallization.

Tempering Chocolate

Tempered chocolate is chocolate that has been melted and then cooled in a controlled environment to achieve the desired crystal structure in the finished, solidified product. Tempering is a very important technique when working with chocolate. If done successfully, it will result in chocolate with a high gloss, resistance to warmth, pleasant aroma, smooth mouthfeel, longer shelf life, good snap, and contraction. "Snap" refers to the sound that the chocolate should make when it is broken, if it has been tempered correctly. Contraction is important for molding chocolates. During the crystallization process, cocoa butter is bound together tightly, which causes it to shrink and makes releasing the chocolate from a mold easy.

If chocolate is not properly tempered before use it will be overly saturated with unstable crystals, which will result in an uneven and streaky appearance sometimes referred to as fat bloom (see page 51). Other characteristics of untempered chocolate include: visible spots on the surface; a dull and matte appearance; and a texture that is soft to the bite or an unpleasant and crumbly texture. The tempering process follows the same principles as the technique for creating stable crystals in pure cocoa butter.

BASIC TEMPERING PROCESS

1   Heat the chocolate above 110°F/43.3°C to melt out any existing crystals.

---

2   Agitate the chocolate to begin the cooling process. This will cause both stable and unstable crystals to form.

3   Rewarm the chocolate to the ideal working temperature to melt out the unstable crystals and start the multiplying of the stable crystals.

4   Test to ensure that the chocolate is tempered. To test, dip a piece of paper or the edge of a scraper into the chocolate and let it sit. If the chocolate is tempered correctly, the chocolate will start to set evenly throughout within a minute. If the test shows any fat bloom or spots, the crystals are not evenly distributed. If the chocolate does not set during the test, the chocolate is not in temper. Milk and white chocolates will take a bit longer than dark chocolate to set up because of the added ingredients.

5   Maintain the chocolate at the ideal working temperature, stirring occasionally to redistribute the crystals.

Methods of Tempering

There are many different methods of tempering chocolate; however, they all consist of the same process of warming and then cooling the chocolate to the ideal working temperature. If done properly, all of the methods described below should yield the same result. The method used to temper is not important; it is more important to create the correct amount of stable crystals in the chocolate in order to achieve perfect crystallization and form.

The Direct Method

The direct method of tempering is done by melting solid chocolate to the proper temperature without taking it out of temper. The temperature required to melt the chocolate depends on the type of chocolate. Melting the chocolate to a higher temperature than necessary will destroy all crystals and force the chocolate out of temper, resulting in wild crystallization and a gray, uneven surface. If the chocolate should reach a higher temperature than recommended, the tempering process must be started over from the beginning.

IDEAL WORKING TEMPERATURES:

Milk chocolate	86°–88°F/30.0°–31.1°C
White chocolate	84°–86°F/28.8°–30.0°C
Dark chocolate	88°–90°F/31.1°–32.2°C

These temperatures are intended as a general guideline. Some brands of chocolate might have to be taken to higher temperatures to achieve the correct temperature for use.

The most commonly used heat sources for the direct method are the oven, microwave, or water bath. Other possible equipment for use in the direct method of tempering includes:

EQUIPMENT	CONSIDERATIONS
Tempering machine	Size and capacity vary greatly; can be costly
Chocolate melter	Can handle 5.5 to 33 lbs/2.5 to 15 kg of chocolate
Chocolate cabinet	Can handle 220 to 440 lbs/100 to 200 kg of chocolate
Directly over flame	Not recommended; requires 100 percent attention

DIRECT METHOD OVEN PROCEDURE

1   Place the chocolate to be tempered in an ovenproof container.

2   Place in the oven and leave for 12 hours, until the chocolate is melted.

RECOMMENDED OVEN TEMPERATURES:
>   Milk chocolate: 86°–88°F/30.0°–31.1°C
>   White chocolate: 84°–86°F/28.8°–30.0°C
>   Dark chocolate: 88°–90°F/31.1°– 32.2 °C

> ADVANTAGES: The chocolate will be heated from all sides, at a low temperature in a controlled environment. This provides a better melting environment than melting on a stovetop, where the chocolate is heated only from the bottom, or in the microwave, where the heat comes from the middle and the rim of the bowl stays cold.
> DISADVANTAGES: If the oven is used for baking, there may be some residual steam inside, which can form condensed water on the chocolate and will change the consistency and smoothness. If the chocolate is warmed in a metal bowl and the bowl is only half full, the bowl will absorb and store an excessive amount of heat, resulting in chocolate that is too warm.

DIRECT METHOD MICROWAVE PROCEDURE

1   Place the chocolate in a microwave-safe container. Warm the chocolate in short intervals of 20 seconds or less, using 50% power if using an industrial microwave, or high power if using a household model. Make sure to stir the chocolate after each interval.

2   Remove from the microwave before all of the chocolate is melted. It is safe to take the chocolate out of the microwave while it has small lumps.

3   These lumps will melt away with stirring and time. Remember that solid chocolate is always in temper; therefore, the remaining pieces of unmelted chocolate will "seed" the newly melted chocolate, helping it to remain in temper. (See page 45 for more information on seeding.)

4   Always be sure to test the chocolate prior to use to be sure the chocolate has the right crystallization. To test, dip a piece of paper or the edge of a scraper into the chocolate and let it sit. If the chocolate is tempered correctly, the chocolate will start to set evenly throughout within a minute.

> ADVANTAGES: This method of tempering is very quick.
> DISADVANTAGES: It is very easy to burn or overheat chocolate in the microwave. To prevent burning, take the chocolate out of the microwave before it is fully melted and stir gently to melt the residual chocolate pieces.

- Warm the chocolate in the microwave.
- Stir to smooth out any remaining lumps.
- Properly tempered chocolate will set quickly and evenly.

DIRECT METHOD WATER BATH PROCEDURE

1   Place water in the bottom half of a double boiler. Be careful not to fill the bottom half so high that the water touches the top part of the double boiler.

2   Place the chocolate in the top half of the double boiler and heat over medium heat. Once the water is simmering, occasionally stir the chocolate gently until it is melted to the desired temperature (see Direct Method Oven Procedure, page 44).

> ADVANTAGES: This is most likely the oldest method of warming chocolate. By using a water bath, the chocolate never comes into direct contact with the water below, which is why it is not necessary to stir it constantly.
>
> DISADVANTAGES: Water is the number one enemy of chocolate. One drop can cause the chocolate to seize up, resulting in chocolate that is not smooth and viscous. Never set up a station to dip chocolates using a water bath to keep the chocolate melted. Steam can also change the surface of tempered chocolate and may result in sugar bloom.

The Seeding Method

The seeding method is a clean and efficient way to retemper chocolate. This technique can be used at any time and in any place, because only minimal equipment is required, and there is no need for a stone or marble slab as in the tabling method (see page 47). This method uses the stable crystals already found in fully set chocolate to cool a larger melted mass of chocolate. By seeding the melted chocolate, which has no crystal structure, you are introducing only the stable beta crystals. Through gentle stirring, those beta crystals will begin to multiply. To ensure that all crystals are melted, white and milk chocolate should be melted at 110° to 115°F/43.3° to 46.1°C, and dark chocolate should be melted at 115°F to 120°F/46.1°C to 48.8°C.

Either coins, grated chocolate, or a large block of chocolate can be used for seeding. All have advantages and disadvantages. For instance, if a large block of chocolate is used to seed, it can be easily removed once the chocolate has been put in temper, and there will be no small lumps remaining as there might be with coins. When using the seeding method with coins, though, it is easy to see the rate at which the coins are melting. At first seeding, the coins will disappear rapidly and easily. Once the new crystals begin to multiply, the chocolate coins will start melting at a slower rate, which indicates that the chocolate has almost reached the ideal working temperature and that there is no need to add any more coins. If using this technique, it is not necessary to bring the temperature below

86°F/30.0°C for milk, 84°F/28.8°C for white, and 88°F/31.1°C for dark, as in the direct method. Remember, only stable crystals are being introduced to the chocolate, and therefore there is no need to reform a crystallized structure. If using a block for seeding, you will have to measure the temperature and test the chocolate to determine whether it is in temper. To test, dip a piece of paper or the edge of a scraper into the chocolate and let it sit. If the chocolate is tempered correctly, the chocolate will start to set evenly throughout within a minute. Regardless of whether blocks or coins are used for seeding, this is a very efficient way to temper chocolate.

- Prepare the chocolate to be used for seeding.
- The larger the pieces of chocolate used, the longer the seeding process will take.
- Stir the seeds into the warmed chocolate to temper.

SEEDING METHOD PROCEDURE

1   If necessary, prepare the seeding chocolate by grating in a food processor. Note that the larger the seeding pieces, the longer it will take to melt and cool the chocolate.

2   Warm milk or white chocolate to 110° to 115°F/43.3° to 46.1°C, and dark chocolate to 115° to 120°F/46.1° to 48.8°C to melt all the existing cocoa butter crystals. It is better to let the chocolate cool down a little bit prior to adding the coins, so less chocolate is needed in the seeding process.

3   Gradually add the coins or grated chocolate, which contain all stable beta crystals. Stir gently to incorporate and distribute the newly added coins without incorporating a lot of air. When the air is humid, the chocolate can easily get thick and airy as a result of overmixing.

4   When the added chocolate seeds have stopped melting, check the temperature and proceed according to that temperature.

5   If the chocolate is still above the ideal working temperature (86° to 88°F/30.0° to 31.1°C for milk, 84° to 86°F/28.8° to 30.0°C for white, and 88° to 90°F/31.1° to 32.2°C for dark), then add more seeds and stir gently. When the proper temperature has been achieved, test the chocolate to verify that it is tempered. To test, dip a piece of paper or the edge of a scraper into the chocolate and let it sit. If the chocolate is tempered correctly, the chocolate will start to set evenly throughout within a minute.

6   If the chocolate is below the ideal working temperature and is a bit lumpy, use an immersion blender to melt the pieces down and get a nice smooth consistency. This is the safest way to bring the temperature back up without the risk of breaking the new crystal structure, because the friction created by the immersion blender will gently warm the chocolate back to the ideal working temperature. The use of a water bath is also

gentle enough to warm the chocolate without breaking the newly formed crystal structure. Another way to rewarm the chocolate is in the microwave or with a heat gun, but with this equipment there is a risk that the chocolate may get too warm and all crystals, both stable and unstable, may melt away. If this happens, the only solution is to start the tempering process over from the beginning.

The Tabling Method

The tabling method is the fastest and most efficient way to temper smaller amounts of chocolate. This method requires the use of a stone slab and good hand skills. The marble or stone slab draws the heat out and away from the chocolate without becoming overly hot itself. Although this is the most efficient way to temper small amounts of chocolate, it requires more hand-eye skill coordination than the other techniques in order to move the chocolate around the table.

Working quickly and cleanly is the key to successful tabling. Keeping the spatulas clean of excess chocolate will help prevent lumps. The steps below should be repeated until the chocolate cools enough to be added back into the bowl. The amount of chocolate used as well as the air and surface temperature will all have an effect on tabling time. As your hand skills improve, you will start to get a feel for the chocolate and will know when it is time to place it back into the bowl. If the chocolate becomes too cold, simply reheat the chocolate and start again.

- Pour two-thirds of the chocolate onto the marble.
- Scrape the chocolate toward the center until it begins to thicken.
- Scrape the tabled chocolate back into the bowl to mix with the remaining chocolate.

TABLING METHOD PROCEDURE

1   Warm white and milk chocolate 110° to 115°F/43.3° to 46.1°C and dark chocolate to 115° to 120°F/46.1° to 48.8°C to ensure that all the crystals, stable and unstable, have melted. It is best to cool the chocolate down a little bit before tabling.

2   Pour two-thirds (²/₃) of the melted chocolate onto the marble.

3   With an offset spatula, spread the chocolate over the marble.

4   With the offset spatula in one hand and a triangle spatula in the other, move or scrape the chocolate toward the center with the triangular spatula.

5   Lift the triangle spatula and slide it against the offset blade edge to remove excess chocolate from the blade. Clean the triangle spatula, first the top and then the bottom, in a fluid motion. Repeat this action, moving to the next portion of chocolate, moving

along the bottom outside edges of the spread chocolate. This is important—otherwise small drops of chocolate may be dragged back over the clean marble and get cold faster than the rest of the chocolate, causing lumps to appear.

6   Continue repeating the steps above until all of the chocolate has been moved to the center. When it starts to thicken, it means that multiplication of the stable crystals has started, and that tabling must be stopped before all of the chocolate starts to set and lump up completely. Scrape the chocolate off the table immediately, into the remaining one-third (⅓) of the melted chocolate in the bowl, and stir gently. It is important to ensure that the crystals are dispersed evenly throughout the chocolate. The perfect tempering occurs when the right proportions of tempered and untempered chocolate reach the ideal working temperature.

7   If the chocolate is too warm, spread a little bit of the chocolate out again and repeat the steps above. Take a test of the chocolate to see that it is in temper. To test, dip a piece of paper or the edge of a scraper into the chocolate and let it sit. If the chocolate is tempered correctly, the chocolate will start to set evenly throughout within a minute.

Troubleshooting for Tempering Chocolate

If the chocolate becomes too cold, lumps may occur. If this happens, use an immersion blender to remove the lumps. The blade will break up the lumps, and the friction of the immersion blender may warm the chocolate and bring it to the right temperature. Gently stir and check for any remaining lumps. Never stir too briskly, as this can cause air bubbles to form. These air bubbles contain moisture that is harmful to the chocolate. Too much stirring will also cause the chocolate to become too thick. Milk and white chocolates are especially vulnerable to this problem, because they contain milk powder and more sugar, which absorb more moisture.

Remember, even if there are no lumps, the temperature may still need to be brought up. To achieve this, warm the surface of the chocolate with a heat gun.

–   Use an immersion blender to remove any lumps.
–   Stir until smooth and free of lumps.
–   Use a heat gun to bring up the temperature of the chocolate.

Dipping Chocolates

Handmade candies are a work of art. When chocolate drips down the sides of a piece of candy and forms a pool of chocolate around the base, the pools are called feet. This occurs when the excess chocolate is not properly removed during the dipping process. A good chocolatier will be able to create beautiful chocolates without feet. Learning this technique will take a lot of practice, but once learned, it will result in chocolates with a beautiful finish.

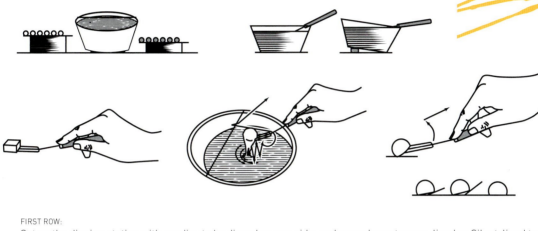

FIRST ROW:
- Set up the dipping station with candies to be dipped on one side, and a parchment paper–lined or Silpat-lined tray for the finished dipped candies on the other.
- The bowl of chocolate for dipping should be tilted toward you.

SECOND ROW:
- Keep your pointer finger on top of the dipping fork for stability.
- Use an up-and-down dipping motion, then slide the candy across the wire to remove excess chocolate.
- Lift the fork up and out from under the finished dipped candy to set it on the tray.

1 Set up the dipping area. If you are right-handed, place the candies to be dipped on the left side of the bowl, raised on a platform, and place a parchment paper– or Silpat-lined tray for the completed candies on the right side, raised on a platform, so you can work from left to right. If you are left-handed, the candies to be dipped should be placed on the right side and the receiving tray on the left.

2 Attach a wire to the top of a bowl using tape or by bending the wire over the rim. Place the bowl with attached wire on a support to tilt the bowl toward you. This will keep the chocolate close to the rim on one side and will allow the fork to remain parallel with the chocolate surface. Not having to tilt the fork allows the candy to stay in place and allows for cleaner dipping. The bowl should be placed on the support so that the wire is opposite you, approximately one-quarter (¼) of the way in from the far side of the bowl, so that it is not in the way of dipping.

3 Hold the fork between your thumb and fingers, keeping your pointer finger on top of the handle for balance, and place the candy three-quarters (¾) of the way onto the fork.

4 Submerge the candy into the chocolate, then quickly dip using a fluid up-and-down

motion. Dip the candy two to three times into the chocolate, decreasing the dipping depth each time. The fast movement will create a sucking motion that pulls the excess chocolate back into the bowl.

5   Lift the candy and slide the bottom of the fork across the wire to remove the excess chocolate from the base of the candy. Using the wire is preferable to using the rim of the bowl, as the small surface area of the wire is easier to keep clean. Using the rim of the bowl is often done, but it is not recommended because the chocolate accumulates, gets cold, and then hardens on the rim.

6   Place the dipped candy on the lined tray. Place the first candies farthest away from you on the tray and subsequent candies closer to you, to avoid dripping on or damaging already dipped candies. Touch the anterior portion of the candy to the paper, lift up slightly, and then ease the fork away, allowing the candy to gently slide off onto the paper.

Troubleshooting for Dipped Chocolates

Using a slightly textured surface such as a Silpat to place the candies on will help to prevent the creation of a foot. The slight texture will allow some of the excess chocolate to fall into the indentations, instead of pooling on a totally flat surface.

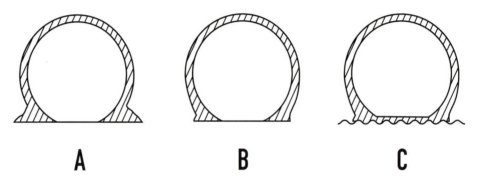

A   **B**   **C**

A: An imperfectly dipped chocolate with a noticeable foot. B: A perfectly dipped chocolate placed on a flat surface. C: A perfectly dipped chocolate placed on a textured surface.

Blow dryers can be used to blow cold air over the chocolates right after dipping to blow away excess chocolate and achieve a thinner coating. This is a particularly nice technique when trying to expose the silhouette of a nut or fruit that is covered with chocolate.

Working and Storage Conditions

The conditions in which chocolate is used and stored can have a major impact on its texture, flavor, and appearance. The major enemies of chocolate include temperature fluctuations, humidity, light and air, odors, and poor hygiene. Handling chocolate properly to prevent contact with these enemies can have a major effect on the shelf life of chocolate products.

Working Temperature Fluctuation

The temperature of the room in which you are working is very important when dealing with chocolate. If the room temperature is too high, the chocolate will take too long to set. When this happens, the cocoa butter stays in a liquid state for too long and travels to the surface of the chocolate, resulting in *fat bloom*. Fat bloom can be identified by streaks of gray or white on the surface of the chocolate, and inconsistent shine. Without its shiny surface, chocolate affected by fat bloom has a soft, crumbly texture on the interior. Chocolate with fat bloom will also feel oily and will melt on contact, because cocoa butter melts at body temperature. The ideal working temperature for a chocolate room should be approximately 20°F/11.1°C cooler than the working temperature of dark chocolate, which is around 88° to 90°F/31.1° to 32.2°C, and therefore the ideal room temperature should be somewhere between 65°F and 70°F/18.3° and 21.1°C.

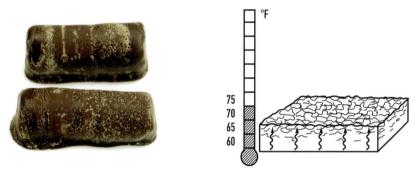

LEFT: Chocolates showing signs of fat bloom.
RIGHT: Fat bloom occurs when cocoa butter travels to the surface of the chocolate

Storage Temperature Fluctuation

Chocolate is an emulsion of cocoa solids and cocoa butter. If it is stored improperly, this integral emulsion breaks down, resulting in bloom. Fat bloom occurs when chocolate is stored at high temperatures (above 75°F/23.8°C) or is exposed to wide fluctuations in temperature, causing the cocoa butter to separate from the emulsion and to crystallize on the surface of the chocolate. The ideal temperature for storing chocolate is between 54° and 68°F/12.2° and 20.0°C. The lower temperatures in this range are less risky, because cocoa butter remains tightly bound at the lower temperatures and only gives up its crystal structure when melted at high temperatures.

Humidity

Humidity is not good for chocolate, because the sugar in the chocolate will absorb moisture. This is especially true for milk and white chocolates, which have a high sugar content. When the chocolate is stirred in a humid room, humidity can be incorporated into the chocolate and cause it to thicken. Sugar is hygroscopic, meaning that it will draw in the moisture from any outside source and hold it until it dissolves. As a result, sugar in chocolate can absorb moisture from the air (humidity), and the sugar will eventually dissolve out of the chocolate and cause *sugar bloom*. Sugar bloom is often caused by the surface moisture that can result from moving chocolate that might have been stored in a refrigerator quickly into a warmer room. Condensation will form on the chocolate, and the sugar in the chocolate will absorb the moisture, which dissolves the sugar and draws it to the surface. Eventually, the moisture will evaporate, leaving behind sugar that recrystallizes on the surface of the chocolate, resulting in a dull white film and chocolate that is dry and hard to the touch. Chocolate should always be stored in a place where the relative humidity is no more than 50 percent.

To distinguish between fat and sugar bloom, rub the affected chocolate on a palm or cheek and feel for texture. Fat bloom will feel smooth against the skin, whereas sugar bloom will have a grainy, sandy texture. Once chocolate has bloomed, it is no longer workable. If it is in the form of pralines, nothing can be done to save it. However, if solid chocolate has bloomed, retempering can be used to save the chocolate.

LEFT: Chocolates showing signs of sugar bloom.
RIGHT: Sugar bloom occurs when moisture is absorbed into the chocolate.

Light and Air

All chocolate should be protected from the light and air by wrapping it in aluminum foil, along with an airtight covering or plastic wrap. If care is not taken to protect chocolate from these elements, chocolate will oxidize quickly and change color and flavor. Dark and milk chocolates naturally contain antioxidants that slow down this oxidation process; however, white chocolate does not contain these antioxidants and is therefore much more susceptible to oxidation. Chocolate that is not going to be used immediately should be stored in a cool, dark place to protect it from exposure to the light and air.

Odors

Chocolate is susceptible to any external odors and/or flavorings. Chocolate contains sugar and fat (in the form of cocoa butter), both of which have a tendency to absorb odors from food or other products. Hand washing is very important when working with chocolate, not only for hygiene but also because of chocolate's tendency to absorb smells from anywhere. Take care not to eat strong-smelling foods or handle any type of cleaning product around chocolate. This tendency to absorb odors is another reason that storing chocolate in a safe place, wrapped tightly, is important. The storage space should be well ventilated and odor free.

Poor Hygiene

There are three critical factors to pay attention to in regard to hygiene:

– The ingredients should be fresh and should be stored correctly.
– The equipment and production room has to be cleaned constantly.
– Attention should be paid to everyone's own hygienic methods.

If these important directives are not followed, it will tremendously shorten the shelf life of the products. In addition, serving products that have not been handled correctly can create a serious risk of food-borne illness.

Shelf Life

The shelf life of a chocolate depends on the conditions in which it was stored. If stored properly in a cool, well-ventilated, dry place, the typical shelf life of milk or white chocolate is 9 to 12 months. Due to its simpler ingredient list, the shelf life of dark chocolate is longer—approximately 12 to 18 months. Good hygiene practices, the correct treatment and storage of ingredients, and the water content in the product will have direct correlation to the product's shelf life. The higher the water content of a product, the shorter its shelf life.

Sugar Boiling

For many confectionary items such as marzipan, liquor-filled bonbons, nougats, and caramels, sugar is used in a dissolved and liquefied form. Sugar may be mixed with water or cream and then boiled to achieve a desired concentration level by evaporating the water. The higher the boiling temperature, the lower the resulting water content.

To ensure that the sugar dissolves completely when boiling, use at least one part water to three parts sugar. If too much water is used, the boiling process will take longer and the sugar may turn yellowish in color. To prevent recrystallization of the sugar, add glucose in a proportion of 20 percent of the weight of the sugar.

1   Mix sugar and cold water together well and place over low heat. Bring to a slow boil to ensure that the sugar dissolves well.

2   The slow boiling process allows any impurities to rise to the surface. These impurities should be removed with a sieve.

3   Keep the rim of the pan clean and prevent sugar crystals from forming by washing down the rim with a brush and a lot of water during the boiling process.

4   Once the sugar mixture is boiling, add the glucose. If the mixture contains any cream, the pot must be stirred constantly to avoid burning.

5   As soon as the mixture has reached the desired temperature (see "Stages of Sugar Boiling," page 54), remove from the heat and shock the pot briefly in cold water to stop the boiling process.

STAGES OF SUGAR BOILING

The temperatures refer to syrups containing 20 percent glucose.

TEMPERATURE	STAGE	RECOGNIZABLE CHARACTERISTICS
223°F/106.1°C	Pearl	Syrup rolls from a sieve and pearls appear
226°F/107.8°C	Thread	Thin thread forms from fingers
230°F/110.0°C	Soft bubble	Small bubbles appear when sugar is blown through an object with a hole, such as a key
232°F/111.1°C	Hard blow	Bigger bubble will appear when blown through an object with a hole
239°F/115.0°C	Soft ball	Soft ball appears when sugar is dropped from a small spoon into cold water
242°F/116.7°C	Firm ball	Firm ball appears when sugar is dropped from a small spoon into cold water
248°F/120.0°C	Hard ball	Hard ball appears when sugar is dropped from a small spoon into cold water
257°F/125.0°C	Soft crack	Sugar feels pliable before breaking when it is dropped into cold water and removed
286°F/141.1°C	Middle crack	Sugar feels firmer before breaking when it is dropped into cold water and removed
310°F/154.4°C	Hard crack	Sugar breaks immediately when dropped into cold water and removed; sugar does not stick to teeth (e.g., hard candy)
320°–338°F/160.0°–170.0°C	Caramel	Sugar becomes dark brown in color

Caramelization

Caramelizing sugar and nuts and storing them properly are simple but important techniques that will be used in countless recipes. Learning these techniques prior to making candies will allow you to progress smoothly through the steps once you get started.

Caramelizing Sugar

Caramelizing sugar is the process of heating sugar in its dry or wet form. For the dry method, melt the sugar with either a little bit of glucose or lemon juice. For the wet method, dissolve the sugar in water and boil to the last stage of sugar boiling, in which all the water is evaporated and the sugar starts to melt. The sugar should be slightly brown and have a slightly toasted caramel flavor.

Melting Sugar in a Copper Pot

Copper is an excellent conductor of heat and makes a superior pot to use when caramelizing. Because copper transfers heat well, the flame should not be larger than the "mirror" of the sugar—the top surface or width of the sugar in the pot. If the flames are too high, the rim and sides of the pot get very hot and the sugar will burn as soon as it comes into contact with those hot areas.

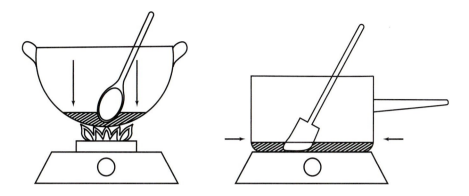

LEFT: When using copper, the entire pot will get hot. The flame should be no wider than the surface of the sugar.

RIGHT: When using an induction burner, only the bottom of the pot will get hot.

Melting Sugar on an Induction Burner

An induction burner works only with pots made from magnetic material. With an induction burner, only the bottom of the pot gets hot. The sides will only get warm; when the sugar hits those areas, the sugar will barely melt and not caramelize. To ensure that the sugar melts evenly, you should stir carefully, being careful not to push the sugar up on the sides of the pot. If this happens, the sugar crystals should be either washed down with a wet brush or scraped down with a heatproof spatula.

Sugar Melting Properties

The sugar charts below and on page 56 are a visual tool to help explain the melting properties of sugar when combined with different substances. Notice in each chart the rise and fall of the sugar temperature. The goal is to have a steady, even rise of temperature in order to attain lump-free, golden caramelization of the sugar. This can be achieved by first adding lemon juice or glucose and by prewarming the sugar before melting.

Melting Sugar in Small Portions

Glucose, invert sugar, or honey can be used with sugar to provide quicker melting properties, but glucose is recommended because of its neutral taste. The water in the glucose will start the melting process of the sugar. To determine the amount of glucose to use, calculate 10 percent of the sugar weight (for example, 1¾ oz/50 g of glucose for 17²/₃ oz/ 500 g sugar).

1   Bring the glucose to a boil.

2   Add small amounts of sugar into the boiling glucose and stir slowly with the spatula. As soon as the sugar is dissolved, add more sugar. The goal is to add small amounts. If too much sugar is added at one time, the temperature of the sugar will fall and lumps will be created. It takes a long time to get these lumps melted, and because of that the sugar may become darker in color.

3   Continue to stir the sugar and glucose, being careful to keep the temperature of the sugar above the melting point of 320°F/160.0°C. An even distribution of heat can be achieved by adding more or less sugar at different intervals. The sugar should reach 347°F/175.0°C when completely melted.

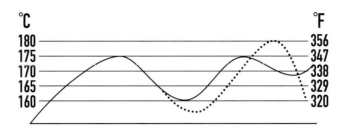

Melting sugar in small portions. Dots represent the change in temperature when too much sugar is added at once.

Melting Sugar with Lemon Juice

Once sugar (sucrose) inverts, it doesn't recrystallize. The combination of acid and heat will create an inversion. Invert sugar is achieved through acid by splitting sucrose into its components: monomers, glucose, and fructose. Creating an inversion will result in a very light-colored liquid caramel. One quick squeeze of lemon should be used for each 3½ oz/100 g of sugar, or the juice of one whole lemon for 35¼ oz/1000 g of sugar. When the lemon juice is added, the mixture will begin to thin out.

1   Combine all the sugar and lemon juice in a pot and bring to a boil.

2   Stir evenly until all the sugar is completely melted and no crystals are visible.

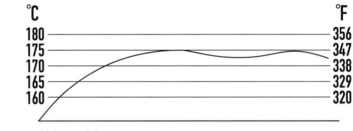

Melting sugar with lemon juice.

Melting Sugar with Prewarmed Sugar

By warming the sugar first, the melting time and manual work will be shortened, and the caramelized sugar will be lighter in color and have a higher viscosity.

1   Spread ½ inch/13 mm of sugar in a loose layer on a sheet pan and warm it in a steam-free oven at 400°F/204.4°C.

2   Proceed with melting the prewarmed sugar using one of the techniques above.

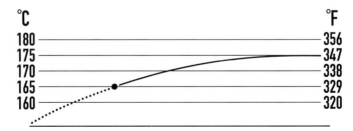

Melting prewarmed sugar. The dot represents the point at which prewarmed sugar is taken from the oven and placed into a pot for melting.

Caramelizing Nuts

Caramelized nuts are mostly used for decorating pralines, small cakes, desserts, and entremets. Caramelizing enhances their flavor and the fine coating of sugar makes their appearance more appealing. When the nuts are roasted first, the color becomes more attractive and the flavor more intense. Not all nuts need to be roasted prior to caramelizing, though, as the nuts actually begin roasting during caramelization. Some nuts retain more flavor if their skins are left on, particularly almonds. However, sometimes skins must be removed because of visual qualities, for example when using the nuts to make marzipan. Roasting and/or blanching will aid in the removal of the skin. Hazelnuts in particular must be roasted in order to remove the skins, while almonds need only to be blanched if their skins are to be removed. To get the nicest, best quality of caramelized nuts, the sugar has to be completely melted, slightly brown, and liquid.

ALMONDS: To remove the skin from almonds, add the nuts to boiling water, allow them to soak for 3 minutes, and then drain the water through a sieve. Press firmly on each nut with the thumb and index finger and squeeze. The clean white nut will slip out of the skin immediately. These nuts have to be roasted lightly in a 340°F/171.1°C oven before caramelizing, because blanching adds moisture that needs to be removed. If too much water is left in the nuts, they can become chewy instead of crunchy.

OTHER NUTS: To remove the skin from all other varieties of nuts, roast them at 340°F/171.1°C, then rub the nuts between your palms or in a clean kitchen towel. The dry skin will come off completely. Always remove the skins from hazelnuts, as they lend a bitter flavor to the product.

METHOD FOR CARAMELIZING NUTS

1   Remove the skins from the nuts, if desired, following the instructions above.

2   Caramelize the sugar using one of the methods described on pages 54 to 56, while keeping the nuts hot in the oven at 320°F/160.0°C.

3   Add the hot nuts into the light brown caramelized sugar and stir well to coat. This will create a light coating of sugar. (If the nuts are added cold, the temperature of the sugar will drop immediately, cooling and thickening the sugar and making a fine coating impossible.)

4   Add some cocoa butter to the nuts. This provides a fine coating of fat on the nuts, allowing them to separate, and keeps them from getting moist and sticky.

5   Empty the nuts onto Silpat, a lightly oiled marble slab, or lightly oiled sheet pan. Some of the nuts will still stick together. Separate them by hand immediately. Once cold, place the nuts into an airtight container and store in a cool area.

Part 2: Making Chocolates and Other Confections

4

Simple Chocolate Methods and Recipes

This chapter includes basic recipes for a variety of mouthwatering products. But before working with even the simplest recipes, it is important to have an understanding of the fundamentals; otherwise you can ruin even the best ingredients. The basic methods in this chapter show how to use quality ingredients to create the foundations for many of the simple recipes that follow.

Basic Methods

With the methods outlined below, you can create the components for a wide range of chocolate confections. From chocolate discs and curls to caramelized nuts, these are the building blocks for many of the simple chocolate recipes that follow.

Chocolate Discs

Chocolate discs are used as a base component for several pralines, including Almond Rosette Pralines, Hidden Hazelnut Pralines, and Kirsch Points.

1 Moisten an acrylic base or other flat surface with a small amount of water. Place down a sheet of acetate and smooth it with a clean, dry cloth. This will remove any air bubbles and will keep the acetate in place.

2 Place a 1⅛-in/29-mm diameter, ¹⁄₁₆-in/1.6-mm deep rubber mat disc template on the acetate.

3 Pour a small amount of couverture onto the template.

4 Spread the couverture evenly, filling each hole and keeping level with the top of the disc. Spread the couverture quickly, with as little motion as possible. (Back-and-forth movement will force crystallization of the couverture, making it difficult to remove the template.)

5 Slightly angle the spatula and carefully scrape across the top to remove excess couverture.

6 Remove the disc template immediately and let the couverture set. Store at room temperature.

- Pour couverture onto the disc template.
- Remove excess couverture from the top of the template.
- Lift up the template to release the chocolate discs.

Small Chocolate Curls

Chocolate curls are commonly used to decorate petit fours, cakes, and plated desserts. Milk, white, and dark couvertures can be used individually or in combination to make curls. The technique of making curls is always the same: spreading the couverture and shaving it off. The shape will vary based on the hand skills of the chocolatier.

1   Using an offset spatula, spread a thin layer of couverture onto a table. Let it set.

2   After the couverture has set, warm it by lightly rubbing your fingertips across the surface.

3   Vertically score the couverture with a knife every ⅛ in/3 mm.

4   With the flat edge of a baker's knife, horizontally shave or push the couverture away, allowing it to curl.

5   Store at room temperature.

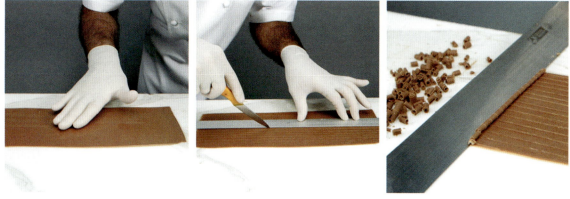

−   Warm the surface of the couverture with your fingertips.
−   Score the couverture with a knife.
−   Shave the couverture to create curls.

Sandy Hazelnuts

The hazelnuts used in the process are lightly roasted to remove the skins. Hazelnuts can be purchased without skins or you can do it yourself.

This technique finishes the roasting process started when the skins were removed. The hazelnuts are coated in sugar before the roasting process continues, which reduces the chance of flavor loss. When nuts are fully roasted in the oven, by contrast, the nuts are openly exposed, and the heat and air blowing in the oven makes them more vulnerable to losing their distinguished flavor.

Use a copper pan to caramelize the hazelnuts, if possible, because nuts roast more easily in copper as the whole pan stays hot.

It is very important that the hazelnuts be warm when added to the sugar. Cold nuts would shock the sugar and slow down the caramelizing process.

INGREDIENTS	METRIC	US	VOLUME
Hazelnuts, whole, skinned	500 g	17.6 oz	3½ cups
Sugar, for the caramel	125 g	4.4 oz	½ cup + 2 tbsp
Water	40 g	1.1 oz	2 tbsp + 1 tsp
Cocoa butter	12 g	0.4 oz	2 tbsp
Sugar, for coating	80 g	2.9 oz	⅜ cup
YIELD	**755 g**	**26.4 oz**	**4¾ cups**

1. Place the hazelnuts in a 320°F/160.0°C oven to warm them.

2. Combine the sugar for the caramel and the water and bring to a boil to slowly dissolve the sugar. Once the syrup reaches 239°F/115.0°C, remove the pan from the heat.

3. Add the warm nuts and stir. It is important to stir constantly, as this will crystallize the sugar. Once the mass is sandy (crystallized) and all the nuts are covered with the white sugar, return the pan to low heat.

4. Continue to stir constantly. The sugar will slowly begin to melt and will caramelize around the nuts and roast them. When the sugar has melted and appears golden brown, remove the pan from the heat and add the cocoa butter to help separate the mass.

5. Mix the cocoa butter into the nuts, then add the coating sugar and toss to coat.

6. Empty the nuts onto a lightly oiled sheet pan or marble, or use a sheet pan covered with a Silpat, and immediately separate by hand.

7. Once the nuts have cooled, place in a sieve and shake gently to remove any excess sugar.

8. Store in an airtight container in a cool, dark place.

NOTE: Normally when cooking sugar in a larger quantity, you would remove any impurities using a sieve. The small amount of sugar in this recipe, however, makes it difficult to do this.

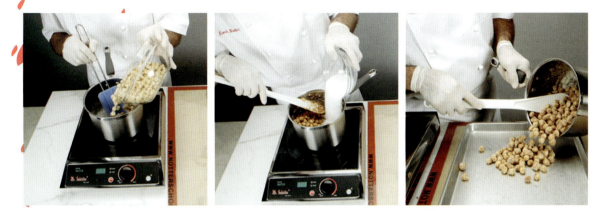

- Add the warmed nuts to the sugar syrup.
- Add the coating sugar to the nuts and cocoa butter.
- Pour out the nuts to be separated by hand.

Sandy Pistachios

It is very important that the nuts be warm when added to the sugar. Cold pistachios would shock the sugar and slow down the caramelizing process. Use a copper pan to caramelize the pistachios, if possible, because nuts roast more easily in copper as the whole pan stays hot.

INGREDIENTS	METRIC	US	VOLUME
Pistachios	500 g	17.6 oz	3 cups
Sugar, for the caramel	150 g	5.3 oz	⅔ cup
Water	50 g	1.8 oz	2 tbsp + 2 tsp
Cocoa butter	16 g	0.6 oz	¼ cup
Sugar, for coating	80 g	2.8 oz	½ cup
YIELD	**796 g**	**28.1 oz**	**4 ⅝ cup**

1   Place the pistachios in a 320°F/160°C oven to warm them.

2   Combine the sugar for the caramel and the water and bring to a boil to slowly dissolve the sugar. (The slow process allows enough time to remove any impurities with a sieve when cooking large quantities.) Once the syrup reaches 239°F/115°C, remove the pan from the heat.

3   Add the warm nuts. Stir constantly, as this will crystallize the sugar. Once the mass is sandy (crystallized) and all the nuts are covered with the white sugar, return the pan to low heat.

4   Continue to stir constantly. The sugar will begin to melt slowly and will caramelize around the nuts and roast them. When the sugar has melted and appears golden brown, remove the pan from the heat and add the cocoa butter to help separate the mass.

5   Mix the cocoa butter into the nuts, then add the coating sugar and toss to coat.

6   Empty the nuts onto a lightly oiled sheet pan or marble, or use a sheet pan covered with a Silpat, and immediately separate by hand.

7   Once the nuts have cooled, place in a sieve and shake gently to remove any excess sugar.

8   Store in an airtight container in a cool, dark place.

NOTE: Normally when cooking sugar in a larger quantity, you would remove any impurities using a sieve. The small amount of sugar in this recipe, however, makes it difficult to do this.

Caramelized Almonds, Wet Method

In the wet method, the sugar crystals are melted in water. With the help of heat, the water evaporates from the sugar solution. When the temperature reaches 293°F/145.0°C, all the water evaporates and the sugar becomes water-free liquid sugar. Because the temperature is not yet past the melting point of sugar, the sugar has neither the color nor the taste of caramel. The sugar is neutral and can be used for all kinds of bonbons, decorations, and pulled, blown, and cast sugar showpieces. As the sugar is boiled a little longer to reach the target temperature of 347°F/175°C, it will start to get yellowish and will develop a pleasant almost-burned caramel sugar flavor.

INGREDIENTS	METRIC	US	VOLUME
Sugar	100 g	3.5 oz	½ cup
Almonds, whole	500 g	17.6 oz	3½ cups
Water	40 g	1.4 oz	2 tbsp + 1 tsp
Cocoa butter	12 g	0.4 oz	2 tbsp
YIELD	**652 g**	**22.9 oz**	**4½ cup**

1 Place the sugar on a sheet pan and warm it in the oven at 320°F/160.0°C. Once the sugar is hot, place it in a container to keep warm.

2 Place the almonds in a 320°F/160.0°C oven to warm them.

3 Place the water and sugar in a pan and stir to dissolve the sugar. Cook the mixture to 347°F/175.0°C, until it turns a golden color. Immediately remove from the heat. (This is important, because the sugar will continue to caramelize from the heat of the pan and can quickly turn dark and bitter.)

4 Add the warmed nuts to the sugar syrup and mix well, being sure to coat all the nuts evenly.

5 Add the cocoa butter to the nuts and mix. (This provides a fine coating of fat on the nuts, allowing them to separate and keeping them from getting moist and sticky.)

6 Empty the nuts onto a lightly oiled sheet pan, Silpat, or marble. Some of the nuts will still stick together; separate them by hand immediately.

7 Once the nuts have cooled, store in an airtight container in a cool, dark place.

Caramelized Almonds, Dry Method

In this method, the sugar is melted with the combination of acid and heat, which creates an inversion. It is important to melt the sugar in small portions so as to not create lumps. Be careful to stir gently and not get sugar onto the sides of the pan.

INGREDIENTS	METRIC	US	VOLUME
Sugar	100 g	3.5 oz	½ cup
Almonds, whole	500 g	17.6 oz	3½ cups
Glucose (or 2 squeezes of lemon juice)	20 g	0.7 oz	2 tbsp
Cocoa butter	12 g	0.4 oz	2 tbsp
YIELD	632 g	22.2 oz	4¼ cups

1   Place the sugar on a sheet pan and warm it in the oven at 320°F/160°C. Once the sugar is hot, place it in a container to keep warm.

2   Place the almonds in a 320°F/160°C oven to warm them.

3   If using glucose, warm it in a pan until bubbling occurs. Add small amount of the warmed sugar and stir to dissolve. If using lemon juice, place it in the pan (it is not necessary to boil), add a small amount of warmed sugar, and stir to dissolve.

4   Continue adding the sugar in small amounts, allowing each addition to melt before adding the next. When the syrup has changed to a golden color (around 347°F/175.0°C), immediately remove from the heat. This is important because the sugar will continue to caramelize from the heat of the pan and can quickly turn dark and bitter.

5   Add the warmed nuts to the sugar mixture and mix well, being sure to evenly coat all the nuts.

6   Add the cocoa butter to the nuts and mix. (This provides a fine coating of fat on the nuts, allowing them to separate and keeping them from getting moist and sticky.)

7   Empty the nuts onto a lightly oiled sheet pan, Silpat, or marble. Some of the nuts will still stick together; separate them by hand immediately.

8   Once the nuts have cooled, store in an airtight container in a cool, dark place.

- Add the warmed sugar to the glucose.
- Add the nuts to the glucose-sugar mixture.
- Separate the caramelized almonds.

Recipes

With a few simple ingredients, you can create delicious and beautiful treats. These recipes are quick and easy and can be made using the basic techniques covered in Chapter 3. For the recipes in this section, any percentage couverture can be used according to taste.

Knackerli

This recipe is versatile, as you can select your own combination of fruits and nuts to place on top. In addition to the suggestions below, dried cherries, chopped dried mango, and chopped candied orange peel are also very good with chocolate.

INGREDIENTS	METRIC	US	VOLUME
Sandy Hazelnuts (page 64), 350 ea	350.0 g	12.3 oz	3 cups
Caramelized Almonds (pages 67–69), 350 ea	500.0 g	17.6 oz	3⅔ cups
Sandy Pistachios (page 66), 350 ea	164.5 g	5.8 oz	1¼ cups
Golden raisins, 350 ea	182.0 g	6.4 oz	1¼ cups
Dried apricots, chopped, 350 ea	327.6 g	11.5 oz	2½ cups
Dried cranberries, 350 ea	227.5 g	8.0 oz	1½ cups
Milk, white, or dark couverture, tempered	2625.0 g	92.6 oz	9 cups
YIELD: 350 PIECES, 1½ in/38 mm each	**4376.6 g**	**154.2 oz**	

1 Have the nuts and fruit ready in bowls.

2 Pipe the tempered couverture onto a Silpat or parchment paper in any desired shape, such as a ring, line, or *S*-shape.

3 Before the couverture sets, arrange the nuts and fruit on top of the couverture.

4 Let sit at room temperature for 30 minutes to allow the couverture to set.

5 Store in an airtight container in a dark and cool room.

– Pipe the couverture into lines, rings, or circles.
– Place nuts and dried fruits onto the piped couverture.
– Knackerli can be made in any shape, such as rounds, rings, or sticks.

Spicy Nut Sticks

This recipe works well with Kirschwasser or simple syrup and with hazelnuts, almonds, pistachios, and pecans.

INGREDIENTS	METRIC	US	VOLUME
Nuts and dried fruits of your choice	500.00 g	17.6 oz	3½ cups
Egg whites	13.00 g	0.5 oz	1 tbsp
Salt	3.25 g	0.1 oz	1 tbsp
Liqueur or simple syrup	65.00 g	2.3 oz	¼ cup
Milk, white, or dark couverture, tempered	3250.00 g	114.6 oz	11 cups
Paprika, regular	to taste	to taste	to taste
Cayenne	to taste	to taste	to taste
YIELD: 248 PIECES, 4 in/100 mm each	**3831.25 g**	**135.1 oz**	

1   Chop the nuts coarsely, moisten with the egg whites, and sprinkle with the salt.

2   Spread the nuts on a sheet pan and roast at 340°F/171.1°C until golden brown. Let cool.

3   Drizzle the liquor into the tempered couverture to thicken it slightly for piping, and pour the mixture into a parchment piping bag or pastry bag without a tip.

4   Pipe the couverture onto a Silpat or parchment paper in 4-in/100-mm stick shapes.

5   Before the couverture sets, sprinkle the chopped nuts and the spices on top of the couverture sticks.

6   Let sit at room temperature for 30 minutes to allow the couverture to set.

7   Store in an airtight container in a cool, dark place.

–   Thicken the couverture with liquor.
–   Pipe the couverture into stick shapes.
–   Sprinkle nuts and spices onto the sticks.

Rochers

This recipe calls for making sugared almonds; Kirschwasser or simple syrup work best with the almonds. In place of the almonds, corn flakes or puffed rice cereal would also work well to add crunch.

INGREDIENTS	METRIC	US	VOLUME
Almonds, slivered	500 g	17.6 oz	2¼ cups
Liqueur or simple syrup	20 g	0.7 oz	1 tbsp + 1 tsp
Confectioners' sugar	50 g	1.8 oz	½ cup
Cocoa butter	70 g	2.5 oz	⅓ cup
Milk, white, or dark couverture, tempered	100 g	3.5 oz	⅓ cup
YIELD: 74 PIECES, 0.4 oz/10 g each	740 g	26.1 oz	

1   Moisten the almonds with the liqueur or simple syrup. Dust the confectioners' sugar over the almonds and mix well, coating all sides.

2   Spread the almonds onto a sheet pan and roast at 340°F/171.1°C until golden brown. Let cool.

3   Warm a bowl either using a torch or by placing it in the oven for 10 seconds at 320°F/160.0°C. (Warming it first will prevent the couverture from setting up in the bowl.) Place the almonds in the warm bowl. Add the cocoa butter, then the tempered couverture, and stir to coat the nuts.

4   Spoon small portions (0.4 oz/10 g each) onto parchment paper.

5   Let sit at room temperature for 30 minutes to allow the couverture to set.

6   Store in an airtight container in a cool, dark place.

Fruit and Nut Clusters

The almonds can be replaced with any other type of nuts, if desired. Cranberries and sour cherries are both good choices for the dried fruit, due to their acidity.

INGREDIENTS	METRIC	US	VOLUME
Almonds, sliced	500 g	17.6 oz	2¼ cups
Liqueur or simple syrup	20 g	0.7 oz	1 tbsp + 1 tsp
Confectioners' sugar	50 g	1.8 oz	½ cup
Milk couverture, tempered	125 g	4.4 oz	½ cup
Cocoa butter	88 g	3.1 oz	½ cup
Dried fruits of your choice, diced	127 g	4.5 oz	1 cup
YIELD: 91 PIECES, 0.4 oz/10 g each	**910 g**	**32.1 oz**	

1   Moisten the almonds with the liqueur or simple syrup.

2   Dust the confectioners' sugar over the almonds and mix well.

3   Spread the almonds onto a sheet pan and roast at 340°F/171.1 °C until golden brown. Let cool.

4   Warm a bowl either using a torch or by placing it in the oven for 10 seconds at 320°F/160°C. (Warming it first will prevent the couverture from setting up in the bowl.) Pour the tempered couverture into the warm bowl and stir in the cocoa butter to thin it. Add the almonds and fruit, stir to coat.

5   Spoon small portions (0.4 oz/10 g each) onto parchment paper.

6   Let sit for 30 minutes at room temperature to allow the couverture to set.

7   Store in an airtight container in a cool, dark place.

Chocolate Nut Blocks

This is similar to the recipe on page 78, but the following provides a nice chocolate-to-nut ratio for an all-nut candy. This recipe is very versatile. You can select any combination of nuts to place in the block molds for bars, or you can place the ingredients on a sheet pan to make fruit and nut bark.

INGREDIENTS	METRIC	US	VOLUME
Hazelnuts, skinned	140 g	4.9 oz	1 cup + 2 tbsp
Almonds	140 g	4.9 oz	2 cups
Pistachios	80 g	2.8 oz	1 cup + 2 tbsp
Milk, white, or dark couverture, tempered	1000 g	35.3 oz	3¼ cups
YIELD: 12 BLOCKS, 5 × 3 in/127 × 76 mm each	**1360 g**	**47.9 oz**	

1 Roast the pistachios, almonds, and hazelnuts at 340°F/171.1°C until golden brown. Be careful with the pistachios, as they roast quickly. Let cool. Chop nuts if needed to fit into molds.

2 Place the nuts in 5 × 3–in/127 × 76–mm block-style molds.

3 Pipe the tempered couverture over the nuts and place in the refrigerator for 5 minutes to set.

4 Flip the mold over, and the chocolate will naturally come out.

5 Store in an airtight container in a cool, dark place.

VARIATIONS

Sprinkle the roasted nuts on a 13 × 18–in/330 × 458–mm half-sheet pan and pipe the tempered couverture over them to create Chocolate Nut Bark.

Replace the nuts with 12.7 oz/360 g of diced candied or dried fruit to create Chocolate Fruit Blocks or Bark. Candied orange peel, dried cherries, dried apricots, and dried cranberries are all good choices.

Chocolate Fruit and Nut Blocks

As in the previous recipe, any combination of fruits and nuts can be used.

INGREDIENTS	METRIC	US	VOLUME
Hazelnuts, skinned	84 g	3.0 oz	2¾ cups
Almonds	108 g	3.8 oz	½ cup
Pistachios	72 g	2.5 oz	½ cup
Dried cranberries	72 g	2.5 oz	½ cup
Dried cherries	72 g	2.5 oz	½ cup
Candied orange peel, chopped	72 g	2.5 oz	½ cup
Milk, white, or dark couverture, tempered	1000 g	35.3 oz	7 cups + 2 tbsp
YIELD: 12 BLOCKS, 5 × 3 in/127 × 76 mm each	**1480 g**	**52.1 oz**	

1 Roast the hazelnuts, almonds, and pistachios at 340°F/171.1°C until golden brown. Be careful with the pistachios, as they roast quickly. Let cool. Chop nuts if needed to fit into molds.

2 Place the nuts and fruits in 5 × 3–in/127 × 76–mm block-style molds.

3 Pipe the tempered couverture over the nuts and fruits and place in the refrigerator for 5 minutes to set.

4 Flip the mold over, and the chocolate will naturally come out.

5 Store in an airtight container in a cool, dark place.

VARIATION

Sprinkle the roasted nuts and fruits on a 13 × 18–in/330 × 458–mm half-sheet pan and pipe the tempered couverture over them to create Fruit and Nut Bark.

Nougat Montélimar

Soft nougat from Montélimar is traditionally made with lavender honey, almonds, pistachios, and dried fruit. More savory than sweet, it has a nutty taste and can be a great snack for any time of day.

INGREDIENTS	METRIC	US	VOLUME
Hazelnuts, whole, skinned	150 g	5.3 oz	1 ½ cup
Almonds, sliced, skinned	100 g	3.5 oz	1 cups + 2 tsp
Pistachios	100 g	3.5 oz	¾cup
Dried apricots, diced	50 g	1.8 oz	⅓ cup
Dried cherries, diced	120 g	4.2 oz	1 cup
Candied orange peel, diced	50 g	1.8 oz	⅓ cup
Cocoa butter	30 g	1.1 oz	¼ cup
Sugar, for the syrup	350 g	12.3 oz	1¾ cups
Water	100 g	3.5 oz	6 tbsp + 2 tsp
Glucose	90 g	3.2 oz	½ cup
Egg whites	50 g	1.8 oz	3 tbsp + 1 tsp
Sugar, for egg whites	35 g	1.2 oz	2 ½ tsp
Honey	200 g	7.1 oz	1¾ cups
Dark couverture, 63%, tempered	225 g	7.9 oz	1 cup
YIELD: 112 PIECES, 0.5 oz/14.7 g each	**1650 g**	**58.2 oz**	

1   Spread the hazelnuts and almonds on a sheet pan and roast in the oven at 340°F/ 171.1°C until golden brown. Add the pistachios and roast for 3 minutes. (Do not roast the pistachios for too long, or they will lose their nice green color.) Remove from the oven.

2   Mix the nuts with the apricots, cherries, and orange peel, and keep warm.

3   To make the syrup, combine the sugar, water, and glucose in a saucepan and heat to 311°F/155.0°C.

4   Meanwhile, combine the egg whites and sugar and whip to soft peaks.

5   Heat the honey to 248°F/120.0°C. With the mixer on low speed, slowly add the honey to the beaten egg whites.

6   Melt the cocoa butter in the microwave.

7   After the honey has been incorporated, add the cooked sugar syrup in a steady stream and whip the mixture on low speed until it cools, about 20 minutes.
Continued on page 82.

THE ART OF THE CHOCOLATIER

8 Pour the melted cocoa butter slowly into the egg whites and mix well.

9 Add the fruit and nut mixture and carefully mix into the egg white mixture using a spatula.

10 Pour into a 10-in/254-mm square frame on a Silpat and cover with another Silpat.

11 Use a rolling pin to level the nougat and push it into the corners of the frame. Leave the nougat to set overnight at room temperature, covered with the Silpat.

12 Remove the frame and Silpat and transfer the nougat slab to a cutting board. Use a clean, sharp knife to cut the nougat into eight strips 1¼ in/32 mm wide, then cut each strip into ¾-in/19-mm pieces.

13 Using a dipping fork, dip the nougat into the melted couverture to coat all sides but the top. Place on parchment paper, and let set for 30 minutes at room temperature.

14 In order to protect the nougat from moisture in humid areas, apply edible lacquer to the exposed side.

FIRST ROW:
- Pour the melted cocoa butter into the egg white mixture.
- Stir in the fruit and nuts.
- Spread the nougat mixture into a frame.

SECOND ROW:
- Level the top of the nougat mixture.
- Slice the nougat into pieces.
- Dip the finished nougat pieces in couverture.

Macadamia Bites

This recipe is a very simple solution for a festive snack for parties. The mixture of chocolate with the subtle tastes of sugar and salt goes well with any drink.

INGREDIENTS	METRIC	US	VOLUME
Macadamia nuts, whole	500 g	17.6 oz	4 cups
Egg whites	13 g	0.5 oz	1 tbsp
Sugar	30 g	1.1 oz	2 tbsp
Sea salt, coarse	18 g	0.6 oz	1 tbsp + 1 tsp
White couverture, tempered	1000 g	35.3 oz	7 cup + 2 tbsp
YIELD: 150 PIECES, 0.4 oz/10 g each	**1561 g**	**55.1 oz**	

1   Moisten the macadamia nuts with the egg whites. Sprinkle the sugar and salt over the nuts and toss to coat.

2   Spread the nuts evenly on a sheet pan and roast at 340°F/171.1°C until golden brown. Let cool.

3   Mix the nuts with the tempered white couverture.

4   Spoon the mixture onto parchment paper and spread with a spatula into an even layer.

5   Let sit for 30 minutes at room temperature to allow the couverture to set.

6   Break or cut into serving-size portions, about 11 g/0.4 oz each.

7   Store in an airtight container in a cool, dark place.

VARIATION

For Hazelnut Bites, which are lower in fat, replace the macademia nuts with skinned hazelnuts and use tempered milk couverture in place of the white couverture. Increase the quantity of egg whites to 20 g/0.7 oz/1 tbsp + 1 tsp, increase the quantity of sea salt to 40 g/1.4 oz/2 tbsp, and omit the sugar.

Granola Mix

This is a healthier option that can be eaten for breakfast or as a snack. The combination of all the nuts and honey makes for a sweet treat.

INGREDIENTS	METRIC	US	VOLUME
Pistachios	70 g	2.5 oz	½ cup
Almonds, slivered	60 g	2.1 oz	½ cup
Oatmeal, rolled oats	50 g	1.8 oz	½ cup
Sugar	40 g	1.4 oz	3 tbsp
Water	30 g	1.1 oz	2 tbsp
Corn syrup, light	70 g	2.5 oz	6 tbsp
Honey	25 g	0.9 oz	2 tbsp
Cocoa butter	23 g	0.8 oz	¼ cup
Sunflower seeds, roasted, unsalted	40 g	1.4 oz	¼ cup
Flaxseed, whole, raw	10 g	0.4 oz	2 tbsp
Wheat germ	10 g	0.4 oz	1 tbsp
Dried cranberries	40 g	1.4 oz	⅓ cup
Dried cherries	40 g	1.4 oz	⅓ cup
Dried apricots, chopped	40 g	1.4 oz	⅓ cup
Raisins	40 g	1.4 oz	⅓ cup
Dark couverture, 63%, tempered	250 g	8.8 oz	1 cup
YIELD: 84 SERVINGS, 0.35 oz/10 g each	**838 g**	**29.7 oz**	

1. Spread the pistachios, almonds, and oatmeal on a sheet pan and roast in a 320°F/160.0°C oven for 3 to 5 minutes until the nuts are lightly roasted. Let cool.

2. Mix the sugar, water, corn syrup, honey, and cocoa butter in a saucepan, and boil until the syrup reaches 240°F/116°C.

3. Combine the roasted nuts and oatmeal, the sunflower seeds, flaxseeds, wheat germ, and dried fruits. Pour the cooked syrup over the nut and fruit mixture and stir to mix.

4. Pour the granola into metal bars measuring 7 × 12 in/178 × 305 mm on a Silpat and cover with another Silpat.

5. Roll out the granola to make a smooth surface.

6. Cut into 1 in/25 mm squares, weighing ¼ oz/7 g each. Let set until cool.

7. Dip each granola square in the tempered dark couverture to coat all sides except the top. Place on parchment paper, and let set for 30 minutes at room temperature.

8. Store in an airtight container in a cool dark room.

Pâte de Fruit

Pâte de fruit is a refreshing fruity treat. The mixture of fruit with some acidity is great to cleanse the palate after a meal. Raspberry pâte de fruit is shown here as an example, but it is possible to produce a wide variety of flavors of pâte de fruit. See the chart on page 89 for the ingredient quantities and desired cooking temperatures for a range of different pâte de fruit flavors. If using a less acidic or flavorful fruit, citric acid can be added to the sugar used to coat the pâte de fruit, to give it a more refreshing mouth feel. Tartaric acid is added to help gel the pectin.

INGREDIENTS	METRIC	US	VOLUME
Sugar, for the pâte	595 g	21.0 oz	2½ cups
Pectin	13 g	0.5 oz	1¼ tbsp
Raspberry puree	510 g	18.0 oz	2½ cups
Glucose	100 g	3.5 oz	½ cup
Tartaric acid	8 g	0.3 oz	½ tbsp
Sugar, for coating	125 g	4.4 oz	½ cup
YIELD: 122 PIECES, 0.4 oz/11 g each	**1351 g**	**47.7 oz**	

1 Whisk together the sugar and pectin. (This will prevent the pectin from forming lumps when it is added to the puree.)

2 Bring the puree to a simmer. Stir in the sugar and pectin mixture. Bring the mixture to a boil, then add the glucose.

3 Cook to 225°F/107.2°C (or to the desired temperature for other flavors, based on the chart on page 89).

4 Meanwhile, mix 1 part tartaric acid with an equal weight of boiling water and bring to a boil.

5 Remove the puree mixture from the heat and stir in the tartaric acid solution. *Continued on page 88.*

– Use a funnel dispenser to fill the mold cavities with the pâte de fruit mixture.
– Umold the hardened pâte de fruit.
– Coat the finished candy with sugar.

6   Pour the mixture into a funnel dispenser and fill the cavities of a silicone mold.

7   Let the cast mixture set at room temperature until hardened, about 2 hours, before unmolding.

8   After the pâte de fruit has hardened, remove the candy from the silicone mold by inverting the mold and pressing on the back of each cavity.

9   Place the candies in a bowl of sugar and toss to fully coat all sides. Store at room temperature.

VARIATIONS

To create a different shape, pour the pâte de fruit mixture between framed metal bars resting on a Silpat instead of dispensing into a mold. Let set until hardened, about 2 hours, then remove the metal bars and sprinkle sugar over the pâte de fruit. Place a metal tray on top of the sugared pâte de fruit, then carefully and quickly flip it over. Remove the Silpat and move the pâte de fruit onto a guitar base. The granulated sugar on the bottom will assist in moving the pâte de fruit. After slicing, slip the tray under the slab, rotate 90 degrees, remove the tray, and slice again to create squares. Alternatively, the pâte de fruit can be cut into other shapes, if desired. Finish by tossing the cut squares in sugar as above.

–   Sprinkle sugar over the slabbed pâte de fruit created using metal bars.
–   Slice the slab on a guitar.
–   Finished slabbed pâte de fruit.

The chart below shows the ratio of ingredients needed to create a wide range of pâte de fruit flavors.

PUREES	PUREE	SUGAR	PECTIN	GLUCOSE	TARTARIC ACID	TEMPERATURE	
	GRAMS	GRAMS	GRAMS	GRAMS	GRAMS	F	C
Apple (Granny Smith) Puree	1000	1114	26	220	18	225	107
Apricot Puree	1000	860	26	200	16	225	107
Banana Puree	1000+750	1655	35	200	30	225	107
Blackberry Puree	1000	1100	26	200	16	225	107
Black Currant Puree	1000	1044	26	200	16	225	107
Blood Orange Puree	1000	1450	44	200	18	228	109
Blueberry Puree	1000	900	25	200	15	225	107
Cherry (Sour) Puree	1000	1100	22	200	18	225	107
Coconut Puree	1000	848	36	235	24	225	107
Exotic Mix Puree	1000	788	20	200	15	225	107
Fig Puree	1000+250	1220	25	200	18	225	107
Grapefruit (Pink) Puree	1000	1145	40	200	21	225	107
Guava Puree	1000	1112	24	232	17	221	105
Lemon Puree	1000+970	1175	25	100	18	225	107
Lime Puree	1000+970	1175	25	100	18	225	107
Lychee Puree	1000	686	40	133	19	225	107
Mandarin Puree	1000	1440	41	200	21	225	107
Mango Puree	1000	1123	24	232	17	221	105
Melon Puree	1000	919	24	213	24	221	105
Mirabelle Plum Puree	1000	1111	24	230	18	225	107
Passion Fruit Puree	1000	1125	51	232	33	226	108
Peach (Ruby) Puree	1000	1060	25	200	15	225	107
Peach (White) Puree	1000	1065	26	200	16	225	107
Pear William Puree	1000	1120	26	220	14	225	107
Pineapple Puree	1000	705	25	250	18	225	107
Raspberry Puree	1000	1110	26	200	16	225	107
Red Currant Puree	1000	1044	26	200	16	225	107
Strawberry Puree	1000	1110	24	200	15	225	107
Strawberry Mar des Bois Puree	1000	1111	24	200	15	225	107
Summer Fruit Puree	1000	1100	25	200	15	225	107

Courtesy of Albert Uster Imports

5

Gianduja, Caramelized Gianduja, and Marzipan

Gianduja, caramelized gianduja, and marzipan are very traditional preparations that are used in making a variety of confections. Gianduja and caramelized gianduja both contain chocolate, while marzipan is made of only sugar and almonds.

Gianduja

Gianduja is a water-free, smooth, cuttable mass usually made of almonds or hazelnuts, sugar, and chocolate. It is mostly used for praline fillings and to flavor crèmes. Gianduja is normally made of equal parts sugar, nuts, and chocolate.

The fat content of gianduja should be at least 30% to ensure quality and smoothness in the product and can be easily more than 30%, resulting in a smoother, better-quality gianduja. The fat content of gianduja is determined by the fat content of the nuts used to make it. If the fat content of the nuts is about 50%, then the basic gianduja mass (the roasted nuts and sugar) will have a fat content of 25%. This amount of fat in the gianduja mass is the minimum needed to achieve the proper oily consistency from the grinding process and to achieve 30% fat content in the finished gianduja, after grinding and adding the chocolate. The quality of the gianduja's consistency depends on the amount of oil that is released during grinding. The oil ensures that all the ingredients—including the sugar, cocoa butter, and dry ingredients in the chocolate—will bind together.

The nuts for gianduja need to be roasted before they are ground. Roasting times can vary depending on the desired flavor. Hazelnuts have to be roasted longer than other varieties, otherwise the skin will not release from the nut. Walnuts, on the other hand, should be roasted for only a short time or not at all. Cool the nuts before grinding in a food processor with the sugar.

When the roasted nuts are ground with sugar, initially a thin powder will be achieved. Then, as the nuts release their oil, the mass will become pasty. Keep grinding until the mixture attains a runny consistency. It is best to use confectioners' (or icing) sugar, as the grinding process will go faster than it would with granulated sugar.

The chocolate for gianduja always has to be melted, but it does not have to be tempered. The ideal mixing temperature for the chocolate is about 90° to 95°F / 32.2° to 35.0°C. If the chocolate is too cold or too thick when it is mixed with the nut paste, the mass may not bind together very well and will fall apart easily.

Mix the runny nut paste with the melted chocolate, then pour the mixture onto marble and table it until the mass begins to set. This will help the gianduja to achieve a nice even crystallization of the fats to ensure a smooth texture.

Gianduja Base

INGREDIENTS	METRIC	US	VOLUME
Hazelnuts, skinned	500 g	17.6 oz	4 cups
Confectioners' sugar	500 g	17.6 oz	3⅔ cups
Dark couverture, 63%, melted	500 g	17.6 oz	3½ cups
YIELD	**1500 g**	**52.8 oz**	**11½ cups**

1 Roast the hazelnuts in a 338°F/170.0°C oven until golden brown. Let cool.

2 Grind the hazelnuts with the sugar in a food processor until the mixture has a runny consistency.

3 Add the nut paste to the melted couverture and stir until combined.

4 Temper the mixture on a marble until it has reached a pipeable consistency.

5 Use immediately or store in an airtight container in a cool, dark place.

— Combine the ground nuts and sugar with melted couverture.
— Stir to evenly combine.
— Table the gianduja to a pipeable consistency.

VARIATIONS

It is possible to modify the ratio of equal parts nuts, sugar, and chocolate to achieve different flavors or textures in the finished gianduja. When adjusting amounts, keep the following tips in mind:

SUGAR: More sugar will make the gianduja sweeter. Using less sugar is advisable if the gianduja is for a praline filling that will be covered with white or milk chocolate. The amount of sugar should not be reduced by more than 20 percent.

NUTS: If the percentage of nuts is reduced, another fat has to be added to make up for the decrease in oils from the nuts. Having too little fat in the mixture could create problems during the grinding process. Cocoa butter can be added to make up for the decreased fat quantity. Adding more nuts to the gianduja will create a rich, intense nut flavor. But because the mixture will contain a lower percentage of chocolate, the gianduja will be softer.

CHOCOLATE: More chocolate can be added to a gianduja recipe without creating any technical problems. However, the gianduja will be firmer and the nut flavor will be weaker.

Different Flavors of Gianduja

The flavor of gianduja is dependent on the ingredients used to make it. The most important factor in determining flavor is choosing the right type of nut. Also important are the roasting process used for the nuts and the type of chocolate used. A variety of nuts can be used, but all should have a fat percentage of 50% or more. Some nuts can be roasted longer for a stronger flavor, while others should be roasted more lightly to achieve the desired flavor. Below are some sample flavor combinations that work well for gianduja.

NUT	FAT %	ROAST	CHOCOLATE
Almonds	45–50	Golden Brown	Dark, 63%
Hazelnuts	50–60	Golden Brown	Dark, 63%
Walnuts	50–55	Lightly Roasted	Dark, 63%
Pistachios	50–54	Lightly Roasted	Dark, 63%
Peanuts	40–50	Golden Brown	Dark, 63%
Coconut	55–65	Lightly Roasted	Dark, 63%

The most commonly recommended chocolate for making gianduja is 63% dark couverture. However, gianduja can also be made with milk chocolate or even white chocolate, using the same method steps listed on page 93. To ensure that the gianduja is firm and not too sweet, the amount of sugar must be reduced slightly and cocoa butter must be added when making milk or white gianduja.

MILK GIANDUJA

INGREDIENTS	METRIC	US	VOLUME
Hazelnuts, skinned	500 g	17.6 oz	4 cups
Confectioners' sugar	450 g	15.9 oz	3⅓ cups
Milk couverture, 37%, melted	500 g	17.6 oz	3½ cups
Cocoa butter	50 g	1.8 oz	2 tbsp
YIELD	**1500 g**	**52.9 oz**	**11 cups**

WHITE GIANDUJA

INGREDIENTS	METRIC	US	VOLUME
Hazelnuts, skinned	500 g	17.6 oz	4 cups
Confectioners' sugar	450 g	15.9 oz	3⅓ cups
White couverture, melted	450 g	15.9 oz	3 cups
Cocoa butter	100 g	3.5 oz	3 tbsp
YIELD	**1500 g**	**52.9 oz**	**10 ½ cups + 1 tsp**

Caramelized Gianduja

Caramelized gianduja is a mixture of roasted almonds or hazelnuts and melted sugar, ground until oily. This mass can be bound with melted chocolate or cocoa butter. Some people prefer this type of gianduja because the sugar is caramelized, giving it more flavor. The coating of the sugar protects the nuts from losing flavor.

Besides the melted sugar and the different roasting process for the nuts, the only other difference between this recipe and the standard gianduja recipe is the addition of water. To ensure accuracy in dissolving the sugar, one part water should be used for every three parts sugar. All the water will evaporate during the boiling and roasting process. The quantities of the other ingredients are the same as in the standard gianduja recipe. If using spices or vanilla, they should be added at the beginning of the boiling process.

For caramelized gianduja, the nuts are coated with caramelized sugar before grinding.

Caramelized Gianduja, Traditional Recipe

INGREDIENTS	METRIC	US	VOLUME
Almonds, whole	150 g	5.3 oz	1¼ cups
Hazelnuts, whole, skinned	150 g	5.3 oz	1¼ cups
Sugar	300 g	10.6 oz	1½ cups
Water	100 g	3.5 oz	6 tbsp + 2 tsp
Dark couverture, 63%, melted	300 g	10.6 oz	2 cups
YIELD	**1000 g**	**35.3 oz**	**6 ½ cups**

1. Place the almonds and hazelnuts in a 320°F/160.0°C oven to warm them.

2. Combine the sugar and water in a saucepan and boil to soft ball stage (239°F/115.0°C).

3. Remove from the heat and add the warmed nuts. Mix continuously with a heatproof spatula until the nuts are completely covered with sugar. (Because of the movement, the sugar will crystallize and stick to the nuts, forming a nice coating.)

4. Return to the heat to begin the actual roasting process. Set the heat at a low temperature, and stir the nuts constantly with the heatproof spatula to allow the sugar to caramelize without burning. At first, the sugar around the nuts will be crystallized and grainy. The heat will cause the sugar to melt and caramelize. Cooking time varies, but the caramelization is complete when the sugar is completely melted around the nuts and the nuts are shiny.

5. Remove from the heat and pour the nuts onto a Silpat. Spread into a single layer and separate as they cool.

6. When cool, place the nuts in a food processor and grind until the mixture has a runny consistency.

7. Add the nut paste to the couverture and stir until combined.

8. If the consistency is too thin or the temperature is too warm, temper the gianduja on a marble until it reaches the correct consistency.

9. Use immediately or store in an airtight container in a cool, dark place.

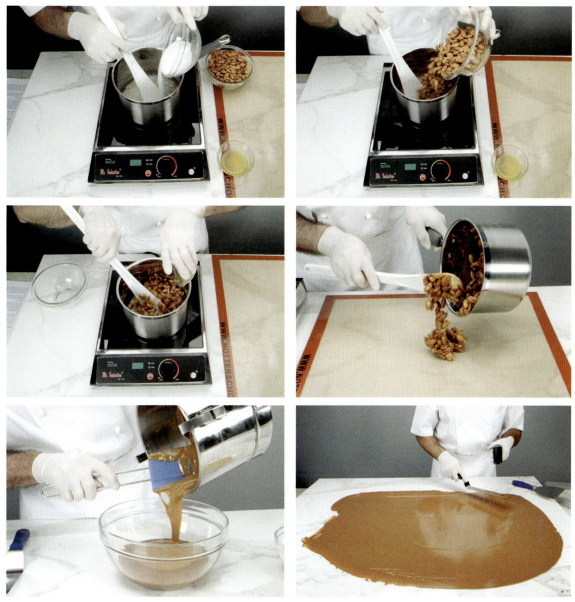

FIRST ROW:
- Melt the sugar.
- Add the nuts to the melted sugar.

SECOND ROW:
- Stir to coat the nuts with the sugar mixture.
- Pour out the roasted nuts to cool and separate.

THIRD ROW:
- After grinding, the nuts should have a runny consistency.
- Table the caramelized gianduja to the proper consistency.

Caramelized Gianduja, Modified Recipe

For a less-sweet gianduja, this recipe reduces the amount of sugar and water to allow the nut and chocolate flavors to be more prevalent. It also uses a mix of half dark and half milk chocolate for a more balanced flavor.

INGREDIENTS	METRIC	US	VOLUME
Almonds, whole	150 g	5.3 oz	1¼ cups
Hazelnuts, whole, skinned	150 g	5.3 oz	1¼ cups
Sugar	150 g	5.3 oz	1½ cups
Water	50 g	1.8 oz	3 tbsp + 1 tsp
Dark couverture, 63%, melted	150 g	5.3 oz	1 cup
Milk couverture, 37%, melted	150 g	5.3 oz	1 cup
YIELD	**800 g**	**28.3 oz**	**6 ½ cups**

1   Place the almonds and hazelnuts in a 320°F/160.0°C oven to warm them.

2   Combine the sugar and water in a saucepan and boil to soft ball stage (239°F/115.0°C).

3   Remove from the heat and add the nuts. Mix continuously with a heatproof spatula until the nuts are completely covered with sugar.

4   Return to low heat, constantly stirring the nuts. You may hear popping sounds, which is normal during the roasting process. Continue to stir until the sugar turns a golden brown. Cooking time varies, but the nuts are done as soon as the color begins to change.

5   Remove from the heat and pour the nuts onto a Silpat. Spread into a single layer and separate as they cool.

6   When cool, place the nuts in a food processer and grind until the mixture has a runny consistency.

7   Add the nut paste to the couverture and stir until combined.

8   If the consistency is too thin or the temperature is too warm, pour onto a marble table and temper the gianduja until it reaches the correct consistency.

9   Use immediately or store in an airtight container in a cool, dark place.

Marzipan

Marzipan is a finely ground, pliable mixture made of almonds and sugar, bound with a liquid. The liquid is typically a syrup of water and sugar, but liqueurs such as Kirschwasser or Williams pear brandy can also be used. There are three primary kinds of marzipan: French, German, and quick marzipan.

While in the United States marzipan never really became popular, it is very popular in Europe and has many applications. It can be found as an ingredient or filling in pralines, doughs, creams, ice creams, cookies, and cakes, or it can be used as a decoration.

Because of its moisture content, marzipan can be vulnerable to bacteria. If it is made and stored under very clean and hygienic conditions, however, marzipan can have a shelf life lasting up to a year. Marzipan should be stored at 50° to 59°F/10.0° to 15.0°C.

If using fresh almonds to make marzipan, the almonds have to be blanched in boiling water for three minutes before they are peeled. These almonds will absorb water, resulting in a softer marzipan. Because the moisture content of blanched almonds will never be exactly the same from one batch to the next, the consistency of marzipan made with fresh almonds is regulated by the water content.

It is easier to achieve a consistent result and control the moisture content of marzipan by using dry almonds. Therefore, the dry method is preferred, because the exact amount of liquid desired can be determined and added. In the dry method, additional liquid such as syrup or flavored liquor must be added during the grinding process.

Grinding the almonds is important because it exposes more surface area, which allows more boiled sugar to be absorbed. The almonds have to be processed until their oils start to release. At this point, the almonds will easily stick together if slightly pressed by hand.

The boiling temperature for the sugar should be between 246° and 257°F/118.9° and 125.0°C. To determine the exact temperature, a thermometer should be used. If using the marzipan for pralines, boil the sugar to the higher end of the temperature range, as this will result in a firmer marzipan that can absorb more liquid.

Bring the sugar and water slowly to a boil, then remove any impurities from the surface with a sieve. Wash any sugar crystals that form down the sides of the pan with a wide brush that has been soaked with water.

Once the sugar has been boiled, always mix the sugar into the almonds, never vice versa. Add the sugar very slowly to the almonds while constantly moving the almonds with a spatula. If too much sugar is added at once, the almonds may heat up too much and become yellow in color. Sugar crystallization will be forced by the constant movement of the sugar and almond mixture. The mixture will become whiter, which will make it easier to add coloring later on.

Once the sugar and nuts are combined, immediately empty the mixture onto a marble and flatten it to cool down. As soon the mixture is cooled, add the remaining liquid to this mass and grind again in a food processor to the desired consistency.

Whenever marzipan gets oily, it is an indication that liquid is missing. If enough liquid is not added to the sugar-almond mixture before grinding, the almonds will release oil. It is very easy to fix this problem by adding liquid (either simple syrup or boiling water) to reemulsify the fat. Use as little liquid as possible, though, because too much liquid will soften the marzipan.

If marzipan becomes too soft, confectioners' sugar can be added to achieve a firmer consistency. However, this will make the marzipan sweeter and will reduce the almond flavor. This marzipan should be used for decoration rather than as an ingredient for pastry or pralines.

If marzipan is flavored you may add some food coloring to match the flavor. For example, if using pistachios to flavor the marzipan and the color of the nuts does not color the marzipan enough, you may knead in some green food coloring immediately after processing to distribute the color evenly throughout the marzipan.

Finished marzipan should be cooled before using. If not using the marzipan immediately, wrap it tightly in plastic and store in the refrigerator.

French Marzipan

The working process for French marzipan is simpler and easier than the procedure for German marzipan. Sugar is boiled, mixed into ground almonds, then cooled and ground again into a fine paste with syrup.

INGREDIENTS	METRIC	US	VOLUME
Almonds (whole fresh or dry sliced; see Note)	150 g	5.3 oz	1 cup, whole, or 1⅔ cups, sliced
Sugar	300 g	11.6 oz	1½ cups
Water	100 g	3.5 oz	6 tbsp + 2 tsp
Glucose	30 g	1.1 oz	1 tbsp + 1 tsp
Simple syrup (as needed; not necessary if using blanched fresh nuts)	30 g	1.1 oz	3 tbsp
YIELD	**610 g**	**22.6 oz**	**3⅔ cups**

1 If using fresh almonds, blanch the almonds in boiling water for 3 minutes, then drain. Press on the almonds to remove the skins. Dry the skinned almonds. If using sliced almonds, soak in boiling water for 3 minutes, then shock the almonds in cold water, and let soak in cold water for 30 minutes, drain, and dry.

2 Coarsely grind the almonds in a food processor and transfer to a bowl.

3 Boil the sugar, water, and glucose in a saucepan to 248°F/120.0°C, skimming off any impurities and washing down the sides of the pan as necessary.

4 Add this sugar syrup to the ground almonds and stir until the sugar crystallizes around the almonds

5 Pour the mixture onto a Silpat and cool. Break the mixture apart to cool faster using a scraper. Do not use a knife, as it could cut through the Silpat.

6 In a food processor, combine the almond mixture and simple syrup, if needed, and grind to a paste on a fast rpm. Remember that, if using fresh blanched almonds, you may not need additional syrup due to the amount of moisture achieved from blanching. For a praline center, you may prefer a coarser texture. In this case do not process the mixture for as long.

7 Empty the marzipan onto a Silpat and knead until the marzipan comes together and holds together. Pack into a tightly closed container, and store at 50° to 59°F/10.0° to 15.0°C.

Note: Prepared sliced almonds may be used instead of fresh almonds. These almonds are dehydrated and will need to be soaked in boiling water for 3 minutes, then shocked in cold water, and soaked for 30 minutes in cold water to achieve their desired state. The water absorption rate will be 10 percent. If using dry sliced almonds, it may be necessary to add simple syrup to achieve the right consistency.

- Blanch the almonds to loosen the skins.
- Remove the almond skins.

SECOND ROW:
- Add sugar syrup to the coarsely ground almonds.
- Cool the almond-sugar mixture before further grinding.

THIRD ROW:
- Add additional syrup as necessary to the ground almonds.
- Pour out the marzipan to be kneaded.

Gianduja Praline Base

German marzipan is more labor-intensive than French marzipan, and the German method is not used very often any more. However, many older praline recipes are based on the raw mass that is created in the first step of the German method. The raw mass is made up of two parts almonds mixed with one part sugar. The mixture is ground, roasted, cooled, and then ground again with syrup.

In the beginning of the grinding process, the almonds have a high water content, and the percentage of sugar in the mixture will be about 30 percent. Once the roasting process begins, the water from the almonds will evaporate and the sugar percentage will rise to 35 percent.

The raw mass is considered a half-finished product and needs further processing to be turned into marzipan. Combining one part raw mass with one part confectioners' sugar results in a finished marzipan.

The German method creates a very intense, flavorful, fine praline, because the relatively dry sugar-almond mixture can absorb a lot more flavored liquid than a raw mass that already contains a lot of syrup.

In this marzipan recipe, a lot of sugar is added to keep the color light and make it easier to color the marzipan for decorations, but this results in a very sweet marzipan. For consumption, less sugar may be used.

RAW MASS

INGREDIENTS	METRIC	US	VOLUME
Almonds (whole fresh)	300 g	10.6 oz	2½ cups
Confectioners' sugar	150 g	5.3 oz	1¼ cups
Simple syrup	45–90 g	1.5–3.2 oz	¼ to ½ cup
YIELD	**495–540 g**	**17.4–19.1 oz**	**4–4¼ cups**

GERMAN MARZIPAN

INGREDIENTS	METRIC	US	VOLUME
Raw Mass	500 g	17.6 oz	4 cups
Confectioners' sugar	500 g	17.6 oz	3¾ cups
YIELD	**1000 g**	**35.2 oz**	**7 ¾ cup**

1   If using fresh almonds, blanch the almonds in boiling water for 3 minutes, then drain. Press on the almonds to remove the skins. Dry the skinned almonds. If using dry sliced almonds, soak in boiling water for 3 minutes, shock the almonds in cold water and let soak for 30 minutes in cold water, drain, and dry.

2   Combine the almonds and sugar in a food processor and grind to a coarse consistency. Be careful not to grind the mixture too fine, as this may cause lumps to form during the roasting process, making it difficult for the water to evaporate.
Continued on page 104.

3 Place the sugar-almond mixture in a bowl set over a water bath and bring the water to a boil. Stir the mixture constantly. The process is completed once the mass appears dry and releases from the rim of the bowl.

4 Empty the mass immediately onto a cold marble or sheet pan. Flatten the mass to cool it quickly and guarantee a rich white color. (If the mass is not pressed flat and thin, the remaining heat may burn the mass or make it yellowish.)

5 Return the mixture to the food processor and add the simple syrup. The amount of liquid to be added depends on how finely the almonds have been processed. The dryer and finer the almonds, the more liquid will be needed. The amount of liquid to be added can range anywhere between 10 and 20 percent of the total weight of the mixture (for every 3.5 oz/100 g of the almond mixture, add 0.4 to 0.7 oz/10 to 20 g syrup). Process the mixture until the mass can hold its own shape. For a better binding of the mass, 50 percent of the syrup can be replaced with glucose.

6 This mixture is called the raw mass. In order to finish and create marzipan, one part sugar must still be added.

7 To create the German marzipan, combine the raw mass and the confectioners' sugar in a bowl and mix well. Empty the marzipan onto a Silpat and knead until the marzipan comes together and holds together.

8 Use immediately or store in an airtight container in a cool, dark place.

Note: Dry sliced almonds may be used instead of fresh almonds. These almonds are dehydrated and will need to be soaked in boiling water for 3 minutes, then shocked in cold water, and soaked for 30 minutes in cold water to achieve their desired state. The water absorption rate will be 10 percent.

Quick Marzipan

This is a very simple method of making marzipan. There is no boiling of sugar or roasting of nuts involved, and the use of dry almonds ensures a long shelf life. The fondant does not have a high enough water content to be used on its own in this recipe, as the resulting marzipan would be too dry. Therefore some liquid (syrup or liquor) must be added at the beginning of the recipe.

INGREDIENTS	METRIC	US	VOLUME
Simple syrup or liquor	as needed	as needed	as needed
Fondant	500 g	17.6 oz	1⅔ cups
Almonds (dry whole peeled or sliced)	500 g	17.6 oz	4 cups whole or 5 cups flakes
Confectioners' sugar	500 g	17.6 oz	3⅔ cups
YIELD	**1500 G**	**52.8 OZ**	**10⅓ CUPS**

1 Stir syrup or liquor into the fondant little by little until a nice smooth consistency is reached. Use enough syrup to make the fondant a bit moist, but not soggy.

2 Mix the fondant with the almonds in a food processor and grind to a fine consistency.

3 Add the confectioners' sugar to the fondant-almond mixture and process to combine. Empty the marzipan onto a Silpat and knead until the marzipan comes together and holds together.

4 Use immediately or store in an airtight container in a cool, dark place.

VARIATION

For a less-sweet marzipan, reduce the quantities of fondant and confectioners' sugar by 25 percent for a ratio of 1 part almonds to 1½ parts sugar.

6

Ganache

Ganache is a mixture made from chocolate and
liquid. Most often, the liquid used is heavy cream,
but ganache can also be made using fruit juices or
purees, butter, eggs, or other liquids. It can be used as
a glaze, a filling for pastries, and in dessert sauces,
but it is best known for its versatility in the production
of chocolate candies. The rich, creamy texture of
ganache makes it ideal for rolling into truffles and
for use as a filling for molded pralines or as a center
for dipped pralines. While the ratio of chocolate to
liquid may vary, the technique for creating ganache
remains the same. This chapter will describe the basic
technique for forming ganache along with guidelines
for adjusting texture, mouthfeel, and flavor.

Emulsions

Ganache is an emulsion, a homogeneous mixture made from two otherwise unmixable products. Another common example of an emulsion is vinaigrette, in which oil and vinegar are combined to make a creamy dressing. The fats in the oil generally do not mix with the water in the vinegar, so if oil is poured into a beaker containing vinegar, the vinegar sinks and the oil rises to the top. However, if the oil is slowly drizzled and whisked vigorously into the vinegar, the result is a creamy blended mixture. In this example, the momentum of stirring breaks the water in the vinegar into smaller molecules, which then become suspended in the fats in the oil. Vinaigrette is a water-in-fat emulsion. In contrast, ganache is a fat-in-water emulsion, made when hot cream combines with chocolate. The heat melts the fats in the chocolate, and careful stirring breaks the fats in the chocolate and the cream into smaller molecules that become suspended in the water of the cream. The resultant mixture is well blended with a high gloss and creamy consistency.

Types of Ganache

As noted in the introduction, ganache is made from chocolate and a liquid. The type of liquid selected will alter the flavor, texture, and mouthfeel of the finished ganache. These variations in finished ganaches are largely related to the fat and water content of the liquids used. Higher-fat liquids will generally produce a creamier ganache.

Cream Ganache

Cream is the most widely used liquid for ganache. Cream contains both butterfat and water, necessary components for the formation of an emulsion. The fat in the cream combines with the cocoa butter in the chocolate, providing a creamy texture and velvety mouthfeel. If the overall percentage of fats is too high, however, the ganache will separate. As a general rule, select cream containing 35 to 40% butterfat for optimum results. Adjustments to ganache formulas may be necessary to achieve the proper balance between fat and water.

Cream also contains milk solids and lactose, which add a characteristic dairy flavor to ganache.

BASIC CREAM GANACHE METHOD

1   Scale (measure out) the couverture and heavy cream. For soft and medium ganache, use solid pieces of chocolate. Chop the couverture into ¼-inch pieces and place in a mixing bowl. Small pieces of couverture will melt more easily and thoroughly than larger chunks. For a firm ganache, however, the ratio of couverture to cream will be too high for the heat of the cream to melt all of the couverture, so warm the couverture gently to soften it before adding the cream. To warm it, place the ¼-inch pieces of couverture in the oven or microwave and heat until it is half melted.

2   Heat the cream just to a boil, then remove from the heat. Be careful not to allow the cream to boil, as water will evaporate and concentrate the total amount of fats in the cream.

3   Pour the cream over the couverture in the mixing bowl, immersing the couverture completely in the cream. Set aside undisturbed for 1 or 2 minutes. (Allowing the mixture to rest provides time for the cream to melt all of the solid pieces of couverture and for the mixture to cool slightly.) The ideal mixing temperature for ganache is 90 to 110°F/32.2 to 43.3°C (see page 122).

4   Using a spatula, begin stirring the ganache in small circles starting in the center of the bowl. Stir in wider circles toward the outer edges of the bowl as the emulsion emerges from the unmixed couverture and cream. (Stirring breaks the fats in the cream and couverture into smaller molecules, which then become suspended in the water of the cream.) Care should be taken not to incorporate too much air into the mixture during stirring, as air bubbles can introduce bacteria into the ganache and shorten its shelf life.

5   Let the ganache cool to 94°F/34.4°C. If adding a liquor to the ganache, add it once the ganache has cooled and mix in either by hand or using an immersion blender. (If the ganache is too warm when the liquor is added, the alcohol will evaporate.)

6   If adding butter to the ganache, let the ganache cool to 92°F/33.3°C, then add the butter. (If the ganache is too warm when the butter is added, the butter will melt completely and the mouthfeel of the ganache will change.) Mix the butter in by hand, or use an immersion blender. When using an immersion blender, care should be taken to keep the blade at the bottom of the container and to gently move the blender in small circles starting at the center of the container. (Keeping the blade at the bottom helps reduce the introduction of unwanted air bubbles into the mixture.)

7   The finished ganache should be smooth and glossy with no visible traces of cream or solid pieces of couverture. If a few solid pieces of couverture remain in the mixture, it can be gently warmed and mixed again to melt all of the pieces.

8   Finish and store the ganache according to its intended use.

–   *For rolled truffles:* Pour the ganache into a bowl or hotel pan and cover the surface with plastic wrap. Allow to rest undisturbed at room temperature, ideally 68°F/20.0°C, for a few hours or until firm enough to pipe or scoop and roll.

–   *For filling truffle shells or molded pralines:* Cover the surface of the ganache with plastic wrap. Allow to rest undisturbed at room temperature, ideally at 68°F/20.0°C, until the ganache reaches 84°F/28.8°C for white chocolate shells, 86°F/30.0°C for milk chocolate shells, or 88°F/31.1°C for dark chocolate shells.

–   *For piped shapes:* Follow the instructions above for ganache for filling truffle shells or molded pralines, but allow the ganache to firm up overnight at room temperature so that it will hold its shape when piped.

–   *For slabbed pralines:* Pour the ganache into frames or between metal bars of the desired height and size. Allow to rest undisturbed at room temperature, ideally 68°F/20.0°C, overnight or until firm enough to cut.

FIRST ROW:
- Pour cream over the couverture and let sit to melt the couverture.
- Stir in small circles from the inside out.

SECOND ROW:
- To avoid the evaporation of alcohol, add the liquor after the ganache has cooled to 94°F/34.4°C.
- Add butter to the cooled ganache.

THIRD ROW:
- Use an immersion blender to fully incorporate the butter.
- The finished ganache should be smooth and shiny.

CREAM GANACHE FORMULAS

PRODUCT/USE	CHOCOLATE VARIETY	RATIO OF CHOCOLATE TO CREAM	AMOUNT OF CHOCOLATE	AMOUNT OF CREAM
Firm ganache for slabbed pralines and truffles	Dark couverture	2:1	35.3 oz/1000 g	17.6 oz/500 g
	Milk couverture	2.5:1	35.3 oz/1000 g	14.1 oz/400 g
	White couverture	2.5:1	35.3 oz/1000 g	14.1 oz/400 g
Medium ganache for piped pralines	Dark couverture	1.5:1	35.3 oz/1000 g	23.5 oz/667 g
	Milk couverture	2:1	35.3 oz/1000 g	17.6 oz/500 g
	White couverture	2:1	35.3 oz/1000 g	17.6 oz/500 g
Soft ganache for molded pralines	Dark couverture	1:1	35.3 oz/1000 g	35.3 oz/1000 g
	Milk couverture	1.5:1	35.3 oz/1000 g	23.5 oz/667 g
	White couverture	1.5:1	35.3 oz/1000 g	23.5 oz/667 g

Butter can be added to achieve a better mouth feel and smoother consistency. The quantity of butter used should be 10 percent of the total ganache weight.

When adding alcohol to the above formulas, to keep the same consistency listed in the table, add an extra 7.1 oz/200 g cream and 5.3 oz/150 g chocolate.

If a sweetener is desired for a dark chocolate ganache because of the bitterness of dark chocolate, fondant is a reasonable choice to use, because it does not contain any hard crystals and the high water content (16 percent) of butter should dissolve the sugar completely. Fondant will also enhance the stability of the ganache. If the fondant is too firm, it can be slightly warmed and softened using simple syrup. The amount of fondant used should not equal more than 50 percent of the quantity of butter.

However, the recipes in this book will not contain fondant as a sweetener, as taste preferences have changed over the last decade and most people do not prefer the sweet taste it provides.

Butter Ganache

Butter can replace cream to make ganache. Butter ganache is more prevalent in Europe than in the United States, and it is often made with liquors. Butter contributes a creamy mouthfeel with dairy flavors. Additionally, butter contains less water (16 percent) than cream (60 to 65 percent) and therefore creates a firmer and more shelf-stable product. While cream ganache is a fat-in-water emulsion, butter ganache is a water-in-fat emulsion due to the higher fat content and lower water content.

Unsalted butter is the best choice for making ganache, and ideally butter containing 85% fat should be used. In the United States, butter is generally 80 to 81% fat, with 15 to 16 percent water and 4 to 5 percent milk solids. In Europe, the fat content can be up to 85%. Like chocolate, butter is susceptible to odors and should be stored in well-wrapped packaging.

Butter ganache is made using melted, tempered chocolate and softened, but not melted butter. Tempered chocolate enhances the texture and mouthfeel of the finished ganache, and when combined with the fat in the butter, it creates a quick-setting and firm product. Using melted butter would increase the risk of separation into butterfat and water and would prevent the formation of a smooth emulsion when the butter is combined with the chocolate. Both the chocolate and the butter should be at similar temperatures when they are combined to ensure even emulsification. Butter ganache is mainly used for piping.

BASIC BUTTER GANACHE METHOD

1   Scale (measure out) the butter and couverture.

2   Temper the couverture and make sure it is at the high end of the working temperature range, 90°F/32.2°C for dark chocolate, 88°F/31.1°C for milk chocolate, and 86°F/30°C for white chocolate.

3   In a mixing bowl, blend the softened butter (at 80° to 90°F/30° to 32°C) until smooth. If the ganache will be used for piped applications, you may whip the butter using a mixer and paddle attachment until light and fluffy. Aerating the butter helps retain the shape of the piped pieces and provides a creamier mouthfeel.

4   Fold in the tempered couverture.

5   Add the liquor, if using (see page 114), and blend with an immersion blender until the ganache is smooth and shiny.

6   Allow the ganache to set up until it is firm enough to pipe.

BUTTER GANACHE FORMULAS

PRODUCT/USE	CHOCOLATE VARIETY	RATIO OF CHOCOLATE TO CREAM	AMOUNT OF CHOCOLATE	AMOUNT OF BUTTER
Firm ganache for slabbed pralines and truffles	Dark couverture	2:1	35.3 oz/1000 g	17.6 oz/500 g
	Milk couverture	2.5:1	35.3 oz/1000 g	14.1 oz/400 g
	White couverture	2.5:1	35.3 oz/1000 g	14.1 oz/400 g
Medium ganache for piped pralines	Dark couverture	1.5:1	35.3 oz/1000 g	23.5 oz/667 g
	Milk couverture	2:1	35.3 oz/1000 g	17.6 oz/500 g
	White couverture	2:1	35.3 oz/1000 g	17.6 oz/500 g
Soft ganache for molded pralines	Dark couverture	1:1	35.3 oz/1000 g	35.3 oz/1000 g
	Milk couverture	1.5:1	35.3 oz/1000 g	23.5 oz/667 g
	White couverture	1.5:1	35.3 oz/1000 g	23.5 oz/667 g

If adding alcohol to the formula, in order to keep the same consistency listed in the table, add an extra 5.3 oz/150 g couverture and 3.5 oz/100 g alcohol.

–   Since they are close in temperature, the butter and chocolate mix very easily.
–   Once the chocolate and butter are blended, carefully add the liquor and create an emulsion.
–   For butter ganache pralines, pipe the set ganache onto chocolate discs.

Egg Ganache

Egg yolks contain lecithin, a natural emulsifier. In the past, egg yolks were added to fruit ganaches to bind the water content. However, as eating uncooked egg products raises health concerns, this type of ganache will not be featured in this text. Currently, invert sugar and apple pectin are used to replace the egg yolks in many fruit ganaches to help control water activity levels.

Additional Ingredients Used in Making Ganache

A variety of other ingredients can be used in producing ganache in order to adjust the flavor, texture, and shelf life.

Flavorings

There are unlimited possibilities for flavoring ganache. Some potential flavoring agents include herbs and flowers, spices, teas, coffees, fruit and vegetable purees, liquors and alcohols, sweeteners, flavor compounds and oils, and nuts and nut pastes. Guidelines for incorporating each of these flavor agents are provided below.

Herbs, Flowers, Spices, Coffees, Teas, and Fruit Peels

Infusing the cream or liquid with one or a combination of these ingredients is an easy way to maximize the flavor in ganache. The amount of flavoring agent and the time required for infusing will vary according to the ingredient and the desired effect. For example, vanilla beans can remain in the cooling cream for hours or even overnight. On the other hand, lavender will become overpowering and will leave a soapy flavor if used in too great a quantity or left to infuse for more than a few minutes. Teas also impart a bitter flavor when infused for longer than 10 to 15 minutes. Remember that the infused liquid should taste stronger than the desired final product, as its flavor will be softened by the addition of chocolate and other ingredients.

TO INFUSE CREAM OR OTHER LIQUIDS WITH A FLAVORING AGENT

1   Heat the cream or liquid just to a boil and remove from the heat.

2   Submerge the flavoring agent in the hot liquid.

3   Cover the pot with plastic wrap to trap the volatile oils. Allow the liquid to infuse for several minutes to several hours, depending on the flavoring agent and the desired result.

4   Strain the infused liquid and remeasure. Some of the liquid may have been absorbed by the flavoring ingredient and must be replaced to achieve the proper formula ratio. Add additional liquid as needed to obtain the original formula amount.

5   Reheat the liquid prior to adding it to the couverture.

Fruit and Vegetable Purees

Fruit and vegetable purees can be substituted for all or part of the cream in preparing ganache. As purees do not contain fats, butter is often added to the ganache formula when purees are used. As a general guideline, the amount of butter should equal 50 percent of the nonfat liquid. For example, if using 3.5 oz/100 g fruit puree, add 1.8 oz/50 g of butter to the formula. When the ganache has cooled to 97°F/37°C, mix in the butter using an immersion blender.

If using fruit or vegetable purees to replace cream entirely, the amount of chocolate in the formula may need to increase to compensate for the increase in water from the puree. The final texture of this ganache will be very firm and lack the characteristic creamy mouthfeel of more traditional ganaches.

Liqueurs and Alcohols

Liqueurs and other alcoholic beverages are popular ganache flavorings. When adding alcohol to a cream ganache formula, use 10 to 20 percent of the volume of cream. As these liquids increase the total water content in the ganache, butter can be added to increase the fat content, as described above for fruit and vegetable purees. The chocolate in the ganache formula may also need to be increased (see pages 111 and 112).

Sweeteners

In addition to their hygroscopic properties, sweeteners can impart flavor to ganache. Honey, maple syrup, and caramel are particularly popular choices. Each of these sugars may crystallize and alter the texture and mouthfeel from smooth to grainy as the ganache ages. To minimize this problem, use only liquid honey or maple syrup and prepare the caramel using the wet method to ensure that all sugar crystals are thoroughly dissolved. Caramel can be added to the cream at the beginning of the process, but if you boil honey, its flavor will be lost. For adding honey or maple syrup, boil the required amount of cream first, then remove it from the heat and add the additional sweetener. As a rule, the amount of added sweetener should not be more than 50 percent of the amount of cream.

Flavor Compounds and Oils

Flavor compounds and oils such as peppermint, orange, or lemon oil can be added after the ganache emulsion is established. The amount needed varies depending upon the strength of the flavoring and the desired flavor impact. As these products are concentrated, only small quantities will be necessary.

Nuts and Nut Pastes

All varieties of nuts and nut pastes can be used to flavor ganache. Toasted nuts can be used to infuse cream, or nuts can be chopped and added to the ganache once it has been fully blended for flavor and texture. Nut pastes provide more concentrated flavor and can be added after the chocolate and cream or butter are blended together. The amount of nut paste required will vary depending on the type of nut, the composition of the paste, and the desired flavor of the finished product.

Ingredients to Enhance Shelf Life of Cream Ganaches

How long cream ganache remains fresh without deterioration in flavor or the development of bacteria and mold depends on the composition of the ganache itself, proper preparation and finishing techniques, and proper packaging and storage. As a general rule of thumb, cream ganache-filled pralines can be kept at room temperature (68°F/20.0°C) for approximately two weeks.

The shelf life of cream ganache is largely determined by the water activity in the mixture. Water activity measurements (A_w) indicate how much water in a mixture is available as a medium for the growth of bacteria and microorganisms. Water activity is based upon a scale of 0 to 100, and lower water activity measures indicate a longer product shelf life.

A number of ingredients can be added to ganache to lower the water activity and improve shelf life. Sugar is hygroscopic, meaning that it helps retain moisture. Consequently, the addition of various forms of sugar helps lower water activity by binding water to the sugar and preventing it from becoming a breeding ground for bacteria and other hazardous organisms. Sucrose (granulated sugar) is not a good choice, as it crystallizes easily and can alter the texture of ganache. Corn syrup, glucose, and invert sugar all work well to maintain the smooth texture of ganache and increase the product's shelf life.

Corn syrup and glucose are added to the cream prior to heating to ensure that they fully dissolve and incorporate into the liquid. Invert sugar, however, should not be boiled with the cream, because boiling will cause it to lose its beneficial properties. It can be added later, when the cream is combined with the chocolate. As a general guideline, the amount of sugar added should equal 7 to 10 percent of the total weight of the ganache.

Other additives such as Sorbitol or potassium sorbate can be added at the beginning of the process to act as a preservative for improving the shelf life of cream ganache. Potassium sorbate is a convenient mold and fermentation inhibitor, formulated to help prevent mold growth from within. This water-based preservative is ideal for all candies and pralines. As a general guideline, use 0.1 percent of the total weight of the ganache. Adding more than 0.2 percent of the total weight of the ganache will affect the product's flavor and texture. For Sorbitol, you may add up to 5 to 7 percent of the ganache's total weight.

Basic Techniques for Using Ganache

Ganache can be used to make a wide variety of truffles and pralines, using the basic techniques below.

Piping Ganache for Hand-Rolled Truffles

Hand-rolled truffles can be finished in many ways. Finishing options include rolling the truffles in confectioners' sugar mixed with fruit powder and corn starch; in ground nuts such as pistachios or coconut; or in chocolate curls, as demonstrated here.

HAND-ROLLED TRUFFLES METHOD

1   Fill a pastry bag with a ½-in/10-mm round tip with ganache. Pipe the ganache into spheres. Try to pipe the ganache into as spherical a shape as possible, to minimize the manual rolling time. This will reduce the likelihood of melting the ganache with body heat.

2   Refrigerate the tray for 1 minute, then roll the ganache by hand if necessary to create nicely rounded balls. Let the ganache set until it becomes firm.

3   Coat the rounded ganache in a fine coating of tempered couverture, and let sit until the couverture is completely set.

4   Coat the truffles with a second coat of couverture, and immediately roll each truffle in chocolate curls or another topping before the couverture sets, so that the topping sticks to the surface. The truffles are coated twice in couverture before the topping is added in order to maintain a firm shape. If they were coated only once, rolling might cause the truffles to lose their round shape.

–   Pipe the ganache into spheres.
–   Give the truffles a second coating with the tempered couverture.
–   Immediately after the second coating, roll the truffles in couverture curls.

Truffles with Shells

For truffles with shells, it is best to use a soft ganache. See page 111 for the cream ganache formulas for softer ganache. The ganache for filling truffle shells should be cooled to 86°F/30.0°C for milk chocolate shells, 84°F/28.8°C for white chocolate shells, or 88°F/31.1°C for dark chocolate shells, because if the ganache is too warm, it will melt the shells.

TRUFFLES WITH SHELLS METHOD

1   Place a filling tray for truffles on top of the truffle shells. Ensure that the holes of the filling tray are aligned with the shell holes.

2   Using a disposable pastry bag with the end snipped off, pipe the ganache into the shells. Make sure to keep the pastry bag halfway into the shells while piping the ganache, and overfill the shells to ensure there are no air bubbles inside the truffles. Air bubbles will cause mold to form.

3   Immediately after filling the shells, scrape the excess ganache off the tray using as little movement as possible. Movement will create more crystals, making it difficult to pipe the ganache back into the shells.

4   Set the filled truffles aside to rest for a day at room temperature (68°F/20.0°C) to allow the ganache to fully crystallize.

5   Once the ganache has fully crystallized and reduced in size, use a slightly warmed capping tray and slightly overwarmed couverture to cap the truffles. Spread the couverture back and forth over the tray. (This will prevent the couverture from setting immediately.

FIRST ROW:
-   Pipe the ganache into shells.
-   Immediately after filling the shells, scrape the excess ganache into a bowl.
-   Rested, fully crystallized ganache, ready to be capped.

SECOND ROW:
-   Use a warmed capping tray and slightly overwarmed couverture to cap the truffles.
-   Dip the truffle in tempered couverture with a round dipping fork.
-   Place the finished truffles in a tray to hold and store.

Using overwarmed couverture will allow the caps to meld into the shells.) Roll the truffles on the cooling tray to fully meld the caps and shells and prevent the caps from tearing off of the truffles.

6   Using a round dipping fork, dip each truffle in tempered couverture and set aside on a cooling tray.

7   Once the couverture begins to set, roll the truffles quickly over a wire cooling rack to create spikes. Too much rolling will cause the couverture to overcrystallize and will turn the couverture spikes dull. It is nice to see some shiny empty space between the spikes.

8   Immediately place the truffles in an empty shell tray.

Slabbed Ganache

When making slabbed ganache, the recommended schedule for production should be spread out over 3 days, as follows:

DAY 1: Make all the ganache, cast or spread it in frames, and let the ganache fully crystallize overnight.
DAY 2: Cut the ganache and separate the pieces to allow the sides of each piece to dry, making it easier to handle the ganache while maintaining its shape.
DAY 3: Enrobe the ganache pieces and package.

In the slabbed technique, the ganache will be poured into a metal or acrylic frame. If two or more ganache layers will be used, an acrylic frame is preferred. Acrylic frames can be custom ordered in designs based on desired measurements and heights. When special ordering a frame, it is better to order two ¼-in /6-mm thick frames instead of one ½-inch/13 mm frame. This allows flexibility to have either two layered fillings or one thick layer. For the thicker filling, the two ¼-in/6-mm frames can be stacked on top of one another to create a ½-in/13-mm frame. Make sure that the frame measurements are small enough to allow the finished slab to be cut with a guitar. If the desired batch size is smaller than the entire frame, an extra divider, such as a vertical bar, can be cut to fit inside the frame and adjusted to partition the frame and make it smaller or narrower, as necessary.

SLABBED GANACHE METHOD

1   Moisten the surface of an acrylic base; a metal tray or the back of a sheet pan can also be used. Press an acetate transfer sheet onto the moist surface. Rub a dry towel or squeegee over the acetate sheet to secure it in place and remove any possible air bubbles.

2   Pour overtempered couverture (very warm, at 95° to 100°F/35.0° to 37.8°C) onto the acetate sheet. Overtempered couverture has a wild crystallization and does not set as fast as properly tempered couverture, allowing more time to spread it. Since the crystallization of the couverture is different, it will also be easier to cut with a guitar and will not crack.

3   Using an offset spatula, spread the couverture into a thin layer on the acetate sheet. This chocolate layer on the bottom of the slabbed ganache will allow ease of movement when working with the ganache. If the ganache were on the bottom, it would stick.

4   Place a frame on top of the spread couverture, and pour the ganache into the frame. Milk chocolate should not be warmer than 86°F/30.0°C; white chocolate should not be warmer than 84°F/28.9°C; and dark chocolate ganache should not be warmer than 88°F/31.1°C.

5   Use a ruler or a straight bar to evenly spread the ganache so that it is the same height as the frame. Let sit for 15 to 30 minutes, until it is tacky to the touch but not completely set.

6   Once the first layer of ganache has crystallized, place the second frame on top of the first frame and pour in the next layer of ganache.

7   Use a ruler or a straight bar to evenly spread the second layer of ganache so that it is the same height as the frame. Let sit until it has fully crystallized (normally for about 1 day).

8   Once the ganache has crystallized, use a nonserrated paring knife to cut around the inside of the frame, then release the frame from the ganache. If the ganache is still soft, place it in the freezer for 5 minutes, then release the frame.

9   Once the frame has been removed, place a sheet of parchment paper on top of the ganache and place another acrylic board on top of that. Then flip the two acrylic boards over.

10   Remove the first acrylic board and carefully peel back the acetate sheet. Place a metal tray on top of the couverture and flip it over again. Remove the second acrylic board and the parchment paper.

11   Slide the ganache slab off the metal tray onto the guitar base. If the slab is smaller than the guitar frame, it is better to place the slab closer to rear of the guitar wires than to the front, to avoid the possibility of compressing the slab against the front of the frame.

12   Press the guitar wires all the way down, cutting through the slab.

13   Slide the metal tray under the slab from the back and remove the slab from the guitar base. Lift the guitar wires up and clean or change them, depending on the desired shape.

14   Slide the cut slab back onto the guitar base from the tray, rotating the slab as necessary to cut the desired shape. Press the guitar wires down to cut through the slab again. Use the metal tray to remove the cut slab from the guitar base.

15   If the ganache is too soft to handle once it has been fully cut, place it in the freezer for a few minutes. Be careful not to leave the ganache in the freezer for too long, as condensation will form and the ganache will absorb moisture.

16   Separate the pieces of ganache and place on a parchment-lined tray, leaving room between each one so that a crust can form on all sides. Group the separated pieces in batches according to how they will be enrobed and decorated. Let them sit at room temperature for several hours to allow the crust to form. Once a crust has formed on the ganache, the pieces are ready to be enrobed, or they can be hand-dipped as shown on page 117.

FIRST ROW:
- Moisten the surface of the acrylic base and press the acetate sheet on the moist surface, then rub dry.
- Pour overtempered couverture onto the acetate.
- Place a frame on the spread couverture.

SECOND ROW:
- Use a ruler or straight bar to evenly spread the ganache into the frame.
- Once the first layer has set, place a second frame on top and pour the next layer of ganache.
- Release the frames around the ganache.

THIRD ROW:
- Remove the acrylic and carefully peel back the acetate sheet.
- Use a metal tray to slide the ganache onto the guitar.
- Separate the pieces, leaving room between each one so that a crust can form.

ENROBING

1   Place the ganache pieces onto the belt of the enrober in batches, leaving enough space between them for each piece to be fully enrobed.

2   Make sure there is a nice curtain of couverture flowing through the enrober and pass the ganache pieces through the machine.

3   Once the ganache pieces are enrobed, they will pass under a blower and a rotator, which will shake the pieces and remove excess couverture (to prevent feet).

4   As soon as the pieces are enrobed, decorate as desired using a transfer sheet (see Chapter 7), colored chocolate squares, or other decorations such as salt, gold leaf, nuts, or cocoa nibs.

–   Make sure there is a nice curtain of tempered couverture flowing to enrobe the pieces.
–   The enrobed candies pass under the blower and the rotator, moving them onto the belt.
–   If using colored chocolate squares to decorate the ganache pieces, place them on immediately after enrobing.

Troubleshooting Ganache

While the steps for creating ganache are simple, a variety of factors can prevent the proper formation of the emulsion. In addition to the fats in the cocoa butter, the percentage of nonfat solids and sugar in the chocolate and the properties of the liquid used, such as the percentage of milk solids and sugars in the cream, can all affect fat crystallization and alter the formation of ganache.

Separation

Separation is the most obvious problem in forming a strong emulsion. In a broken ganache, the fats do not remain suspended in the water and instead form separate layers in the chocolate mixture. The resultant mixture appears oily and grainy or curdled, rather than shiny and smooth. A partially broken ganache will have oily streaks on the top surface or oily areas around the edges, even though the chocolate mass may seem homogenous and blended.

The factors contributing to separation include:

HIGH FAT CONTENT

Couverture contains cocoa butter (fat) and nonfat cocoa solids, but the percentage of each varies depending on the manufacturer's formula. Cream and other liquids also have varying fat contents. When the fat content of the ganache is too high, the fat molecules are pressed close together in a small amount of water, forming larger molecules that cannot be held in suspension. These big molecules then break out of the emulsion and rise to the top.

TEMPERATURE VARIATIONS

The ideal temperature for mixing ganache is 90° to 110°F/32.2° to 43.3°C. Stirring the chocolate and cream builds the emulsion, but it also cools the mixture. If the mixture reaches a temperature between 74° to 85°F/23.3° to 29.4°C, the fats will not easily break into small enough molecules for suspension and will separate from the mixture.

How to Fix Broken Ganache

Once broken, a ganache will taste oily and unpleasant and will not achieve the desired degree of firmness. Consequently, steps must be taken to repair the mixture. There are several different procedures that will restore the emulsion:

1   If the temperature has fallen between 74° and 85°F/23.3° to 29.4°C, gently warm the ganache over steam or in the microwave, using short bursts of heat. Reheating the mixture to 90°F/32.2°C will melt the fats sufficiently to break them into small enough molecules for suspension. Once warm, stir the mixture in small circles starting in the center and expanding to the outer edges of the bowl as the emulsion forms.

2   If the step above does not work, rebuild the emulsion as follows:

- Heat a small amount (a few tablespoons) of cream to a simmer and pour into a clean bowl large enough to hold the entire batch of ganache.
- Drizzle in small amounts of the broken ganache while stirring constantly.
- Continue adding small amounts of broken ganache to the new mixture, stirring thoroughly between each addition, until all the broken ganache has been added.

Improper Crystallization

To achieve the desired texture, ganache must be carefully handled. Care must be taken to allow the cocoa butter crystals to form in a stable manner, similar to tempered chocolate. A ganache containing unstable fat crystals will be too soft and will have a gritty texture. If a ganache has not crystallized properly, there is nothing you can do to repair it.

Some chefs prefer to table ganache in the same way they table chocolate to temper it and ensure the formation of stable crystals. Follow these guidelines to ensure proper crystallization:

- Use tempered chocolate in either solid or melted form when creating ganache.
- Stir the mixture vigorously to promote formation of stable crystals.
- Monitor the temperature of the mixture when developing the emulsion. The ideal temperature is 90° to 110°F/32.2° to 43.3°C.
- Allow the ganache to set undisturbed at room temperature (ideally 68°F/20.0°C). Unnecessary motion can disrupt crystal formation as the mixture cools.

7
Decorating Techniques

When decorating chocolates, it is essential to use the correct techniques to create eye appeal. While decoration does not make a product taste better, it can be used to indicate to the consumer, through color and form, what is about to be experienced. However, there is a fine line in using décor on chocolate products—a good product can be ruined by over-decorating.

Creating Transfer Sheets

Transfer sheets are used to give chocolates a lively or dramatic look. They are versatile and have many decorative applications. They can be used with magnetic molds, on slabbed ganaches, on enrobed or molded candies, and to make showpiece components.

Getting Started

Equipment for creating transfer sheets, CLOCKWISE FROM BOTTOM LEFT: Paintbrushes, plastic comb, rubber comb, offset spatula, clear acetate, paint roller, wood grain comb, plastic comb, Exacto knife, Colour Shaper, metal comb, metal ruler.

To create your own transfer sheets, you will need a sheet of acetate, an acrylic base, tempered and colored cocoa butter or chocolate, and an offset spatula, as well as a variety of tools such as paint rollers, paintbrushes, and combs to achieve different designs.

STEP 1: Dampen the acrylic base.

Dampen the acrylic base with water or oil. Water is better, since it is easier to clean off. However, if preparing the base ahead of time, oil should be used, since the coat of oil will last, unlike water, which will evaporate over time.

An acrylic base is not required, but it is useful since it is transparent. Alternatives include the back of a new sheet pan or a metal tray.

STEP 2: Smooth the acetate on the acrylic base.

The acetate should adhere to the dampened base. Use a dry towel to rub the acetate sheet on the base and smooth out any bubbles.

STEP 3: Temper the colored cocoa butter or chocolate and place on Styrofoam.

Once the cocoa butter or chocolate is tempered, do not lay it directly on the marble slab, as its temperature will fall. Instead, place the cocoa butter on a warming plate or a piece of Styrofoam to regulate the temperature.

STEP 4: Create the desired design on the acetate sheet.

Spread, roll, or brush a thin layer of colored cocoa butter or chocolate on the acetate sheet and use one of the techniques outlined below to create the desired design.

STEP 5: Use the finished transfer sheet to decorate chocolates using any of the methods described below.

If the transfer sheet is not needed immediately, it can be stored for weeks at room temperature in a box protecting it from light.

- Moisten the acrylic base with water or oil.
- Rub the acetate on the acrylic base with a dry towel.
- To regulate temperature, place the tempered cocoa butter on top of Styrofoam.

Decorating Techniques

Transfer sheets can be decorated using a number of techniques to create a variety of unique and colorful chocolate designs.

Wood Grain Technique

Using an offset spatula, evenly spread a thin layer of tempered cocoa butter or chocolate on the acetate. Press a wood grain comb along the cocoa butter, rocking back and forth, to create a wood grain pattern. *(Below left)*

Chocolate Wave Technique

Using an offset spatula, evenly spread a thin layer of tempered cocoa butter or chocolate on the acetate. Press a textured comb in a side-to-side motion along the cocoa butter or chocolate to create a wave effect. *(Above right)*

Thin-Line Radio Wave Technique

Using an offset spatula, evenly spread a thin layer of tempered cocoa butter or chocolate on the acetate. Press a textured comb through the cocoa butter or chocolate, alternating pressing down on the left side, then the right, to create a radio wave effect. *(Below left)*

Paintbrush Technique

Using an offset spatula, evenly spread a thin layer of tempered cocoa butter or chocolate on the acetate. Use a wide paintbrush to brush along the layer of cocoa butter or chocolate. Stop brushing before the chocolate completely sets to avoid over crystallization. *(Above right)*

Roller Technique

Using an offset spatula, evenly spread a thin layer of tempered cocoa butter or chocolate on the acetate. Roll a paint roller along the layer of cocoa butter or chocolate. Stop rolling before the chocolate completely sets to avoid over crystallization. *(Below left)*

Spatula Wave Technique

Using an offset spatula, evenly spread a thin layer of tempered cocoa butter or chocolate on the acetate. Then press the offset spatula over the cocoa butter or chocolate, pressing down to the left and right in a waving motion. *(Above right)*

Spatula Smear Technique

Pour or pipe a thin stream of tempered dark chocolate or colored cocoa butter on the acetate, then pour or pipe a thin stream of tempered white chocolate or contrasting-colored cocoa butter on the acetate.

Before the chocolates crystallize, take an offset spatula and spread the chocolates along the acetate, creating a smeared effect. *(Below left)*

Spoon Splatter Technique

Using a spoon, splatter tempered cocoa butter in the desired colors on the acetate. *(Above right)*

Mars Decoration/Moonscape

Using a spoon, splatter cocoa butter in the desired colors on the acetate. Before the cocoa butter crystallizes, take an offset spatula and smear the cocoa butter along the acetate to blend the colors together. *(Below left)*

Lay another acetate sheet on top of the smeared cocoa butter and use a towel to evenly press down on the top acetate. Remove the top acetate sheet before the cocoa butter sets and set aside. Use the bottom sheet for transfer decoration. *(Below right)*

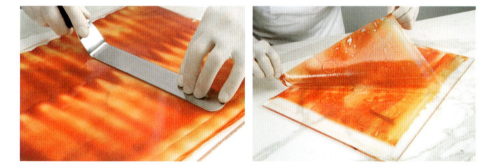

Splatter Spatula Technique

Using a spoon, splatter tempered cocoa butter in the desired colors on the acetate and then spread with an offset spatula. If this transfer sheet is to be finished with dark chocolate, spread a thin layer of white cocoa butter over the colored cocoa butters. This will enable the colors to show through once the dark chocolate is added. If desired, press down to the left and right with the spatula to make a wave design. *(Below left)*

Splatter Paintbrush Technique

Using a paintbrush, splatter tempered cocoa butter in the desired colors on the acetate, then spread with the brush. In order to create stripes, splatter a darker color over the first color and brush again with the paintbrush. *(Above right)*

TIP: To create a dark green stripe on a green base, use blue cocoa butter.

Silver/Gold Splatter and Spray Technique

Using a brush, splatter tempered silver and/or gold cocoa butter on the acetate. After the splattered cocoa butter has set, airbrush the first desired color over the splatters. Once that has set, spray on the next color. *(Below left)*

Swirling Technique

Using an airbrush, spray a thin layer of tempered cocoa butter on the acetate. Before it sets, use a Colour Shaper or the dull end of a skewer to create the desired design. *(Above right)*

After the first sprayed color has set, spray on the next color.

Using Transfer Sheets

Transfer sheets made with any of the techniques above can be used to decorate chocolate shapes, curls, plaques, and enrobed or molded chocolates. There are also many varieties of premade transfer sheets available on the market, including designs for holidays and for different seasons. It is also very common to have a logo or specific design made by companies for upcoming special events.

APPLYING TRANSFER SHEETS TO CHOCOLATE SHAPES AND PLAQUES

1   Place a transfer sheet print side up on the work surface. Spread a layer of tempered chocolate over the transfer sheet and let set.

2   Cut the chocolate into the desired shapes without cutting through the acetate sheet. For curls, place a piece of parchment paper on the chocolate, peel the acetate off the acrylic, and shape or roll the acetate parchment "sandwich" into the desired form. For plaques, place a piece of parchment paper on the chocolate and place another acrylic base on top to prevent the chocolate from curling up. See Chapter 11 for more information on creating cut-out shapes and curls.

3   Place the chocolate into the refrigerator for a few minutes to force crystallization.

4   Remove from the refrigerator and let it set at room temperature until needed. Do not remove the acetate from the chocolate until right before you use it. The acetate serves as a protective coating from dust and light. Chocolate should be stored with the acetate in a box completely protected from light.

APPLYING TRANSFER SHEETS TO ENROBED CONFECTIONS

1   Cut the transfer sheet into pieces slightly larger than the surface to which they will be applied. As soon as the praline has been enrobed, place a transfer sheet print side down on top of it. Use a dipping fork to gently press the transfer sheet down on the praline.

2   Once the chocolate enrobing has completely crystallized, carefully remove the transfer sheet. To guarantee a nice shine, do not remove the transfer sheet too soon. Let the sheet rest for at least an hour before removing. If the pralines are needed immediately, they can be refrigerated to expedite the crystallization process before removing the transfer sheet.

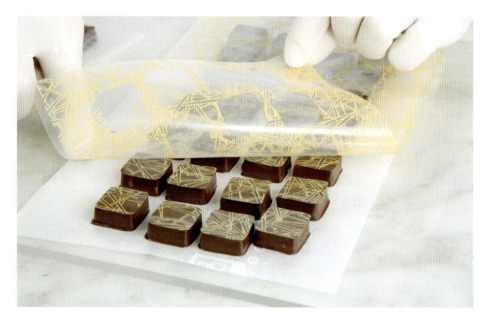

APPLYING TRANSFER SHEETS TO POLYCARBONATE MAGNETIC MOLDS

1   Place a transfer sheet on the steel sheet that goes between the bottom and side parts of the magnetic mold.

2   Cast, fill, and cap the mold as you would any other mold (see pages 138 to 141). A magnet will hold the mold together.

3   Carefully release the transfer sheet and unmold the chocolates. The design from the transfer sheet should appear on the surface.

Colored Shell-Molded Chocolates

Colored molded chocolate has become very trendy in the United States. It is an easy way to start out making visually different chocolates without requiring a large upfront investment. For people who are not in a position to afford an enrobing machine or don't have the hand skills or time to hand-dip chocolates, shell molding can be an ideal solution. Still, creating thin-shelled molded candies takes practice, and coloring molds requires a keen eye. If handled correctly, shell-molded chocolates will have a better sheen than dipped chocolates because of the smooth surface of the mold.

Using the techniques outlined below, it is easy to create your own unique colored mold designs for shell-molded chocolates.

Mold Preparation

In addition to correctly tempered chocolate, a completely clean mold is essential to ensure a shiny, smooth surface on your chocolate products. Chocolate molds are very delicate and should be handled with care. When not in use, they should be placed face down to avoid dust falling in the cavities.

Molds can be washed with hand-washing soap and warm water. When washing acrylic molds, the water temperature should be no hotter than 140°F/60.0°C. It is important to dry molds well, as dried-on water stains can leave lime marks that are difficult to remove and can mar the appearance of the chocolates. Metal molds should be rubbed out with chalk powder and absorbent cotton, then polished.

If using molds several times in a week, it is not necessary to wash the molds every day. Instead, leave the residual cocoa butter in the molds, as it will aid in creating a shiny surface on the chocolates.

If using new molds, there are a few ways to prepare the molds to yield shiny finished chocolates.

- Pipe tempered chocolate into the molds, let it set, then unmold. This will leave a thin film of cocoa butter in the molds.
- Spray a fine layer of a mixture of two parts chocolate and one part cocoa butter into the molds before casting the shells.
- Smear or spray colored cocoa butter in the molds before casting. This will create the same effect as the chocolate–cocoa butter mixture described above and will allow you to create decorative patterns on the finished molded chocolates (see Mold Decorating Techniques, page 135).

Room and Mold Temperature

When working with molds, the room temperature should be 68° to 72°F/20.0° to 22.2°C. The mold temperature could be a little warmer, approximately 80°F/26.7°C. The molds can be warmed slightly using a blow dryer or placed in a warming cabinet.

Cocoa Butter Temperature

The required temperature of the cocoa butter used to color molds depends on the technique to be used. To smear cocoa butter into molds, the cocoa butter must be slightly warmer, about 88°F/31.1°C, since there will be additional motion to accelerate the crystallization process. If using the airbrushing or splattering techniques, the opposite is true. Since the technique requires no additional motion, the cocoa butter needs to be slightly cooler, about 86°F/30.0°C.

Mold Decorating Techniques

Molds can be decorated with cocoa butter in a number of ways to create beautiful patterns and color combinations. Some of the most common decorating techniques include airbrushing, smearing or finger-painting, and splattering cocoa butter into the molds. These techniques can also be combined to create layers of color in a mold.

NOTE: In order to bring out the color of the decoration when casting with dark chocolate, spray white cocoa butter as the last layer before casting.

Airbrushing

The popularity of airbrushing has increased over the last several years. The method is much faster than finger-painting color into the molds. Obviously, airbrushing provides a more consistent look; however, it is nice to have a variety of effects using both the finger-painting and the airbrushing technique. For this reason, I do not recommend spending a lot of money on an airbrush.

1   Use an airbrush to spray the first color of cocoa butter into the molds. Let this color set completely.

2   Use the airbrush to spray in the second color. To create a pattern, use a piece of cardboard to cover half of each cavity while spraying the second color.

–   To achieve this effect, spray the mold with red cocoa butter and cast with milk chocolate.
–   To achieve this effect, spray the mold with yellow cocoa butter, then cover one half with cardboard and spray with red. Cast with white chocolate.
–   To achieve this effect, spray the mold with yellow and red cocoa butter and cast with white chocolate.

- To achieve this effect, spray the mold with yellow cocoa butter, then cover one half with cardboard and spray with red and white. Cast with dark chocolate.
- To achieve this effect, spray the mold with red cocoa butter, then cover one half with cardboard and spray with white. Cast with white chocolate.
- To achieve this effect, spray the mold with yellow, red, and white cocoa butter. Cast with milk chocolate.

Smearing or Finger-Painting

For a unique look, molds can be smeared or finger-painted with colored cocoa butter. To help your customers identify the content of the chocolates, it is a good idea to use colors that correspond to the flavors inside.

1   Wearing gloves, dip your finger into slightly warm cocoa butter and smear it into each cavity of the mold. Let the cocoa butter set completely.

2   Repeat using additional colors as desired.

- Use your finger to swirl colored cocoa butter into the mold cavities.
- To achieve this effect, swirl the mold with yellow cocoa butter first, then cover with red cocoa butter and cast with dark chocolate.
- To achieve this effect, smear the mold with yellow cocoa butter and cast with white chocolate.

Splattering

Splattering colored cocoa butter in molds creates a festive look in the finished chocolates.

1   Take a brush and dip it into colored cocoa butter. Splatter the cocoa butter into each cavity of the molds.

2   Scrape off any excess drops with a triangle scraper.

3   If desired, use an airbrush to spray on a second color.

FIRST ROW:
–   Use a paintbrush to splatter the mold cavities with colored cocoa butter.
–   To achieve this effect, splatter the mold with gold cocoa butter, then spray with red and cast with milk chocolate.

SECOND ROW:
–   To achieve this effect, splatter the mold with dark chocolate, then spray with red cocoa butter and cast with white chocolate.
–   To achieve this effect, splatter the mold with dark chocolate, then spray with green cocoa butter and cast with white chocolate.
–   To achieve this effect, splatter the mold with white cocoa butter, then spray with yellow and cast with white chocolate.

Using Decorated Molds

It takes time and practice to gain the hand skills for casting molds. Using a variety of types of chocolate with different setting points and different tempering methods can be a challenge. It can also be difficult to judge and accommodate important considerations like room temperature and humidity.

Once molds have been colored using the techniques described on pages 135 to 137 and the cocoa butter has set, the molds are ready to be cast, filled, capped, and finally unmolded.

Casting

Make sure the cocoa butter used to color the mold has fully set. If it has not set, the chocolate used for casting will smear the design.

1   Grip the bar under the frame of the mold to avoid warming the cavities with your body heat. Hold the mold at an angle over the bowl of chocolate, and use a ladle to pour tempered chocolate into the cavities of the mold. Pouring the chocolate in lines into each row of cavities, rather than over the entire mold, will help facilitate the cleanup process.

2   Use an offset spatula to scrape off excess chocolate from the top of the mold, and use a triangle spatula to remove excess chocolate from the sides.

3   Let the molds sit in order to create a thin shell of chocolate. The amount of time to let the cast molds sit depends on the fluidity of the chocolate. If the chocolate is very fluid, it can sit for a couple of minutes before the excess chocolate should be poured out. If the chocolate is thicker, it should not sit very long, and sometimes should even be poured out immediately after casting. The excess chocolate must be poured out before the chocolate begins to crystallize on the edges of the cavities.

4   Once the molds have sat long enough, pour out the excess chocolate to leave a thin shell in each cavity. Use the wooden handle of a spatula to tap the mold to assist in removing the excess chocolate. Be careful not to use metal to tap on the molds, as metal could damage them.

5   Use a triangle spatula to clean the molds by removing any excess chocolate from the top and sides.

6   Place the molds face down on a cooling rack or on a piece of parchment paper or newsprint, and let sit just until the chocolate starts to crystallize.

7   As soon as the chocolate has begun to crystallize, lift up the molds and use a triangle spatula to scrape off any excess chocolate that may have poured out while the molds were face down.

8   If making chocolates with nuts, the nuts should be added at this point, before the shells have fully set and before the molds are refrigerated. Place the nut pieces in the shells and seal the nuts by piping chocolate over them, which will keep them crunchy. Add the chocolate over the nuts right away to avoid cracking the shells. If it is added too late, the cast shells may crack because the chocolate piped over the nuts will contract.

The piped chocolate will not only seal the nuts but also secure them in place so that they do not move around during the filling and capping process.

9   Place the molds in the refrigerator for a few minutes to accelerate the crystallization process. Take the molds out of the refrigerator before the molds release the shells completely. Otherwise, you may have difficulty filling the shells as they might release when piping.

FIRST ROW:
- Hold the decorated and cleaned mold at a tilt and ladle chocolate into the cavities.
- Use an offset spatula to scrape off excess chocolate.
- Once the chocolate starts to crystallize, pour out the excess.

SECOND ROW:
- Lift up the mold from the paper.
- Use a triangle spatula to scrape off any excess chocolate.
- Refrigerate the molds to quicken the crystallization process.

Preventing a lip

There are a few techniques that can be used to help prevent the formation of a lip on the chocolates:

-   If you are not experienced in working with molds, it is best to use a cooling rack instead of parchment paper to rest the filled molds, face down, to allow the excess chocolate to pour out during the casting process.

-   After tapping and cleaning the mold but before placing it face down, flip the mold over and tap twice on the side of the mold so that the chocolate starts to run back inside toward the center of the mold. Then place the mold face down on the paper or cooling rack.

-   If it seems that a lip has begun to form on the paper, release the molds from the paper before the chocolate has crystallized. This will cause the excess chocolate to break off the mold and stick to the paper.

Filling

Ganache used for filling shell-molded chocolates must be between 86° and 88°F/30.0° and 31.1°C. If the ganache is too warm, it can melt the shells.

1   Fill a disposable pastry bag with the desired type of ganache. Cut a small opening in the bag. If the opening is too big, the ganache may be dragged from one cavity to the next, making it impossible to cleanly cap the molds.

2   Pipe the ganache into each cavity of the mold. Do not fill the cavities all the way to the top. Leave ⅛ in/2 mm at the top for capping the mold. If the ganache is too firm, you may get a pointy tip coming out of each mold cavity. To fix this, dip your finger in a glass of alcohol such as Kirschwasser, rum, or vodka and press down to flatten the tips. If any of the cavities are overfilled, a pipette can be used to extract the excess ganache.

3   Let the filled molds sit at room temperature for several hours until the ganache has fully crystallized. The ganache may contract a little. It is important to let the ganache fully crystallize, because if it is capped too soon, the bottom will not stay flat and it will cave in.

TIP: If the ganache is runny, use an airbrush to spray a thin layer of chocolate over the fillings to hold the ganache in place. Let the chocolate completely set before starting the capping process.

Capping and Unmolding

Once the shells have been filled to the appropriate level and the ganache has fully crystallized, the chocolates are ready to be capped.

1   Tilt the mold over the chocolate bowl, in the same fashion as when casting, and pour a small quantity of chocolate over the cavities.

2   Use an offset spatula to remove the excess chocolate from the top of the molds. If the ganache is still runny, it is necessary to use the offset spatula solely in an upward direction to hold the ganache in place. Rotate the mold to maintain the upward stroke. If a downward stroke is used, the ganache will slip out.

3   Once the molds are clean, place in the refrigerator for 3 to 5 minutes to accelerate the crystallization process. The molds should be removed from the refrigerator as soon as the chocolate releases from the mold. If the molds are left in the refrigerator for too long, condensation will form on the chocolate. If this occurs, remove the molds from the refrigerator and let the chocolates sit in the molds at room temperature until they warm up, then release from the molds. This will salvage the shiny look of the chocolates.

4   When the chocolates are fully set, tap the molds on the table to release the chocolates from the molds.

–   Once the ganache is completely set, cover the cavities with a small amount of chocolate.
–   Tap the mold on the table to release the chocolates.

8

Chocolate Praline Recipes

Using the techniques and basic recipes outlined in the previous chapters, it is possible to create a wide range of recipes, including gianduja and marzipan pralines, truffles, and molded and slabbed pralines in different colors, shapes, and flavors.

Gianduja and Marzipan Pralines

Almond Rosette Pralines

INGREDIENTS	METRIC	US	VOLUME
Gianduja Base (page 93)	1000 g	35.3 oz	4½ cups
Chocolate Discs (page 62)	190 g	6.7 oz	125 ea
Caramelized Almonds (page 67 or 68)	150 g	5.3 oz	125 ea
YIELD: 125 PRALINES	**1340 g**	**47.3 oz**	

1 Using an open star tip, pipe a gianduja rosette onto each chocolate disc.

2 Finish the candies by adding an almond on top of each.

3 Store in an airtight container at 57° to 61°F/13.9° to 16.1°C in a dark, dry place.

- Once the gianduja starts to crystallize, pipe onto a plain chocolate disc.
- Immediately place a caramelized almond on the praline.

AT RIGHT:
- Finished Almond Rosette Pralines and Hidden Hazelnut Pralines, page 146.

Hidden Hazelnut Pralines

INGREDIENTS	METRIC	US	VOLUME
Sandy Hazelnuts (see page 64)	150 g	5.3 oz	125 ea
Chocolate Discs (page 62)	120 g	4.2 oz	125 ea
Dark couverture, 63%, melted	25 g	0.9 oz	2 tbsp
Gianduja Base (page 93)	1000 g	35.3 oz	4½ cups
Gold leaf	as needed	as needed	as needed
YIELD: 125 PRALINES	**1295 g**	**45.7 oz**	

1   Secure 1 hazelnut onto each chocolate disc with a dot of couverture to hold it in place. Let set.

2   Using an open star tip, pipe a rosette of gianduja over each hazelnut.

3   Finish the candies by placing a small piece of gold leaf on the top of each. Let the gianduja set completely.

4   Store in an airtight container at 57° to 61°F/13.9° to 16.1°C in a dark, dry place.

–   Pipe the gianduja over the caramelized hazelnut on the disc.
–   Place a piece of gold leaf onto the piped rosette.

Duchess

INGREDIENTS	METRIC	US	VOLUME
Pistachios	60 g	2.1 oz	½ cup
Sliced almonds	80 g	2.8 oz	1 cup
Gianduja Base (page 93)	500 g	17.6 oz	2 cups
Milk couverture, 37%, tempered	200 g	7.1 oz	1 cup
Dark couverture, 63%, tempered	200 g	7.1 oz	1 cup
Candied orange peel, diced	200 g	7.1 oz	1¼ cups
Milk couverture, 37%, tempered, for precoating	52 g	1.8 oz	¼ cup
Milk couverture, 37%, tempered, for dipping	250 g	8.8 oz	1¼ cups
Dark couverture, 63%, tempered, for decoration (optional)	as needed	as needed	as needed
YIELD: 160 PIECES	**1542 g**	**54.4 oz**	

1   Cover an acrylic base with parchment paper or an acetate sheet and create an 8 × 14 in/200 × 356 mm rectangle using ½-in/13-mm metal bars.

2   Preheat oven to 340°F/171.1°C. Spread the pistachios and almonds on a baking sheet and roast for 5 minutes. Let cool.

3   Combine the tempered milk and dark couverture and the gianduja in a bowl and mix to incorporate well.

4   The mixture should be thick yet pourable. If it is too warm and runny, pour onto a marble and temper until it reaches the correct consistency.

5   Add the nuts and orange peel to the gianduja mixture and mix gently.

6   Using a triangle spatula, spread the mixture into the rectangle between the metal bars. Place a piece of parchment paper or a Silpat on top of the gianduja and use a rolling pin to roll the mass into the corners. Let set at room temperature until firm.

7   Remove the bars. Precoat the slab with a thin layer of tempered milk couverture.

8   Once the couverture has set, flip the slab over and use a knife to mark guidelines along the 14-in/36-mm side at 1 in/25 mm intervals. Using the lines as a guide, cut the candy into 8-in/20-mm bars.

9   Using a dipping fork, dip each bar into the milk couverture and place on a cooling rack.

10   Level off any excess couverture with an offset spatula, and tap the cooling rack so the excess runs down the sides of the bar.
Continued on page 148.

Continued on page 148.

11 While the couverture is wet, use a knife to mark the tops of the bars with diagonal lines or pipe decorative designs on top with dark couverture. Before the couverture completely sets, trim the ends of the bars to expose the gianduja mixture. Cut the bars into ¾-in/20-mm pieces. Let the couverture set completely.

12 Store in an airtight container at 57° to 61°F/13.9° to 16.1°C in a dark, dry place.

FIRST ROW:
- Spread the gianduja mixture between metal bars and let crystallize.
- Remove the metal bars and evenly spread a layer of couverture on top.
- Cut into bars.

SECOND ROW:
- Dip each bar in tempered milk couverture.
- Place the bars on a cooling rack and level off any excess couverture.
- Decorate the bars with either a knife or piped tempered couverture.

VARIATIONS

Sweet and Silky Duchess

Omit the dark couverture and increase the quantity of tempered milk couverture to 450 g/15.9 oz/1⅔ cups.

Opulent Duchess

Omit the tempered milk couverture and increase the quantity of dark couverture to 350 g/12.3 oz/1¼ cups.

Branches

INGREDIENTS	METRIC	US	VOLUME
Skinned almonds, coarsely ground	85 g	3.0 oz	⅔ cup
Kirschwasser or similar alcohol	as needed	as needed	as needed
Confectioners' sugar	15 g	0.5 oz	2 tbsp
Caramelized Gianduja (page 95)	15 g	17.6 oz	2 cups
Dark couverture, 63%, tempered	15 g	6.0 oz	¾ cup
YIELD: 85 PIECES	**130 g**	**27.1 oz**	

1 Preheat oven to 340°F/171.1°C. Moisten the almonds with the Kirsch and mix well. Add the confectioner's sugar and mix to cover the almonds. Spread the almond mixture on a baking sheet and roast until golden brown, about 4 minutes. Remove from oven and stir to break up clumps. Let cool.

2 In a bowl, combine the gianduja and the almond mixture.

3 Using ½-in/13-mm round tip, pipe logs the length of a parchment paper–lined sheet pan.

4 Let set overnight at room temperature or place in a cooler until firm.

5 Cut into 1¼-in/32-mm pieces.

6 Using a dipping fork, dip the candies in the dark couverture, place on a tray, and let set at room temperature.

7 Store in an airtight container at 57° to 61°F/13.9° to 16.1°C in a dark, dry place.

– Pipe the gianduja mixture onto parchment paper and let sit overnight.
– Once completely crystallized, cut into 1¼-in/32-mm pieces.
– Dip into dark couverture with a three-pronged dipping fork.

Honey Nougat

INGREDIENTS	METRIC	US	VOLUME
Sliced almonds	75 g	2.6 oz	½ cup
Heavy cream	150 g	5.3 oz	⅔ cup
Honey	150 g	5.3 oz	¾ cup
Glucose	15 g	0.5 oz	¾ tbsp
Gianduja Praline Base (page 103)	500 g	17.6 oz	3½ cups
Milk couverture, 37%, tempered, for dipping	200 g	7.1 oz	1 cup
YIELD: 100–110 PIECES	**1090 g**	**38.4 oz**	

1 Preheat oven to 340°F/171.1°C. Spread the almonds on a baking sheet and roast for 5 minutes.

2 Combine the cream, honey, and glucose and cook to 248°F/120°C.

3 When the honey mixture reaches the proper temperature, stir in the almonds.

4 Using an offset spatula, spread the nougat on parchment paper into a 6½ × 10 in/ 165 × 250 mm rectangle. Let cool to room temperature.

5 Cut into ¾-in/15-mm wide strips.

6 If necessary, place the gianduja in the oven to warm it to a piping consistency.

7 Using a 9/16-in/14-mm round piping tip, pipe the gianduja down the length of the nougat strip.

8 Cut each strip into 1 in/25 mm segments.

9 Using a dipping fork, dip each piece into the milk couverture. Let set at room temperature.

10 Store in an airtight container at 57° to 61°F/13.9° to 16.1°C in a dark, dry place.

Marzipan Pralines

INGREDIENTS	METRIC	US	VOLUME
French, German, or Quick Marzipan (pages 101, 103, and 105)	300 g	10.6 oz	1 cup
Dark couverture, 63%, tempered, for dipping	60 g	2.1 oz	¼ cup
Dark couverture, 63%, tempered, for piping	20 g	0.7 oz	2 tbsp
Sliced almonds, toasted	30 g	1.1 oz	⅓ cup
YIELD: 30 PRALINES	**410 g**	**14.5 oz**	

1 Roll the marzipan into a rectangle 3⅛ × 7½ in/80 mm × 190 mm, ½ in/12.7 mm thick.

2 Using a caramel cutter or a ruler and a knife, score the marzipan into pieces ⅝ × 1¼ in/15 × 30 mm.

3 Using the scored lines as a guide, cut the marzipan into rectangles.

4 Dip each piece of marzipan into the tempered couverture only far enough to cover the sides with couverture. Be careful to avoid covering the top surface with couverture.

5 Place each dipped praline on parchment paper.

6 Using a pastry bag, pipe a dot of dark couverture onto each piece and top each with a toasted almond slice or other garnish as desired.

7 Let the chocolates set at room temperature. Store in an airtight bag in a cool, dark place.

– Mark the marzipan with a caramel cutter.
– Cut the marked marzipan into pieces.
– Dip each piece in the tempered dark couverture, keeping the top level so it does not get covered with couverture.

Truffles

Cream Truffles

INGREDIENTS	METRIC	US	VOLUME
Heavy cream	250 g	8.8 oz	1 cup
Glucose	25 g	0.9 oz	1 tbsp + 1 tsp
Milk couverture, 37%, chopped or coins	375 g	13.2 oz	2½ cups
Unsalted butter, softened	50 g	1.8 oz	3 tbsp + 1 tsp
Milk chocolate truffle shells	250 g	8.8 oz	87 ea
Milk couverture, 37%, tempered, for capping and dipping	260 g	9.2 oz	1¼ cups
YIELD: 87 TRUFFLES	**1210 g**	**42.7 oz**	

1. In a medium pot, combine the cream and glucose and bring to a boil over medium heat.

2. Pour the hot cream mixture over the chopped couverture and set aside undisturbed for 1 minute.

3. Using a spatula, stir in small circles at first, then gradually in wider circles to form a ganache.

4. Cool the mixture to 90°F/32.2°C. Blend in the butter using an immersion blender.

5. Cover with plastic wrap and let cool to 86°F/30°C.

6. When the mixture reaches the proper temperature, place in a pastry bag with a small hole cut in the tip and pipe into the shells. Let set overnight at room temperature.

7. Cap the truffles with the milk couverture once the ganache has completely set.

8. Use a dipping fork to dip the truffles in the milk couverture.

9. Before the couverture sets, place the truffles on a cooling rack and roll in a Z motion, using a dipping fork, to create spikes. Let set at room temperature.

10. Store in an airtight container at 57° to 61°F/13.9° to 16.1°C in a dark, dry place.

Dark Chocolate Truffles

INGREDIENTS	METRIC	US	VOLUME
Heavy cream	250 g	8.8 oz	1 cup
Glucose	30 g	1.1 oz	1½ tbsp
Dark couverture, 63%, chopped or coins	250 g	8.8 oz	1¾ cups
Unsalted butter, softened	50 g	1.8 oz	3 tbsp + 1 tsp
Dark chocolate truffle shells	196 g	6.9 oz	96 ea
Dark couverture, 63%, tempered, for capping and dipping	216 g	7.6 oz	2 cups
YIELD: 96 TRUFFLES	**992 g**	**35.0 oz**	

1. In a medium pot, combine the cream and glucose and bring to a boil over medium heat.

2. Pour the hot cream mixture over the chopped couverture and set aside undisturbed for 1 minute.

3. Using a spatula, stir in small circles at first, then gradually in wider circles to form a ganache.

4. Cool the mixture to 90°F/32.2°C. Blend in the butter using an immersion blender.

5. Cover with plastic wrap and let cool to 88°F/31.1°C.

6. When the mixture reaches the proper temperature, place in a pastry bag with a small hole cut in the tip and pipe into the shells. Let set overnight at room temperature.

7. Cap the truffles with the dark couverture once the ganache has completely set.

8. Use a dipping fork to dip the truffles in the dark couverture.

9. Before the couverture sets, place the truffles on a cooling rack and roll in a Z motion, using a dipping fork, to create spikes. Let set at room temperature.

10. Store in an airtight container at 57° to 61°F/13.9° to 16.1°C in a dark, dry place.

White Chocolate Truffles

INGREDIENTS	METRIC	US	VOLUME
Heavy cream	250 g	8.8 oz	1 cup
Glucose	25 g	0.9 oz	1 tbsp + 1 tsp
White couverture, chopped or coins	375 g	13.2 oz	2½ cups
Kirschwasser	20 g	0.7 oz	1 tbsp + 1 tsp
Unsalted butter, softened	50 g	1.8 oz	3 tbsp + 1 tsp
White chocolate truffle shells	252 g	8.9 oz	90 ea
White couverture, tempered, for capping and dipping	270 g	9.5 oz	1¾ cups
YIELD: 90 TRUFFLES	**1242 g**	**43.8 oz**	

1   In a medium pot, combine the cream and glucose and bring to a boil over medium heat.

2   Pour the hot cream mixture over the chopped couverture and set aside undisturbed for 1 minute.

3   Using a spatula, stir in small circles at first, then gradually in wider circles to form a ganache.

4   Cool the mixture to 92°F/33.3°C. Fold in the Kirsch. Blend in the butter using an immersion blender.

5   Cover with plastic wrap and let cool to 86°F/30.0°C.

6   When the mixture reaches the proper temperature, place in a pastry bag with a small hole cut in the tip and pipe into the shells. Let set overnight at room temperature.

7   Cap the truffles with the white couverture once the ganache has completely set.

8   Use a dipping fork to dip the truffles in the white couverture.

9   Before the couverture sets, place the truffles on a cooling rack and roll in a Z motion, using a dipping fork, to create spikes. Let set at room temperature.

10 Store in an airtight container at 57° to 61°F/13.9° to 16.1°C in a dark, dry place.

Caramel Truffles

INGREDIENTS	METRIC	US	VOLUME
Sugar	150 g	5.3 oz	2¼ cups
Honey	30 g	1.1 oz	3 tbsp
Heavy cream	270 g	9.5 oz	2 cups
Vanilla bean	5 g	0.2 oz	1 ea
Milk couverture, 37%, chopped or coins	210 g	7.4 oz	2½ cups
Dark couverture, 63%, chopped or coins	150 g	5.3 oz	1¾ cups
Unsalted butter, softened	42 g	1.5 oz	5 tbsp
Milk chocolate truffle shells	300 g	10.6 oz	106 ea
Milk couverture, 37%, tempered, for dipping and capping	215 g	7.6 oz	1¾ cups
Cocoa powder or ground hazelnuts, for garnishing	102 g	3.6 oz	2 cups
YIELD: 106 TRUFFLES	**1474 g**	**52.1 oz**	

1   Warm the sugar in the oven at 400°F/204.4°C.

2   In a pot over medium heat, warm the honey and melt the sugar in small batches until it turns medium amber.

3   Place the cream in a separate pot. Split the vanilla bean, scrape out the seeds, and add the pod and seeds to the cream. Bring to a boil over medium heat.

4   Slowly strain the cream into the caramelized sugar and stir to combine.

5   Combine the chopped milk and dark couverture. Pour the hot caramel mixture over the couverture, and set aside undisturbed for 1 minute.

6   Using a spatula, stir in small circles at first, then gradually in wider circles to form a ganache.

7   Cool the mixture to 90°F/32.2°C. Blend in the butter using an immersion blender to create a smooth, shiny ganache.

8   Cover with plastic wrap and let cool to 86°F/30.0°C.

9   When the mixture reaches the proper temperature, place in a pastry bag with a small hole cut in the tip and pipe into the shells. Let set overnight at room temperature.

10   Cap the truffles with the milk couverture once the ganache has completely set.

11   Coat the truffles in the milk couverture by hand.

12   Before the couverture sets, roll the truffles in cocoa powder or ground hazelnuts. Let set at room temperature.

13   Store in an airtight container at 57° to 61°F/13.9° to 16.1°C in a dark, dry place.

Lemongrass Truffles

INGREDIENTS	METRIC	US	VOLUME
Heavy cream	200.0 g, plus additional as needed	7.1 oz, plus additional as needed	⅔ cup + 2 tbsp, plus additional as needed
Lemongrass, chopped	150.0 g	5.3 oz	1½ cups
Invert sugar	40.0 g	1.4 oz	1½ cups
White couverture, chopped or coins	300.0 g	10.6 oz	2 cups
Unsalted butter, softened	50.0 g	1.8 oz	3 tbsp + 1 tsp
Cocoa butter, melted	30.0 g	1.1 oz	¼ cup
White chocolate truffle shells	252.0 g	8.9 oz	90 ea
White couverture, tempered, for capping and dipping	180.0 g	6.3 oz	2¾ cups
Finishing Powder (recipe follows)	252.5 g	8.9 oz	1⅔ cup
YIELD: 90 TRUFFLES	**1454.5 g**	**51.4 oz**	

1   In a medium pot, combine the cream and lemongrass and bring to a boil over medium heat.

2   Once the cream has come to a boil, remove from the heat and immediately cover with plastic wrap.

3   Let steep for 10 minutes, then strain to remove the lemongrass.

4   Add additional cream as needed to return the quantity to 7.1 oz/200 g.

5   Return the cream to the heat and return to a boil.

6   Combine the invert sugar and chopped couverture. Pour the hot cream mixture over the couverture mixture, and set aside undisturbed for 1 minute.

7   Using a spatula, stir in small circles at first, then gradually in wider circles to form a ganache.

8   Cool the mixture to 90°F/32°C. Blend in the butter and melted cocoa butter with an immersion blender to create a smooth, shiny ganache.

9   Cover with plastic wrap and let cool to 86°F/30°C.

10 When the mixture reaches the proper temperature, place in a pastry bag with a small hole cut in the tip and pipe into the shells. Let set overnight at room temperature.

11 Cap the truffles with the white couverture once the ganache has completely set.

12 Coat the truffles in the white couverture by hand.

13 Before the couverture sets, roll the truffles in the Finishing Powder for a surprise mouthfeel. Let set at room temperature.

14 Store in an airtight container at 57° to 61°F/13.9° to 16.1°C in a dark, dry place.

Finishing Powder

INGREDIENTS	METRIC	US	VOLUME
Confectioners' sugar	200.0 g	7.1 oz	1⅓ cups
Citric acid	2.5 g	0.1 oz	¼ tsp
Cornstarch	50.0 g	1.8 oz	⅓ cup
YIELD	**252.5 g**	**9.0 oz**	**1⅔ cups**

Sift all the ingredients together to combine.

NOTE: You will have excess finishing powder after rolling the truffles. You may store the excess powder in an airtight container at room temperature (68°F/20°C).

Pistachio Truffles

INGREDIENTS	METRIC	US	VOLUME
Heavy cream	225 g	7.9 oz	1 cup
Salt	2 g	0.1 oz	¼ tsp
Glucose	30 g	1.1 oz	1½ tbsp
Invert sugar	30 g	1.1 oz	1 tbsp
Pistachio paste	125 g	4.4 oz	½ cup
White couverture, chopped or coins	250 g	8.8 oz	1¾ cups
Unsalted butter, softened	45 g	1.6 oz	3 tbsp
Cocoa butter, melted	50 g	1.8 oz	⅓ cup + 1 tbsp
White chocolate truffle shells	260 g	9.2 oz	94 ea
Dark couverture, 63%, tempered, for capping and coating	200 g	7.1 oz	2 cups
Ground pistachios, for garnishing	90 g	3.2 oz	⅔ cup
YIELD: 94 TRUFFLES	**1307 g**	**46.3 oz**	

1 In a medium pot, combine the cream, salt, and glucose and bring to a boil over medium heat.

2 Combine the invert sugar, pistachio paste, and chopped couverture. Pour the hot cream over the mixture and set aside undisturbed for 1 minute.

3 Using a spatula, stir in small circles at first, then gradually in wider circles to form a smooth, shiny ganache.

4 Cool to 90°F/32.2°C.

5 Blend in the butter and cocoa butter using an immersion blender. Cover with plastic wrap and let cool to 84°F/28.9°C.

6 When the mixture reaches the proper temperature, place in a pastry bag with a small hole cut in the tip and pipe into the shells. Let set overnight at room temperature.

7 Cap the truffles with the dark couverture once the ganache has completely set.

8 Coat the truffles in dark couverture by hand.

9 Before the couverture sets, roll the truffles in the ground pistachios to coat. Let set at room temperature.

10 Store in an airtight container at 57° to 61°F/13.9° to 16.1°C in a dark, dry place.

Raspberry Truffles

INGREDIENTS	METRIC	US	VOLUME
Heavy cream	200 g	7.1 oz	⅔ cup + 2 tbsp
Confectioners' sugar	40 g	1.4 oz	⅓ cup
Raspberry puree	260 g	9.2 oz	½ tbsp
Invert sugar	55 g	1.9 oz	1 tbsp + 1 tsp
Milk couverture, 37%, chopped or coins	230 g	8.1 oz	1½ cups
Dark couverture, 63%, chopped or coins	230 g	8.1 oz	1½ cups
Lemon juice	6 g	0.2 oz	1 tsp
Unsalted butter, softened	90 g	3.2 oz	7 tbsp
Dark chocolate truffle shells	350 g	12.3 oz	124 ea
Dark couverture, 63%, tempered, for capping and dipping	250 g	8.8 oz	1 cup
Raspberry Finishing Powder (recipe follows)	300 g	10.6 oz	2 cups + 1 tbsp
YIELD: 125 TRUFFLES	**2011 g**	**70.9 oz**	

1   In a medium pot, combine the cream, confectioners' sugar, and raspberry puree and bring to a boil over medium heat.

2   Combine the milk and dark couverture and the invert sugar. Pour the hot cream mixture over the couverture mixture, and set aside undisturbed for 1 minute.

3   Using a spatula, stir in small circles at first, then gradually in wider circles to form a ganache.

4   Cool the mixture to 94°F/34.5°C. Blend in the lemon juice and butter using an immersion blender.

5   Cover with plastic wrap and let cool to 88°F/31.1°C.

6   When the mixture reaches the proper temperature, place in a pastry bag with a small hole cut in the tip and pipe into the shells. Let set overnight at room temperature.

7   Cap the truffles with the dark couverture once the ganache has completely set.

8   Coat the truffles in the dark couverture by hand.

9   Before the couverture sets, roll the truffles in the Raspberry Finishing Powder. Let set at room temperature.

10   Store in an airtight container at 57° to 61°F/13.9° to 16.1°C in a dark, dry place.

Raspberry Finishing Powder

INGREDIENTS	METRIC	US	VOLUME
Confectioners' sugar	200 g	7.1 oz	1⅓ cups
Raspberry powder	50 g	1.8 oz	⅓ cup + ½ tbsp
Cornstarch	50 g	1.8 oz	⅓ cup + ½ tbsp
YIELD	300 g	10.7 oz	2 cups + 1 tbsp

Sift all the ingredients together to prevent lumping.

NOTE: You will have excess Raspberry Finishing Powder after rolling the truffles. You may store the excess powder in an airtight container at room temperature (68°F/20.0°C) for future use.

Strawberry-Mint Truffles

INGREDIENTS	METRIC	US	VOLUME
Heavy cream	200 g, plus additional as needed	7.1 oz, plus additional as needed	⅔ cup + 2 tbsp, plus additional as needed
Mint leaves	8 g	0.3 oz	½ tsp
Raspberry puree	50 g	1.8 oz	2½ tbsp
Strawberry puree	200 g	7.1 oz	⅔ cup
Glucose	30 g	1.1 oz	1½ tbsp
Confectioners' sugar	50 g	1.8 oz	½ cup
Pectin	6 g	0.2 oz	½ tbsp
Lemon juice	20 g	0.7 oz	1 tbsp + 1 tsp
Citric acid	2 g	0.1 oz	½ tsp
White couverture, chopped or coins	300 g	10.6 oz	2¼ cups
Unsalted butter, softened	30 g	1.1 oz	2 tbsp
Cocoa butter, melted	25 g	0.9 oz	2½ tbsp
Milk chocolate truffle shells	300 g	10.6 oz	108 ea
Milk couverture, 37%, tempered, for capping and dipping	200 g	7.1 oz	1 cup
Strawberry Finishing Powder (recipe follows)	300 g	10.6 oz	2 cups + 1 tbsp
YIELD: 108 TRUFFLES	**1721 g**	**61.1 oz**	

1   In a medium pot, combine the cream, and mint leaves and bring to a boil over medium heat.

2   Once the cream has come to a boil, remove from the heat and immediately cover it with plastic wrap.

3   Let steep for 10 minutes, then strain to remove the mint leaves.

4   Add additional cream, if necessary, to return the total quantity to 7.1 oz/200 g. Add the raspberry puree, strawberry puree, and glucose. Mix the confectioner's sugar and pectin together and add to the cream mixture.

5   Whisk in the lemon juice and citric acid and return the mixture to a boil.

6   Pour the hot cream mixture over the chopped couverture, and set aside undisturbed for 1 minute.

7   Using a spatula, stir in small circles at first, then gradually in wider circles to form a ganache.

8 Cool the ganache to 90°F/32.2°C.

9 Blend in the butter and liquid cocoa butter with an immersion blender to form a smooth, shiny ganache. Cover with plastic wrap and let cool to 86°F/30.0°C.

10 When the mixture reaches the proper temperature, place in a pastry bag with a small hole cut in the tip and pipe into the shells. Let set overnight at room temperature.

11 Cap the truffles with the milk couverture once the ganache has completely set.

12 Coat the truffles in the milk couverture by hand.

13 Before the couverture sets, roll the truffles in the Strawberry Finishing Powder to coat. Let set at room temperature.

14 Store in an airtight container at 57° to 61°F/13.9° to 16.1°C in a dark, dry place.

Strawberry Finishing Powder

INGREDIENTS	METRIC	US	VOLUME
Confectioners' sugar	200 g	7.1 oz	1⅓ cups
Strawberry powder	50 g	1.8 oz	⅓ cup + ½ tbsp
Cornstarch	50 g	1.8 oz	⅓ cup + ½ tbsp
YIELD	**300g**	**10.7 oz**	**2 cups + 1 tbsp**

Sift all the ingredients together to prevent lumping.

NOTE: You will have excess Strawberry Finishing Powder after rolling the truffles. You may store the excess powder in an airtight container at room temperature (68°F/20.0°C) for future use.

Molded, Filled Chocolates

Apricot Pralines

INGREDIENTS	METRIC	US	VOLUME
Colored cocoa butter and/or couverture, for decoration	as needed	as needed	as needed
Milk couverture, 37%, tempered, for casting and capping	200 g	7.1 oz	¾ cup
Apricot puree	290 g	10.2 oz	1 cup + 2 tbsp
Glucose	30 g	1.1 oz	1½ tbsp
Apple pectin	9 g	0.3 oz	1 tbsp
Sugar	40 g	1.4 oz	2 tbsp + 2 tsp
Lemon juice	40 g	1.4 oz	2 tbsp + 2 tsp
Milk couverture, 37%, chopped or coins	345 g	12.2 oz	2½ cups
Unsalted butter, softened	60 g	2.1 oz	4 tbsp
Brandy	60 g	2.1 oz	5 tbsp
YIELD: 96 MOLDED PRALINES	**1074 g**	**37.9 oz**	

1 Prepare 4 molds with twenty-four 0.4 oz/11 g cavities or 3 molds with thirty-two 0.4 oz/11 g cavities with the desired colors of cocoa butter or couverture.

2 Cast the molds with the milk couverture.

3 In a medium pot, combine the apricot puree and glucose and bring to a boil over medium heat.

4 Whisk together the pectin and sugar and add to the apricot puree mixture.

5 Whisk in the lemon juice.

6 Pour the hot puree mixture over the chopped couverture, and set aside undisturbed for 1 minute.

7 Using a spatula, stir in small circles starting in the middle at first, then gradually in wider circles to make an emulsion.

8 Cool to 94°F/34.5°C.

9 Blend in the butter and brandy using an immersion blender. Cover with plastic wrap and let cool to 88°F/31.1°C

10 When the mixture reaches the proper temperature, place in a pastry bag with a small hole cut in the tip and pipe into the prepared molds. Let set overnight at room temperature.

11 Once the filling has completely set, cap with milk couverture. Place in the refrigerator for 3 to 5 minutes to set.

12 Tap the molds on the table to release the chocolates.

13 Store in an airtight container at 57° to 61°F/13.9° to 16.1°C in a dark, dry place.

RECOMMENDED MOLD DÉCOR

1 Using a pastry brush, flick red-brown cocoa butter onto the molds.

2 Using an airbrush, spray each cavity entirely with orange cocoa butter.

3 Spray one side of each cavity only with red-brown cocoa butter.

Coconut Rum Pralines

INGREDIENTS	METRIC	US	VOLUME
Colored cocoa butter and/or couverture, for decoration	as needed	as needed	as needed
White couverture, tempered, for casting and capping	200 g	7.1 oz	¾ cup
COCONUT RUM GANACHE			
Heavy cream	150 g	5.3 oz	⅔ cup
Glucose	13 g	0.5 oz	2 tsp
Dark couverture, 63%, chopped or coins	115 g	4.1 oz	¾ cup
Milk couverture, 37%, chopped or coins	45 g	1.6 oz	⅓ cup
Unsalted butter, softened	13 g	0.5 oz	1 tbsp
Coconut-flavored rum	15 g	0.5 oz	1 tbsp
WHITE GANACHE			
Coconut puree	150 g	5.3 oz	1 cup
Invert sugar	35 g	1.2 oz	1½ tbsp
White couverture, chopped or coins	250 g	8.8 oz	2 cups
Coconut flakes, unsweetened	43 g	1.5 oz	1¾ cups
Coconut-flavored rum	35 g	1.2 oz	3 tbsp
YIELD: 96 MOLDED PRALINES	**1064 g**	**37.6 oz**	

1 Prepare 4 molds with twenty-four 0.4 oz/11 g cavities or 3 molds with thirty-two 0.4 oz/11 g cavities with the desired cocoa butter or couverture.

2 Cast the molds with the white couverture.

3 To make the coconut rum ganache: In a medium pot, combine the cream and glucose and bring to a boil over medium heat.

4 Combine the chopped dark and milk couvertures. Pour the hot cream mixture over the couverture mixture, and set aside undisturbed for 1 minute.

5 Using a spatula, stir in small circles starting in the center of the bowl, then gradually in wider circles, to make an emulsion.

6 Cool the ganache to 94°F/34.5°C.

7 Blend in the butter and rum using an immersion blender. Cover with plastic wrap and let cool to 88°F/31.1°C.

8 When the ganache reaches the proper temperature, pipe into the prepared molds using a pastry bag with a small hole cut in the tip. Only fill the molds halfway up, leaving enough room for the white ganache. Set aside at room temperature.
Continued on page 174.

Continued on page 174.

9 To make the white ganache: In a medium pot, combine the coconut puree and invert sugar and bring to a boil over medium heat.

10 Combine the chopped white couverture and the coconut flakes. Pour the hot puree mixture over the couverture mixture, and set aside undisturbed for 1 minute.

11 Using a spatula, stir in small circles starting in the middle at first, then gradually in wider circles, to make an emulsion.

12 Cool to 94°F/34.5°C.

13 Blend in the rum using an immersion blender. Cover with plastic wrap and let cool to 88°F/31°C.

14 When the ganache reaches the proper temperature, pipe into the molds on top of the coconut rum ganache, using a pastry bag with a small hole cut in the tip. Let set overnight at room temperature.

15 Once the ganache has completely set, cap with white couverture. Place in the refrigerator for 3 to 5 minutes to set.

16 Tap the molds on the table to release the chocolates.

17 Store in an airtight container at 57° to 61°F/13.9° to 16.1°C in a dark, dry place.

RECOMMENDED MOLD DÉCOR

1 Using an airbrush, spray the molds with yellow cocoa butter.

2 Spray a layer of dark couverture over the yellow.

Coffee Pralines

INGREDIENTS	METRIC	US	VOLUME
Colored cocoa butter and/or couverture, for decoration	as needed	as needed	as needed
Milk couverture, 37%, tempered, for casting and capping	200 g	7.1 oz	¾ cup
Coffee beans, raw	36 g	1.3 oz	⅓ cup
Heavy cream	300 g, plus additional as needed	10.6 oz, plus additional as needed	1⅓ cup, plus additional as needed
Glucose	45 g	1.6 oz	2 tbsp
Instant coffee powder	9 g	0.3 oz	2 tbsp
Invert sugar	90 g	3.2 oz	¼ cup
Dark couverture, 63%, chopped or coins	210 g	7.4 oz	1½ cups
Milk couverture, 37%, chopped or coins	150 g	5.3 oz	1 cup
Unsalted butter, softened	30 g	1.1 oz	2 tbsp
YIELD: 96 MOLDED PRALINES	**1070 g**	**37.9 oz**	

1   Prepare 4 molds with twenty-four 0.4 oz/11 g cavities or 3 molds with thirty-two 0.4 oz/11 g cavities with cocoa butter or couverture as desired.

2   Cast the molds with the milk couverture.

3   Preheat the oven to 350°F/176.7°C. Spread the coffee beans on a sheet pan and roast for 10 minutes. Let cool slightly.

4   Crush the roasted beans with a rolling pin.

5   In a medium pot, combine the cream and the crushed beans and bring to a boil over medium heat.

6   Once the cream has come to a boil, remove from the heat and immediately cover with plastic wrap.

7   Let steep for 10 minutes, then strain to remove the coffee beans.

8   Add cream as needed to bring the total amount back to 10.6 oz/300g. Add the glucose and instant coffee and return the mixture to a boil.

9   Combine the invert sugar and the chopped dark and milk couvertures. Pour the hot cream mixture over the couverture mixture, and set aside undisturbed for 1 minute.

10 Using a spatula, stir in small circles starting in the middle at first, then gradually in wider circles, to make an emulsion.

11 Cool to 94°F/34.5°C.

12 Blend in the butter using an immersion blender. Cover with plastic wrap and let cool to 88°F/31.1°C.

13 When the mixture reaches the proper temperature, place in a pastry bag with a small hole cut in the tip and pipe into the prepared molds. Let set overnight at room temperature.

14 Once the ganache has completely set, cap with milk couverture. Place in the refrigerator for 3 to 5 minutes to set.

15 Tap the molds on the table to release the chocolates.

16 Store in an airtight container at 57° to 61°F/13.9° to 16.1°C in a dark, dry place.

RECOMMENDED MOLD DÉCOR

1 Using an airbrush, spray one side of the molds with red cocoa butter.

2 Spray the entire mold with dark couverture so that the red fades into the dark couverture.

Key Lime Pralines

INGREDIENTS	METRIC	US	VOLUME
CRACKER CRUST SQUARES			
Milk couverture, 37%, tempered	30.0 g	1.1 oz	2 tbsp
Cocoa butter	25.0 g	0.9 oz	2 tbsp
Feuilletine or corn flakes	45.0 g	1.6 oz	¾ cup
Unsalted butter, softened	3.0 g	0.1 oz	½ tsp
KEY LIME GANACHE			
Colored cocoa butter and/or couverture, for decoration	as needed	as needed	as needed
White couverture, tempered, for casting and capping	190.0 g	6.7 oz	¾ cup
Sugar	145.0 g	5.1 oz	¾ cup
Pectin	2.2 g	0.1 oz	½ tsp
Heavy cream	90.0 g	3.2 oz	¾ cup + 2 tbsp
Unsalted butter	125.0 g	4.4 oz	½ cup + 1 tbsp
Invert sugar	50.0 g	1.8 oz	2 tbsp
Milk couverture, 37%, chopped or coins	265.0 g	9.3 oz	2 cups
Cocoa butter, melted	13.0 g	0.5 oz	1 tbsp
Key lime juice	90.0 g	3.2 oz	¾ cup
Grated lime zest	2.5 g	0.1 oz	1½ tsp
YIELD: 96 MOLDED PRALINES	**1075.7 g**	**38.1 oz**	

1   For the cracker crust squares: Cover an acrylic base with parchment paper or an acetate sheet and create an 5⅜ × 6 ½–in/135 × 165–mm rectangle using ⅛-in/3-mm metal bars.

2   Melt the couverture and cocoa butter separately, then combine and stir to mix well.

3   Mix in the feuilletine flakes thoroughly.

4   Add the liquid cocoa butter and mix in with a spatula, but do not allow to cool. The mixture should be at 92°F/33.3°C.

5   Spread the mixture, using an offset spatula, between the metal bars on top of the acetate sheet.

6   Using a plastic roller, roll the mixture to an even, smooth layer. Let set for approximately 5 to 10 minutes, until it is partially set but can still be cut cleanly.

7   Using a knife, cut the crust away from the bars. Remove the bars.

8   Use a rolling cutter to create ⅝-in/15-mm squares. Remove any excess pieces.
    Continued on page 180.

9 Place the crackers in the refrigerator for about 5 minutes to set completely.

10 For the ganache and pralines: Prepare 4 molds with twenty-four 0.4 oz/11 g cavities or 3 molds with thirty-two 0.4 oz/11 g cavities with cocoa butter or couverture as desired.

11 Cast the molds with the white couverture.

12 Combine the pectin and the sugar and stir together to prevent lumps.

13 In a medium pot, bring the cream, butter, and sugar-pectin mixture to a boil over medium heat.

14 Combine the invert sugar and chopped couverture. Pour the hot cream mixture over the couverture mixture, and stir lightly to incorporate into a smooth mixture.

15 Add the melted cocoa butter.

16 Stir in the key lime juice and lime zest. Cover with plastic wrap and let cool to 84°F/28.9°C.

17 When the mixture reaches the proper temperature, place in a pastry bag with a small hole cut in the tip and pipe into the prepared molds leaving enough room for the crust as well as capping.

18 Place one cracker on top of the piped ganache in each cavity. Let set overnight at room temperature.

19 Once the ganache has completely set, cap with white couverture. Place in the refrigerator for 3 to 5 minutes to set.

20 Tap the molds on the table to release the chocolates.

21 Store in an airtight container at 57° to 61°F/13.9° to 16.1°C in a dark, dry place.

RECOMMENDED MOLD DÉCOR

1 Wearing gloves, use your finger to swirl the molds with yellow cocoa butter.

2 Repeat the same swirling technique with green cocoa butter.

Lemon Pralines

INGREDIENTS	METRIC	US	VOLUME
Colored cocoa butter and/or couverture, for decoration	as needed	as needed	as needed
Milk couverture, 37%, tempered, for casting and capping	190 g	6.7 oz	¾ cup
Heavy cream	180 g	6.3 oz	⅔ cup + 1 tbsp
Grated lemon zest	4 g	0.1 oz	2 tsp
Glucose	40 g	1.4 oz	2 tbsp
Invert sugar	50 g	1.8 oz	2 tbsp
Milk couverture, 37%, chopped or coins	430 g	15.2 oz	3 cups
Lemon puree	140 g	4.9 oz	⅔ cup
Unsalted butter, softened	35 g	1.2 oz	3 tbsp
YIELD: 96 MOLDED PRALINES	**1069 g**	**37.6 oz**	

1 Prepare 4 molds with twenty-four 0.4 oz/11 g cavities or 3 molds with thirty-two 0.4 oz/11 g cavities with colored cocoa butter or couverture as desired.

2 Cast the molds with the milk couverture.

3 In a medium pot, combine the cream, lemon zest, and glucose and bring to a boil over medium heat.

4 Combine the invert sugar and chopped milk couverture. Pour the hot cream mixture over the couverture mixture, and set aside undisturbed for 1 minute.

5 Using a spatula, stir in small circles starting in the center of the bowl, then gradually in wider circles, to create an emulsion.

6 Add the lemon puree and stir to combine. Cool to 94°F/34.5°C.

7 Blend in the butter using an immersion blender. Cover with plastic wrap and let cool to 88°F/31.1°C

8 When the mixture reaches 88°F/31.1°C, place in a pastry bag with a small hole cut in the tip and pipe into the prepared molds. Let set overnight at room temperature.

9 Once the ganache has completely set, cap with milk couverture. Place in the refrigerator for 3 to 5 minutes to set.

10 Tap the molds on the table to release the chocolates.

11 Store in an airtight container at 57° to 61°F/13.9° to 16.1°C in a dark, dry place.

RECOMMENDED MOLD DÉCOR

1 Using a brush, splatter yellow colored cocoa butter into the molds.

2 Using a spray gun, spray dark couverture into the molds.

Macadamia Pralines

INGREDIENTS	METRIC	US	VOLUME
Colored cocoa butter and/or couverture, for decoration	as needed	as needed	as needed
Milk couverture, 37%, tempered, for casting and capping	200 g	7.1 oz	¾ cup
Heavy cream	300 g	10.6 oz	1⅓ cups
Salt	3 g	0.1 oz	⅓ tsp
Glucose	35 g	1.2 oz	1½ tbsp
Vanilla bean	3 g	0.1 oz	⅓ ea
Invert sugar	35 g	1.2 oz	1 tbsp + 1 tsp
Macadamia paste	160 g	5.6 oz	1 cup
Milk couverture, 37%, chopped or coins	300 g	10.6 oz	2 cups
Cocoa butter, melted	45 g	1.5 oz	3 tbsp
YIELD: 96 MOLDED PRALINES	**1081 g**	**38.0 oz**	

1   Prepare 4 molds with twenty-four 0.4 oz/11 g cavities or 3 molds with thirty-two 0.4 oz/11 g cavities with colored cocoa butter or couverture as desired.

2   Cast the molds with the milk couverture.

3   Combine the cream, salt, and glucose in a medium pot. Split the vanilla bean, scrape the seeds, add the pod and seeds to the cream, and bring to a boil over medium heat.

4   Combine the invert sugar, macadamia paste, and chopped milk couverture. Strain the hot cream mixture into the couverture mixture, and set aside undisturbed for 1 minute.

5   Using a spatula, stir in small circles starting in the center of the bowl, then gradually in wider circles, to create an emulsion.

6   Cool to 94°F/34.5°C. Add the melted cocoa butter and stir to combine. Cover with plastic wrap and let cool to 88°F/31.1°C.

7   When the mixture reaches 88°F/31.1°C, place in a pastry bag with a small hole cut in the tip and pipe into the prepared molds. Let set overnight at room temperature.

8   Once the ganache has completely set, cap with milk couverture. Place in the refrigerator for 3 to 5 minutes to set.

9   Tap the molds on the table to release the chocolates.

10   Store in an airtight container at 57° to 61°F/13.9° to 16.1°C in a dark, dry place.

RECOMMENDED MOLD DÉCOR

1   Using an airbrush, lightly spray the molds with yellow cocoa butter.

2   Spray a touch of red cocoa butter into one side of each cavity.

Maple Pecan Pralines

INGREDIENTS	METRIC	US	VOLUME
Colored cocoa butter and/or couverture, for decoration	as needed	as needed	as needed
Milk couverture, 37%, tempered, for casting and capping	190 g	6.7 oz	¾ cup
Pecans, shelled	115 g	4.1 oz	1 cup
Salt	2 g	0.1 oz	¼ tsp
Whole milk	17 g	0.6 oz	1 tbsp + ½ tsp
Heavy cream	85 g	3.0 oz	⅓ cup
Invert sugar	40 g	1.4 oz	1½ tbsp
Maple syrup	180 g	6.3 oz	½ cup
Milk couverture, 37%, chopped or coins	400 g	14.1 oz	3 cups
Unsalted butter, softened	35 g	1.2 oz	3 tbsp
YIELD: 96 MOLDED PRALINES	**1064 g**	**37.5 oz**	

1   Prepare 4 molds with twenty-four 0.4 oz/11 g cavities or 3 molds with thirty-two 0.4 oz/11 g cavities with colored cocoa butter or couverture as desired.

2   Cast the molds with the milk couverture.

3   Preheat oven to 340°F/171.1°C. Spread the pecans on a sheet pan and roast until golden brown.

4   Allow to cool, then place in a food processor with the salt and chop until fine enough to pipe.

5   In a medium pot, combine the milk, cream, invert sugar, and maple syrup and bring to a boil over medium heat.

6   Pour the hot cream mixture over the chopped couverture, and set aside undisturbed for 1 minute.

7   Using a spatula, stir in small circles starting in the middle of the bowl at first, then in gradually wider circles, to create a smooth, shiny ganache.

8   Cool to 90°F/32°C.

9   Blend in the butter using an immersion blender. Lightly stir in the pecans. Cover with plastic wrap and let cool to 88°F/31.1°C.

10   When the mixture reaches the proper temperature, place in a pastry bag with a small hole cut in the tip and pipe into the prepared molds. Let set overnight at room temperature.

11   Once the ganache has completely set, cap with milk couverture. Place in the refrigerator for 3 to 5 minutes to set.

12 Tap the molds on the table to release the chocolates.

13 Store in an airtight container at 57° to 61°F/13.9° to 16.1°C in a dark, dry place.

RECOMMENDED MOLD DÉCOR

1 Using a pastry brush, splatter dark couverture and red cocoa butter into the molds.

2 Using an airbrush, spray the molds with yellow.

3 Spray with red cocoa butter.

4 Lightly spray the molds with white cocoa butter.

Mint Pralines

INGREDIENTS	METRIC	US	VOLUME
MINT CRACKER CRUST			
Dark couverture, 63%, tempered	30.0 g	1.06 oz	2 tbsp
Cocoa butter	25.0 g	0.88 oz	2 tbsp
Feuilletine or corn flakes	45.0 g	1.59 oz	¾ cup
Unsalted butter, softened	3.0 g	0.11 oz	1 tsp
MINT GANACHE			
Colored cocoa butter and/or couverture, for decoration	as needed	as needed	as needed
Dark couverture, 63%, tempered, for casting and capping	190.0 g	6.70 oz	¾ cup
Heavy cream	300.0 g	10.58 oz	1⅓ cups
Glucose	70.0 g	2.47 oz	3 tbsp + 1 tsp
White couverture, chopped or coins	440.0 g	15.52 oz	3 cups
Cocoa butter, melted	43.0 g	1.52 oz	3½ tbsp
Mint oil	1.4 g	0.05 oz	¼ tsp
YIELD: 96 MOLDED PRALINES	**1147.4 g**	**40.48 oz**	

1 For the mint cracker crust: Cover an acrylic base with parchment paper or an acetate sheet and create an 5⅜ × 6 ½–in/135 × 165–mm rectangle using ⅛-in/3-mm metal bars.

2 Melt the couverture and cocoa butter separately, then combine and stir to mix well.

3 Mix in the feuilletine flakes thoroughly.

4 Add the liquid cocoa butter and mix by with spatula but do not allow to cool. The mixture should be at 92°F/33.3°C.

5 Spread the mixture, using an offset spatula, between the metal bars on top of the acetate sheet.

6 Using a plastic roller, roll the mixture to an even, smooth layer. Let set for approximately 5 to 10 minutes, until it is partially set but can still be cut cleanly.

7 Using a knife, cut the crust away from the bars. Remove the bars.

8 Use a rolling cutter to create ⅝ in/15 mm squares. Remove any excess pieces.

9 Place the crackers in the refrigerator for about 5 minutes to set completely.

10 For the mint ganache: Prepare 4 molds with twenty-four 0.4 oz/11 g cavities or 3 molds with thirty-two 0.4 oz/11 g cavities with colored cocoa butter or couverture as desired.

11 Cast the molds with the dark couverture.

12 In a medium pot, combine the glucose and cream and bring to a boil over medium heat.

13 Pour the hot cream mixture over the chopped couverture, and set aside undisturbed for 1 minute.

14 Using a spatula, stir in small circles starting in the center of the bowl, then gradually in wider circles, to create an emulsion.

15 Blend in the melted cocoa butter using an immersion blender.

16 Add the mint oil and blend until combined. Cover with plastic wrap and let cool to 88°F/31.1°C.

17 When the mixture reaches the proper temperature, place in a pastry bag with a small hole cut in the tip and pipe into the prepared molds, leaving enough room for the crust as well as capping.

18 Place one cracker on top of the piped ganache in each cavity. Let set overnight at room temperature.

19 Once the ganache has completely set, cap with dark couverture. Place in the refrigerator for 3 to 5 minutes to set.

20 Tap the molds on the table to release the chocolates.

21 Store in an airtight container at 57° to 61°F/13.9° to 16.1°C in a dark, dry place.

RECOMMENDED MOLD DÉCOR

1 Using a pastry brush, splatter dark couverture into the molds.

2 Using an airbrush, lightly spray the molds with green cocoa butter.

3 Spray the molds with white cocoa butter.

Passion Fruit Pralines

INGREDIENTS	METRIC	US	VOLUME
Colored cocoa butter and/or couverture, for decoration	as needed	as needed	as needed
White couverture, tempered, for casting and capping	190 g	6.7 oz	¾ cup
Heavy cream	150 g	5.3 oz	⅔ cup
Passion fruit puree	150 g	5.3 oz	½ cup + 1 tbsp
Sugar	100 g	3.5 oz	½ cup
Lemon juice	9 g	0.3 oz	½ tbsp
Invert sugar	50 g	1.8 oz	2 tbsp
Milk couverture, 37%, chopped or coins	185 g	6.5 oz	1½ cups
Dark couverture, 63%, chopped or coins	140 g	4.9 oz	1 cup
Unsalted butter, softened	75 g	2.6 oz	5 tbsp
YIELD: 96 MOLDED PRALINES	1049 g	36.9 oz	

1 Prepare 4 molds with twenty-four 0.4 oz/11 g cavities or 3 molds with thirty-two 0.4 oz/11 g cavities with colored cocoa butter or couverture as desired.

2 Cast the molds with the white couverture.

3 In a medium pot, combine the cream, passion fruit puree, sugar, and lemon juice and bring to a boil over medium heat.

4 Combine the invert sugar and milk and dark couvertures. Pour the hot cream mixture over the couverture mixture, and set aside undisturbed for 1 minute.

5 Using a spatula, stir in small circles starting in the center of the bowl, then gradually in wider circles, until you get a shiny consistency.

6 Cool to 92°F/33.3°C. Blend in the butter using an immersion blender. Cover with plastic wrap and let cool to 88°F/31.1°C.

7 When the mixture reaches the proper temperature, place in a pastry bag with a small hole cut in the tip and pipe into the prepared molds. Let set overnight at room temperature.

8 Once the ganache has completely set, cap with the white couverture. Place in the refrigerator for 3 to 5 minutes to set.

9 Tap the molds on the table to release the chocolates.

10 Store in an airtight container at 57° to 61°F/13.9° to 16.1°C in a dark, dry place.

RECOMMENDED MOLD DÉCOR

1 Using an airbrush, spray the molds with yellow cocoa butter.

2 Spray the molds with red cocoa butter.

Exotic Curry Pralines

INGREDIENTS	METRIC	US	VOLUME
Colored cocoa butter and/or couverture, for decoration	as needed	as needed	as needed
Dark couverture, 63%, tempered, for casting and capping	200.0 g	7.05 oz	¾ cup
Heavy cream	160.0 g	5.64 oz	⅔ cup
Curry powder	0.5 g	0.02 oz	⅛ tsp
Passion fruit puree	70.0 g	2.47 oz	¼ cup
Mango puree	50.0 g	1.76 oz	2 tbsp + 1 tsp
Coconut puree	90.0 g	3.17 oz	⅓ cup
Milk couverture, 37%, chopped or coins	500.0 g	17.64 oz	3 ⅔ cups
Invert sugar	50.0 g	1.76 oz	1 tbsp + 1 tsp
Unsalted butter	40.0 g	1.41 oz	3 tbsp
YIELD: 96 MOLDED PRALINES	**1160.5 g**	**40.92 oz**	

1   Prepare 4 molds with twenty-four 0.4 oz/11 g cavities or 3 molds with thirty-two 0.4 oz/11 g cavities with colored cocoa butter or couverture as desired.

2   Cast the molds with the dark couverture.

3   In a medium pot, combine the cream, curry powder, passion puree, mango puree, and coconut puree and bring to a boil over medium heat.

4   Combine the chopped milk couverture and invert sugar. Pour the hot mixture over the couverture mixture and set aside undisturbed for 1 minute.

5   Using a spatula, stir in small circles starting in the center of the bowl, then gradually in wider circles, to make an emulsion.

6   Cool the ganache to 94°F/34.5°C. Blend in the butter using an immersion blender. Cover with plastic wrap and let cool to 88°F/31.1°C.

7   When the mixture reaches the proper temperature, place in a pastry bag with a small hole cut in the tip and pipe into the prepared molds. Cool for 5 minutes in the refrigerator. Let set overnight at room temperature.

8   Once the ganache has completely set, cap with the dark couverture. Place in the refrigerator for 3 to 5 minutes to set.

9   Tap the molds on the table to release the chocolates.

10   Store in an airtight container at 57° to 61°F/13.9° to 16.1°C in a dark, dry place.

RECOMMENDED MOLD DÉCOR

1   Wearing gloves, use your finger to rub the mold with yellow cocoa butter. Let set, then rub the mold with red cocoa butter.

Raspberry Orange Pralines

INGREDIENTS	METRIC	US	VOLUME
Colored cocoa butter and/or couverture, for decoration	as needed	as needed	as needed
Dark couverture, 63%, tempered, for casting and capping	190 g	6.70 oz	¾ cup
RASPBERRY COULIS			
Raspberry puree	190 g	6.70 oz	½ cup + 2 tbsp
Sugar, for the puree	50 g	1.76 oz	¼ cup
Glucose	30 g	1.06 oz	1½ tbsp
Pectin	9 g	0.32 oz	1 tbsp
Sugar, for the pectin	15 g	0.53 oz	1 tbsp
Lemon juice	1 g	0.04 oz	⅛ tsp
ORANGE GANACHE			
Orange juice	200 g	7.05 oz	½ cup + 2 tbsp
Heavy cream	100 g	3.53 oz	½ cup
Grated orange zest	2 g	0.07 oz	1 tbsp
Glucose	27 g	0.95 oz	1 tbsp + 1 tsp
Invert sugar	40 g	1.41 oz	1 tbsp + 1 tsp
Dark couverture, 63%, chopped or coins	175 g	6.17 oz	1⅓ cups
Unsalted butter, softened	30 g	1.06 oz	3 tbsp
YIELD: 96 MOLDED PRALINES	**1059 g**	**37.35 oz**	

1   Prepare 4 molds with twenty-four 0.4 oz/11 g cavities or 3 molds with thirty-two 0.4 oz/11 g with colored cocoa butter or couverture as desired.

2   Cast the molds with the dark couverture.

3   For the raspberry coulis: In a medium pot, combine the raspberry puree, 1.76 oz/50 g sugar, and glucose and bring to a boil over medium heat.

4   Combine the pectin and the 15 g sugar and add to the puree, then add the lemon juice.

5   Boil for 3 minutes or until the mixture coats the back of a spatula.

6   Cool to 88°F/31°C.

7   When the mixture reaches the proper temperature, place in a pastry bag with a small hole cut in the tip and pipe into the prepared molds. Fill the molds only one-third full, leaving room for the orange ganache. Set aside at room temperature.
Continued on page 192.

8   For the orange ganache: Place the orange juice in a pot over medium heat and reduce by half, until the final weight is 5.82 oz/165 g.

9   Add the cream, orange zest, and glucose to the reduced orange juice and return to a boil.

10   Combine the invert sugar and chopped dark couverture. Pour the hot mixture over the couverture mixture, and set aside undisturbed for 1 minute.

11   Using a spatula, stir in small circles starting in the center of the bowl, then gradually in wider circles, to create a smooth, shiny ganache.

12   Cool to 94°F/34.5°C.

13   Blend in the butter using an immersion blender. Cover with plastic wrap and let cool to 88°F/31.1°C.

14   When the mixture reaches the proper temperature, place in a pastry bag with a small hole cut in the tip and pipe into the prepared molds on top of the raspberry coulis. Let set overnight at room temperature.

15   Once the ganache has completely set, cap with dark couverture. Place in the refrigerator for 3 to 5 minutes to set.

16   Tap the molds on the table to release the chocolates.

17   Store in an airtight container at 57° to 61°F/13.9° to 16.1°C in a dark, dry place.

RECOMMENDED MOLD DÉCOR

1   Dip a brush in white cocoa butter and flick it over the molds to splatter them with the white color.

2   Using an airbrush, spray the molds with red cocoa butter.

3   Spray couverture over the cocoa butter.

Salted Caramel Pralines

INGREDIENTS	METRIC	US	VOLUME
Almonds, whole, skin on	56.0 g	1.98 oz	½ cup
Egg whites	5 0 g	0.18 oz	1 tsp
Salt	3.0 g	0.11 oz	1 tsp
Colored cocoa butter and/or couverture, for decoration	as needed	as needed	as needed
Dark couverture, 63%, tempered, for casting, covering the nuts, and capping	280.0 g	9.88 oz	1 cup + 1 tbsp
Heavy cream	345.0 g	12.17 oz	1½ cups
Vanilla bean	15.0 g	0.53 oz	2 ea
Glucose	70.0 g	2.47 oz	3 tbsp
Sugar	280.0 g	9.88 oz	1¼ cups
Unsalted butter, softened	70.0 g	2.47 oz	3 tbsp
Maldon sea salt	1.3 g	0.05 oz	Pinch
YIELD: 96 MOLDED PRALINES	1125.3 g	39.72 oz	

1 Coarsely chop the almonds in a food processor. Remove and place in a bowl.

2 Stir in the egg whites to lightly coat the nuts.

3 Add the salt and stir to evenly distribute.

4 Preheat oven to 340°F/171.1°C. Spread the almonds on a sheet pan and roast until slightly browned. Remove and cool on the tray, stirring to break up any clumps.

5 Store in an airtight container until needed.

6 Prepare 4 molds with twenty-four 0.4 oz/11 g cavities or 3 molds with thirty-two 0.4 oz/11 g cavities with colored cocoa butter or couverture as desired.

7 Cast the molds with the dark couverture.

8 Immediately after casting, divide the almonds among the cavities evenly, before the chocolate has completely crystallized so that the nuts adhere to the shells.

9 Using a pastry bag, cover the nuts with a small amount of the dark couverture.

10 Place the cream in a pot. Split the vanilla bean, scrape out the seeds, and add the pod and seeds to the cream. Bring to a boil over medium heat. Remove from the heat and keep warm.

11 In a copper pot (if possible), warm the glucose over medium heat until it becomes soft and liquid.

12 Add the sugar in small batches, stirring constantly, to caramelize.
Continued on page 194.

13 Once the sugar is fully caramelized and dissolved, slowly strain the cream into the sugar mixture. Cook to 230°F/110.0°C, then remove from the heat and let cool.

14 When the mixture has cooled to 92°F/33.3°C, blend in the butter using an immersion blender. Fold in the sea salt. Cover with plastic wrap and let cool to 88°F/31.1°C.

15 When the caramel reaches the proper temperature, place in a pastry bag with a small hole cut in the tip and pipe into the prepared molds. Let set overnight at room temperature.

16 Once the caramel has completely set, cap the molds with dark couverture. Place in the refrigerator for 3 to 5 minutes to set.

17 Tap the molds on the table to release the chocolates.

18 Store in an airtight container at 57° to 61°F/13.9° to 16.1°C in a dark, dry place.

RECOMMENDED MOLD DÉCOR

1 Using a brush, splatter yellow cocoa butter into the molds.

2 Using an airbrush, spray dark couverture over the yellow.

Tropical Chocolate Pralines

INGREDIENTS	METRIC	US	VOLUME
Colored cocoa butter and/or couverture, for decoration	as needed	as needed	as needed
Dark couverture, 63%, tempered, for casting and capping	190 g	6.7 oz	¾ cup
Heavy cream	170 g	6.0 oz	¾ cup
Passion fruit puree	65 g	2.3 oz	¼ cup
Mango puree	65 g	2.3 oz	¼ cup
Lemon juice	26 g	0.9 oz	1 tbsp + 2 tsp
Lime juice	13 g	0.5 oz	2¾ tsp
Coconut-flavored rum	17 g	0.6 oz	1 tbsp + ¼ tsp
Banana	35 g	1.2 oz	⅓ cup
Invert sugar	52 g	1.8 oz	2 tbsp
Dark couverture, 63%, chopped or coins	170 g	6.0 oz	1¼ cups
Milk couverture, 37%, chopped or coins	170 g	6.0 oz	1¼ cups
Unsalted butter, softened	80 g	2.8 oz	6½ tbsp
YIELD: 96 MOLDED PRALINES	**1053 g**	**37.1 oz**	

1   Prepare 4 molds with twenty-four 0.4 oz/11 g cavities or 3 molds with thirty-two 0.4 oz/11 g cavities with colored cocoa butter or couverture as desired.

2   Cast the molds with the dark couverture.

3   In a medium pot, combine the cream, passion fruit puree, and mango puree and bring to a boil over medium heat.

4   Combine the lemon juice, lime juice, and coconut rum.

5   In a separate bowl, mash the banana and stir in the lemon juice mixture.

6   Combine the invert sugar and the chopped dark and milk couvertures. Pour the hot cream mixture over the couverture mixture, and set aside undisturbed for 1 minute.

7   Using a spatula, stir in small circles starting in the center of the bowl, then gradually in wider circles to form a smooth, shiny ganache. Stir in the banana mixture.

8   Cool to 92°F/33.3°C.

9   Blend in the butter using an immersion blender.

10   Allow the ganache to cool to 88°F/31°C, then pipe into the prepared molds using a pastry bag with a small hole cut in the tip. Let set overnight at room temperature. *Continued on page 196.*

11 Once the ganache has completely set, cap the molds with dark couverture. Place in the refrigerator for 3 to 5 minutes to set.

12 Tap the molds on the table to release the chocolates.

13 Store in an airtight container at 57° to 61°F/13.9° to 16.1°C in a dark, dry place.

RECOMMENDED MOLD DÉCOR

1 Wearing gloves, use your finger to smear the molds with yellow and red cocoa butter. Let set.

2 Wearing gloves, use your finger to smear white cocoa butter over the colored cocoa butter.

Yuzu Ginger Pralines

INGREDIENTS	METRIC	US	VOLUME
Colored cocoa butter and/or couverture, for decoration	as needed	as needed	as needed
White couverture, tempered, for casting and capping	190 g	6.7 oz	¾ cup
Heavy cream	250 g	8.8 oz	1 cup + 1 tbsp
Ginger, chopped, fresh	40 g	1.4 oz	⅓ cup
Milk couverture, 37%, chopped or coins	320 g	11.2 oz	2⅓ cups
Dark couverture, 63%, chopped or coins	75 g	2.6 oz	½ cup
Honey	75 g	2.6 oz	¼ cup
Yuzu juice	75 g	2.6 oz	5 tbsp
Unsalted butter	37 g	1.3 oz	2 tbsp + 1½ tsp
YIELD: 96 MOLDED PRALINES	**1062 g**	**37.2 oz**	

1   Prepare 4 molds with twenty-four 0.4 oz/11 g cavities or 3 molds with thirty-two 0.4 oz/11 g cavities with colored cocoa butter or couverture as desired.

2   Cast the molds with the white couverture.

3   In a medium pot, combine the cream and ginger and bring to a boil. Remove from the heat and cover immediately with plastic wrap. Let sit for 30 minutes to infuse.

4   Strain out the ginger and add additional cream as needed to bring the total amount back to 8.8 oz/250 g. Return the cream to a boil.

5   Combine the milk and dark couvertures and the honey. Pour the hot cream over the couverture mixture, and set aside undisturbed for 1 minute.

6   Using a spatula, stir in small circles starting in the center of the bowl, then gradually in wider circles to create a smooth and shiny ganache.

7   Cool to 94°F/34.5°C. Blend in the yuzu and butter with an immersion blender. Cover with plastic wrap and let cool to 88°F/31.1°C.

8   When the mixture reaches 88°F/31.1°C, place in a pastry bag with a small hole cut in the tip and pipe into the prepared molds. Let set overnight at room temperature.

9   Once the ganache has completely set, cap with the white couverture. Place in the refrigerator for 3 to 5 minutes to set.

10   Tap the molds on the table to release the chocolates. Store in an airtight container at 57° to 61°F/13.9° to 16.1°C in a dark, dry place.

RECOMMENDED MOLD DÉCOR

1   Using an airbrush, spray the molds with yellow cocoa butter.

2   Spray green cocoa butter over the yellow.

Slabbed Pralines

Cinnamon Pralines

INGREDIENTS	METRIC	US	VOLUME
Couverture, milk, 37%, overwarmed, for the acetate sheet	as needed	as needed	as needed
Heavy cream	220 g, plus additional as needed	7.8 oz, plus additional as needed	1 cup, plus additional as needed
Cinnamon sticks	55 g	1.9 oz	10 sticks
Invert sugar	45 g	1.6 oz	2 tbsp
Milk couverture, 37%, half melted	440 g	15.5 oz	3 cups
Cocoa butter, melted	35 g	1.2 oz	¼ cup
Unsalted butter, softened	55 g	1.9 oz	¼ cup
Colored cocoa butter, for the transfer sheet	as needed	as needed	as needed
Milk couverture, 37%, tempered, for making plaques and dipping	256 g	9.0 oz	1 cup
YIELD: 136 PRALINES	**1106 g**	**38.9 oz**	

1   Prepare an acetate sheet on an acrylic base and cover with overwarmed couverture (see page 118). On the sheet, place a 15-in/380-mm square acrylic frame, ½ in/13 mm high. Place a divider or bar inside the frame to split it in half. (The recipe makes enough ganache for a half-frame, 7½ × 15 in/190 × 380 mm.)

2   In a medium pot, bring the cream and cinnamon sticks to a boil over medium heat.

3   Remove from the heat, immediately cover with plastic wrap, and let steep for 10 minutes.

4   Strain to remove the cinnamon sticks, and add cream as needed to return the total amount to 7.8 oz/220 g.

5   Return the cream to the heat and bring back to a boil.

6   Combine the invert sugar and milk couverture. Pour the hot cream over the couverture mixture, and set aside undisturbed for 1 minute.

7   Using a spatula, stir in small circles starting in the center of the bowl, then gradually in wider circles to create a ganache.

8   Add the melted cocoa butter and mix with the spatula to create a shiny, smooth ganache. Cool to 92°F/33.3°C.

9 Blend in the butter using an immersion blender.

10 Spread the ganache into the prepared acrylic frame, and let set overnight at room temperature.

11 Remove the frame, flip the slab over, and remove the acetate sheet. Place the slab on a guitar cutter and cut into ⅞-in/22 mm squares.

12 Transfer the pieces to a parchment paper–lined sheet tray, separate them, and let them rest at room temperature for 2 hours to form a crust before finishing.

13 To finish the pralines with plaques, decorate a transfer sheet as desired, spread with a thin layer of milk couverture, and let set.

14 Using an Exacto knife or a paring knife, cut the couverture into ¾-in/20-mm square plaques.

15 Using a dipping fork, dip each praline in the milk couverture. Place a plaque on top before the couverture has fully set.

16 Let set overnight at room temperature, then carefully peel off the acetate from each praline before storing. If you want to peel off the acetate sooner, place the pralines in the refrigerator for 5 to 10 minutes first.

17 Store in an airtight container at 57° to 61°F/13.9° to 16.1°C in a dark, dry place.

RECOMMENDED TRANSFER SHEET DÉCOR

1 Lightly brush yellow cocoa butter onto a piece of acetate in vertical streaks.

2 Brush red cocoa butter onto the acetate following the same streaks.

3 Repeat the process with brown cocoa butter.

Kumquat–Passion Fruit Pralines

INGREDIENTS	METRIC	US	VOLUME
Couverture, milk, 37%, overwarmed, for the acetate sheet	as needed	as needed	as needed
Heavy cream	115 g	4.1 oz	½ cup
Kumquat puree	115 g	4.1 oz	½ cup
Passion fruit puree	115 g	4.1 oz	½ cup
Invert sugar	70 g	2.5 oz	2 tbsp
Milk couverture, 37%, half melted	200 g	7.1 oz	1⅓ cups
Dark couverture, 63%, half melted	200 g	7.1 oz	1⅓ cups
Dark couverture, 63%, tempered, for dipping	256 g	9.0 oz	1 cup
Colored cocoa butter, for the transfer sheet	as needed	as needed	as needed
Dark couverture, 63%, tempered, for plaques	65 g	2.3 oz	¼ cup
YIELD: 136 PRALINES	**1136 g**	**40.3 oz**	

1. Prepare an acetate sheet on an acrylic base and cover with overwarmed couverture (see page 118). On the sheet, place a 15-in/380-mm square acrylic frame, ½ in/ 13 mm high. Place a divider or bar inside the frame to split it in half. (The recipe makes enough ganache for a half-frame, 7½ × 15 in/190 × 380 mm.)

2. In a medium pot, bring the cream, kumquat puree, and passion fruit puree to a boil over medium heat.

3. Combine the invert sugar and the milk and dark couvertures. Pour the hot cream over the couverture mixture, and set aside undisturbed for 1 minute.

4. Mix with an immersion blender to create a smooth, shiny ganache.

5. Spread the ganache in the prepared acrylic frame and allow to set overnight at room temperature.

6. Remove the frame, flip the slab over, and remove the acetate sheet. Place the slab on a guitar cutter and cut into ⅞-in/22-mm squares.

7. Transfer the pieces to a parchment paper–lined sheet tray, separate them, and let them rest at room temperature for 2 hours to form a crust before finishing.

8. To finish the pralines with plaques, decorate a transfer sheet as desired, spread with a thin layer of dark couverture, and let set.

9. Using an Exacto knife or a paring knife, cut the couverture into ¾-in/20-mm square plaques.

10 Using a dipping fork, dip each praline in the dark couverture. Place a plaque on top before the couverture has fully set.

11 Let set overnight at room temperature, then carefully peel off the acetate from each praline before storing. If you want to peel off the acetate sooner, place the pralines it in the refrigerator for a short period of time first.

12 Store in an airtight container at 57° to 61°F/13.9° to 16.1°C in a dark, dry place.

RECOMMENDED TRANSFER SHEET DÉCOR

1 Using a brush, lightly splatter red cocoa butter onto a piece of acetate.

2 Using an airbrush, spray a layer of orange cocoa butter over the red.

Tea Pralines

INGREDIENTS	METRIC	US	VOLUME
Dark couverture, 63%, overwarmed, for the acetate sheet	as needed	as needed	as needed
Heavy cream	230 g, plus additional as needed	8.1 oz, plus additional as needed	1 cup, plus additional as needed
Kusmi black tea	12 g	0.4 oz	2 tbsp + 1 tsp
Glucose	45 g	1.6 oz	2½ tbsp
Invert sugar	45 g	1.6 oz	2½ tbsp
Dark couverture, 63%, half melted	240 g	8.5 oz	1¾ cups
Milk couverture, 37%, half melted	180 g	6.3 oz	1¼ cups
Unsalted butter, softened	60 g	2.1 oz	¼ cup
Colored cocoa butter, for the transfer sheet	as needed	as needed	as needed
Dark couverture, 63%, tempered, for dipping	256 g	9.0 oz	1 cup
YIELD: 136 PRALINES	**1068 g**	**37.6 oz**	

1   Prepare an acetate sheet on an acrylic base and cover with overwarmed couverture (see page 118). On the sheet, place a 15-in/380-mm square acrylic frame, ½ in/ 13 mm high. Place a divider or bar inside the frame to split it in half. (The recipe makes enough ganache for a half-frame, 7½ × 15 in/190 × 380 mm.)

2   In a medium pot, bring the cream and Kusmi tea to a boil over medium heat.

3   Once the cream comes to a boil, remove it from the heat and immediately cover with plastic wrap. Let steep for 12 minutes.

4   Strain to remove the tea, and add cream as needed to return the total quantity to 8.1 oz/230 g. Add the glucose to the cream and return to a boil.

5   Combine the invert sugar and the dark and milk couvertures. Pour the hot cream mixture over the couverture mixture, and set aside undisturbed for 1 minute.

6   Using a spatula, stir in small circles starting in the center of the bowl, then gradually in wider circles to create an emulsion.

7   Cool to 92°F/33.3°C.

8   Blend in the butter using an immersion blender.

9   Spread the ganache in the prepared acrylic frame and allow to set overnight at room temperature.

10 Remove the frame, flip the slab over, and remove the acetate sheet. Place the slab on a guitar cutter and cut into ⅞-in/22-mm squares.

11 Transfer the pieces to a parchment paper–lined sheet tray, separate them, and let them rest at room temperature for 2 hours to form a crust before finishing.

12 Decorate a transfer sheet as desired.

13 Using a dipping fork, dip each praline in the dark couverture. Before the couverture sets, cover with a printed transfer sheet.

14 Let set completely before removing the transfer sheet.

15 Store in an airtight container at 57° to 61°F/13.9° to 16.1°C in a dark, dry place.

RECOMMENDED TRANSFER SHEET DÉCOR

1 Lightly brush green cocoa butter onto a piece of acetate in vertical streaks.

2 Brush red cocoa butter onto the acetate following the same streaks.

3 Repeat the process with white cocoa butter.

Lemon-Thyme Pralines

INGREDIENTS	METRIC	US	VOLUME
Milk couverture, 37%, overwarmed, for the acetate sheet	as needed	as needed	as needed
Heavy cream	240 g, plus additional as needed	8.5 oz, plus additional as needed	1 cup, plus additional as needed
Fresh thyme leaves	4 g	0.1 oz	1 tbsp
Invert sugar	45 g	1.6 oz	2 tbsp
Milk couverture, 37%, half melted	250 g	8.8 oz	2 cups
Dark couverture, 63%, half melted	110 g	3.9 oz	⅓ cup
Lemon juice	55 g	1.9 oz	¼ cup
Cocoa butter, melted	33 g	1.2 oz	¼ cup
Unsalted butter	55 g	1.9 oz	¼ cup
Dark couverture, 63%, tempered, for dipping	256 g	9.0 oz	1 cup
Colored cocoa butter, for the transfer sheet	as needed	as needed	as needed
Milk couverture, 37%, tempered, for plaques	65 g	2.3 oz	¼ cup
YIELD: 136 PRALINES	**1113 g**	**39.2 oz**	

1   Prepare an acetate sheet on an acrylic base and cover with overwarmed couverture (see page 118). On the sheet, place a 15-in/380-mm square acrylic frame, ½ in/13 mm high. Place a divider or bar inside the frame to split it in half. (The recipe makes enough ganache for a half-frame, 7½ × 15 in/190 × 380 mm.)

2   In a medium pot, bring the cream and thyme to a boil over medium heat.

3   Once the cream has boiled, remove it from the heat, immediately cover with plastic wrap, and let steep for 10 minutes.

4   Strain to remove the thyme, and add additional cream as needed to return the total quantity to 7.8 oz/220 g. Return the cream to a boil.

5   Combine the invert sugar and the milk and dark couvertures. Pour the hot cream over the couverture mixture, and set aside undisturbed for 1 minute.

6   Add the lemon juice and cocoa butter. Using a spatula, stir in small circles starting in the center of the bowl, then gradually in wider circles to create a shiny, smooth ganache.

7   Cool to 92°F/33.3°C.

8   Blend in the butter using an immersion blender.
Continued on page 206.

9 Spread the ganache into the prepared acrylic frame and allow to set overnight at room temperature.

10 Remove the frame, flip the slab over, and remove the acetate sheet. Place the slab on a guitar cutter and cut into ⅞-in/22-mm squares.

11 Transfer the pieces to a parchment paper–lined sheet tray, separate them, and let them rest at room temperature for 2 hours to form a crust before finishing.

12 To finish the pralines with plaques, decorate a transfer sheet as desired, spread with a thin layer of milk couverture, and let set.

13 Using an Exacto knife or a paring knife, cut the couverture into ¾-in/20-mm square plaques.

14 Using a dipping fork, dip each praline in the dark couverture. Place a plaque on top before the couverture has fully set.

15 Let set overnight at room temperature, then carefully peel off the acetate from each praline before storing. If you want to peel off the acetate sooner, place the pralines in the refrigerator for a short period of time first.

16 Store in an airtight container at 57° to 61°F/13.9° to 16.1°C in a dark, dry place.

RECOMMENDED TRANSFER SHEET DÉCOR

1 Brush yellow cocoa butter onto a piece of acetate in horizontal streaks.

2 Brush green cocoa butter onto the acetate following the same streaks.

3 Repeat the process with brown cocoa butter.

Palet d'Or

INGREDIENTS	METRIC	US	VOLUME
Dark couverture, 63%, overwarmed, for the acetate sheet	as needed	as needed	as needed
Heavy cream	320 g	11.3 oz	⅔ cup + 2 tbsp
Vanilla bean	15 g	0.5 oz	1 ea
Dark couverture, 72%, half melted	390 g	13.7 oz	1¼ cups
Invert sugar	54 g	1.9 oz	2 tbsp
Unsalted butter, softened	80 g	2.8 oz	3 tbsp + 1 tsp
Dark couverture, 72%, tempered, for dipping	256 g	9.0 oz	1 cup
Gold leaf	as needed	as needed	as needed
YIELD: 136 PRALINES	**1115 g**	**39.2 oz**	

1   Prepare an acetate sheet on an acrylic base and cover with overwarmed couverture (see page 118). On the sheet, place a 15-in/380-mm square acrylic frame, ½ in/ 13 mm high. Place a divider or bar inside the frame to split it in half. (The recipe makes enough ganache for a half-frame, 7½ × 15 in/190 × 380 mm.)

2   Place the cream in a medium pot. Split the vanilla bean, scrape out the seeds, and add the pod and seeds to the cream. Bring to a boil over medium heat.

3   Combine the 63% dark couverture and invert sugar. Pour the hot cream over the couverture mixture, and set aside undisturbed for 1 minute.

4   Using a spatula, stir in small circles starting in the center of the bowl, then gradually in wider circles to form an emulsion.

5   Cool to 92°F/33.3°C.

6   Blend in the butter with an immersion blender.

7   Spread the ganache into the prepared acrylic frame and allow to set overnight at room temperature.

8   Remove the frame, flip the slab over, and remove the acetate sheet. Place the slab on a guitar cutter and cut into ⅞-in/22-mm squares.

9   Transfer the pieces to a parchment paper–lined sheet tray, separate them, and let them rest at room temperature for 2 hours to form a crust before finishing.

10 Using a dipping fork, dip each praline into the 73% dark couverture. Before the couverture sets, place a small piece of gold leaf on each praline. Let set completely at room temperature.

11 Store in an airtight container at 57° to 61°F/13.9° to 16.1°C in a dark, dry place.

Spearmint Pralines

INGREDIENTS	METRIC	US	VOLUME
Dark couverture, 63%, overwarmed, for the acetate sheet	as needed	as needed	as needed
Heavy cream	290 g, plus additional as needed	10.2 oz, plus additional as needed	1¼ cups, plus additional as needed
Spearmint leaves	10 g	0.4 oz	1 tbsp
Honey	43 g	1.5 oz	3 tbsp
Milk couverture, 37%, half melted	200 g	7.1 oz	1½ cups
Dark couverture, 63%, half melted	200 g	7.1 oz	1½ cups
Unsalted butter, softened	43 g	1.5 oz	3 tbsp
White crème de menthe	11 g	0.4 oz	1 tbsp
Colored cocoa butter, for the transfer sheet (optional)	as needed	as needed	as needed
Dark couverture, 63%, tempered, for dipping	256 g	9.0 oz	1 cup
YIELD: 136 PRALINES	**1053 g**	**37.2 oz**	

1. Prepare an acetate sheet on an acrylic base and cover with overwarmed couverture (see page 118). On the sheet, place a 15-in/380-mm square acrylic frame, ½ in/ 13 mm high. Place a divider or bar inside the frame to split it in half. (The recipe makes enough ganache for a half-frame, 7½ × 15 in/190 × 380 mm.)

2. In a medium pot, bring the cream and mint to a boil over medium heat.

3. Once the cream has boiled, remove it from the heat, immediately cover with plastic wrap, and let steep for 10 minutes.

4. Strain to remove the mint, and add additional cream as needed to return the total quantity to 10.2 oz/290 g. Add the honey and return the cream to a boil.

6. Combine the milk and dark couvertures. Pour the hot cream mixture over the couverture mixture, and set aside undisturbed for 1 minute.

7. Using a spatula, stir in small circles starting in the center of the bowl, then gradually in wider circles to form a smooth, shiny ganache.

8. Cool to 92°F/33°C. Blend in the butter and crème de menthe with an immersion blender.

9. Spread the ganache into the prepared acrylic frame and allow to set overnight at room temperature.

10. Remove the frame, flip the slab over, and remove the acetate sheet. Place the slab on a guitar cutter and cut into ⅞-in/22-mm squares.

11 Transfer the pieces to a parchment paper–lined sheet tray, separate them, and let them rest at room temperature for 2 hours to form a crust before finishing.

12 Decorate a transfer sheet as desired.

13 Using a dipping fork, dip each praline into the dark couverture. Before the couverture sets, place the transfer sheet on top.

14 Let the couverture completely set before removing the transfer sheet.

15 Store in an airtight container at 57° to 61°F/13.9° to 16.1°C in a dark, dry place.

RECOMMENDED TRANSFER SHEET DÉCOR

1 Using a brush, splatter white cocoa butter onto a piece of acetate.

2 Using an airbrush, spray a layer of yellow cocoa butter, then a layer of green cocoa butter over the white splatters.

3 Spray a layer of white-colored cocoa butter over the yellow and green cocoa butter.

Vanilla Pralines

INGREDIENTS	METRIC	US	VOLUME
Dark couverture, 63%, overwarmed, for the acetate sheet	as needed	as needed	as needed
Heavy cream	310 g, plus additional as needed	10.9 oz, plus additional as needed	1⅓ cups, plus additional as needed
Glucose	45 g	1.6 oz	2 tbsp
Vanilla bean	14 g	0.5 oz	1 ea
White couverture, half melted	450 g	15.9 oz	3 ⅓ cups
Cocoa butter, melted	45 g	1.6 oz	⅓ cup
Colored cocoa butter, for the transfer sheet	as needed	as needed	as needed
Dark couverture, 63%, tempered, for dipping	256 g	9.0 oz	1 cup
YIELD: 136 PRALINES	**1120 g**	**39.5 oz**	

1   Prepare an acetate sheet on an acrylic base and cover with overwarmed couverture (see page 118). On the sheet, place a 15-in/380-mm square acrylic frame, ½ in/13 mm high. Place a divider or bar inside the frame to split it in half. (The recipe makes enough ganache for a half-frame, 7½ × 15 in/190 × 380 mm.)

2   Place the cream and glucose in a medium pot. Split the vanilla bean, scrape out the seeds, and add the pod and seeds to the cream. Bring to a boil over medium heat.

3   Strain to remove the bean, and add additional cream as needed to return the total quantity to 10.9 oz/310 g. Return the cream to a boil.

4   Pour the hot cream over the white couverture and set aside undisturbed for 1 minute.

5   Add the cocoa butter and use a spatula to stir in small circles starting in the center of the bowl, then gradually stir in wider circles to form a smooth, shiny ganache.

6   Spread the ganache into the prepared acrylic frame and allow to set overnight at room temperature.

7   Remove the frame, flip the slab over, and remove the acetate sheet. Place the slab on a guitar cutter and cut into ⅞-in/22-mm squares.

8   Transfer the pieces to a parchment paper–lined sheet tray, separate them, and let them rest at room temperature for 2 hours to form a crust before finishing.

9   Decorate a transfer sheet as desired. Using a dipping fork, dip each praline into the dark couverture. Before the couverture sets, cover with the transfer sheet.

10   Let the couverture completely set before removing the transfer sheet. Store in an airtight container at 57° to 61°F/13.9° to 16.1°C in a dark, dry place.

NOTE: The vanilla praline recipe can be used along with any other slabbed praline to create a double-layer praline, shown opposite.

Butter Ganache Pralines

Cognac

INGREDIENTS	METRIC	US	VOLUME
Milk couverture, 37%	500 g	17.6 oz	2 cups
Unsalted butter, softened	200 g	7.1 oz	1 cup
Cognac	100 g	3.5 oz	½ cup
Dark Chocolate Discs (page 62)	90 g	3.2 oz	90 ea
Dark couverture, 63%, tempered, for dipping	180 g	6.3 oz	¾ cup
YIELD: 90 PRALINES	**1070 g**	**37.7 oz**	

1 Melt the milk couverture in the oven at 88° to 90°F/31.1° to 32.2°C, or use tempered couverture.

2 In a bowl, blend the butter by hand with a spatula until smooth.

3 Mix the butter and couverture together by hand using a spatula or a stand mixer fitted with the paddle attachment. The closer the temperatures of the butter and the couverture, the easier it will be to blend them together. Stir to a smooth consistency.

4 Add the Cognac. Blend in the Cognac very well, by hand, using a spatula, or stand mixer to create a smooth ganache.

5 Pipe the ganache onto the chocolate discs using a pastry bag with a plain size-12 tip. If the ganache is too soft, let it set before piping. If the ganache is too cold, it can be warmed in a water bath or stirred. Stirring will aerate the ganache, leaving a lighter mouthfeel.

6 Let the piped ganache set for 1 hour at room temperature.

7 Once the ganache is fully crystallized, dip the pieces in the dark couverture using a dipping fork. Let the couverture completely set.

8 Store in an airtight container at 57° to 61°F/13.9° to 16.1°C in a dark, dry place.

Cointreau

INGREDIENTS	METRIC	US	VOLUME
Dark couverture, 63%	400 g	14.1 oz	1½ cups
Unsalted butter, softened	200 g	7.1 oz	1 cup
Grated orange zest	1 ea	1 ea	1 ea
Cointreau	100 g	3.5 oz	¼ cup
Dark Chocolate Discs (page 62)	80 g	2.8 oz	80 ea
Dark couverture, 63%, tempered, for dipping	160 g	5.6 oz	⅔ cup
YIELD: 80 PRALINES	**940 g**	**33.1 oz**	

1   Melt the dark couverture in the oven at 90°F/32.2°C, or use tempered couverture.

2   In a bowl, blend the butter and orange zest by hand with a spatula until smooth.

3   Mix the butter-zest mixture and the couverture together either by hand, using a spatula, or in a stand mixer fitted with the paddle attachment. The closer the temperatures of the butter and the couverture, the easier it will be to blend them together. Stir to a smooth consistency.

4   Add the Cointreau. Blend in the Cointreau very well using a spatula or a stand mixer fitted with the paddle attachment to create a smooth ganache.

5   Pipe the ganache onto the chocolate discs using a pastry bag with a plain size-12 tip. If the ganache is too soft, let it set before piping. If the ganache is too cold, it can be warmed in a water bath or stirred. Stirring will aerate the ganache, leaving a lighter mouthfeel.

6   Allow the piped ganache to set for 1 hour at room temperature.

7   Once the ganache is fully crystallized, dip the pieces in the dark couverture using a dipping fork. Let the couverture completely set.

8   Store in an airtight container at 57° to 61°F/13.9° to 16.1°C in a dark, dry place.

Kirsch Points

INGREDIENTS	METRIC	US	VOLUME
Milk couverture, 37%	400 g	14.1 oz	1½ cups
Unsalted butter	200 g	7.1 oz	1 cup
Kirschwasser	100 g	3.5 oz	⅔ cup
Dark Chocolate Discs (page 62)	80 g	2.8 oz	80 ea
Milk couverture, 37%, tempered, for dipping	160 g	5.6 oz	⅔ cup
YIELD: 80 PRALINES	940 g	33.1 oz	

1   Melt the milk couverture in the oven at 88°F/31.1°C, or use tempered couverture.

2   In a bowl, blend the butter by hand with a spatula until smooth.

3   Mix the couverture and butter together either by hand, using a spatula, or in a stand mixer fitted with the paddle attachment. The closer the temperatures of the butter and the couverture, the easier it will be to blend them together. Stir to a smooth consistency.

4   Add the Kirsch. Blend in the Kirsch very well using a spatula or a stand mixer fitted with the paddle attachment to create a smooth ganache.

5   Pipe the ganache onto the chocolate discs using a pastry bag with a plain size-12 tip. If the ganache is too soft, let it set before piping. If the ganache is too cold, it can be warmed in a water bath or stirred. Stirring will aerate the ganache, leaving a lighter mouthfeel.

6   Allow the piped ganache to set for 1 hour at room temperature.

7   Once the ganache is fully crystallized, dip the pieces in the milk couverture using a dipping fork. Let the couverture completely set.

8   Store in an airtight container at 57° to 61°F/13.9° to 16.1°C in a dark, dry place.

Port Wine

INGREDIENTS	METRIC	US	VOLUME
Milk couverture, 37%	200 g	7.1 oz	¾ cup
Dark couverture, 63%	160 g	5.6 oz	⅔ cup
Unsalted butter	200 g	7.1 oz	1 cup
Ruby Port Wine	120 g	4.2 oz	⅔ cup
Dark Chocolate Discs (page 62)	80 g	2.8 oz	80 ea
Dark couverture, 63%, tempered, for dipping	160 g	5.6 oz	⅔ cup
YIELD: 78 PRALINES	**920 g**	**32.4 oz**	

1 Melt the milk and dark couverture in the oven at 88°F/31.1°C, or use tempered couverture.

2 In a bowl, blend the butter by hand with a spatula until smooth.

3 Mix the milk and dark couvertures and the butter together with a spatula or in a stand mixer fitted with the paddle attachment. The closer the temperatures of the butter and the couvertures, the easier it will be to blend them together. Stir to a smooth consistency.

4 Add the wine. Blend in the wine very well using a spatula or a stand mixer fitted with the paddle attachment to create a smooth ganache.

5 Pipe the ganache onto the chocolate discs using a pastry bag with a plain size-12 tip. If the ganache is too soft, let it set before piping. If the ganache is too cold, it can be warmed in a water bath or stirred. Stirring will aerate the ganache, leaving a lighter mouthfeel.

6 Allow the piped ganache to set 1 hour at room temperature.

7 Once the ganache is fully crystallized, dip the pieces in the dark couverture using a dipping fork. Let the couverture completely set.

8 Store in an airtight container at 57° to 61°F/13.9° to 16.1°C in a dark, dry place.

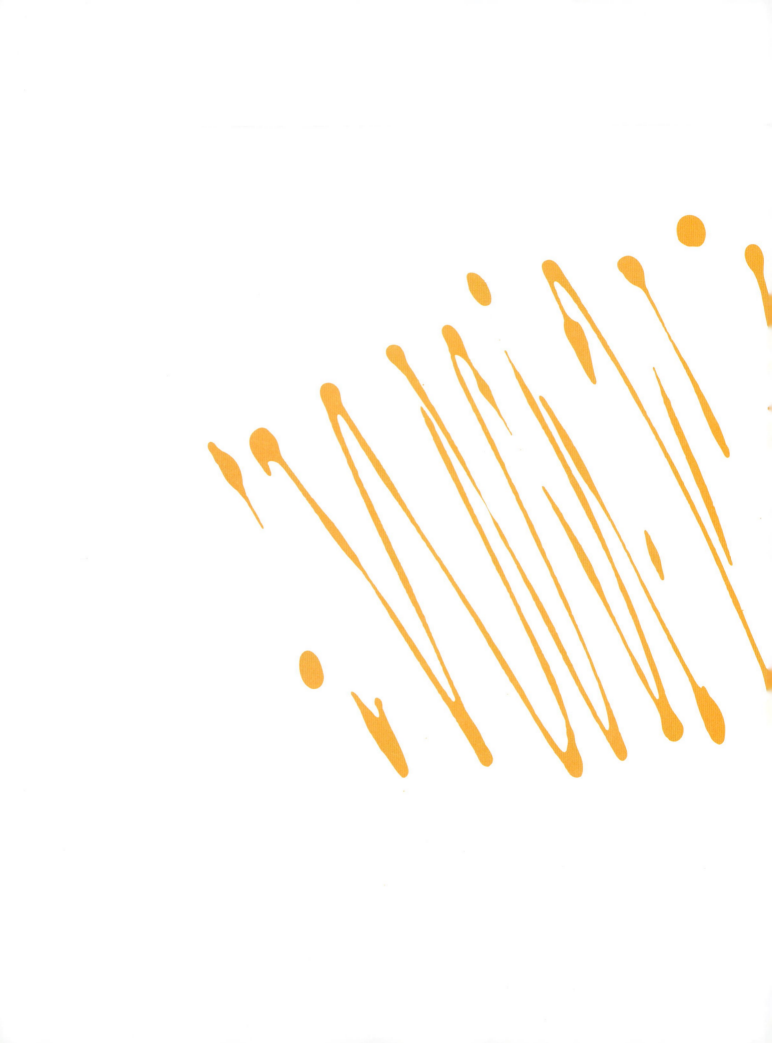

9

Sugar-Crusted Alcohol Pralines

Sugar-crusted alcohol pralines are not as common in the United States as they are in Europe. When these unique treats are sold in Europe, they are usually wrapped in paper or foil to warn customers that they are filled with alcohol. Be sure to warn your customers to place the entire praline in their mouth, so that they do not bite into it and cover themselves in the alcohol.

Making the Molds

The first step in creating sugar-crusted alcohol pralines is to make a mold. Simple shapes and forms without a lot of detail and depth should be chosen, because they will allow the sugar to crystallize more easily, providing a better mouthfeel. The easiest way to create a mold for these pralines is to make a mold of an already existing mold.

1. Pipe tempered chocolate into a chocolate candy mold with simple shapes. After filling the molds, refrigerate the tray for about 5 minutes to speed up the crystallization process.

2. Once the chocolate has set, unmold the chocolates onto a very flat surface such as an acrylic base. Place the base on a hot tray to warm slightly and get the chocolates to stick onto the base. This way the chocolates will not move, and the silicone used in the next step will not seep under the chocolates (see "Gelatin Molds," page 245). Make sure to place the chocolates close together on the base to minimize the amount of silicone needed.

3. Create a sturdy frame around the chocolates and carefully pour silicone into the frame, ensuring that the chocolates are fully covered. Let the silicone set for 24 hours.

4. Once the silicone has set, remove the mold and discard the chocolate.

5. Pipe plaster of Paris into the silicone molds using a pastry bag. Let the plaster set for 1 hour.

6. Once the plaster has set, turn the silicone mold over and unmold the plaster shapes.

7. Use a hot-glue gun to glue the plaster shapes to a wooden stick and let dry. Make sure the wooden stick is longer than the length of the sheet tray that will be used for making the pralines. The plaster shapes should not be placed too close to one another, as that could cause excessive compression and eventually caving in of the starch.

8. Combine two parts wheat starch and one part corn starch, and blend them together with a whisk to loosen the starch. Dry the starch in the oven at 200°F/93.3°C for a few hours, and then completely fill a sheet pan with the starch blend. Smooth the surface with a straightedge to level the starch.

9. Holding both ends of the wooden stick, firmly press the plaster shapes into the powder to make an impression, then carefully pull the stick back up, leaving only the print of the stamp in the powder.

TOP ROW:
- Pipe tempered chocolate into the candy mold.
- Unmold the chocolates onto an acrylic base.
- Frame the chocolates with metal bars and pour the silicone mixture over the chocolates.

CENTER ROW:
- Once the silicone has set, remove the mold and discard the chocolate.
- Mix plaster of Paris with water and pipe into the molds.
- Once the plaster has set, unmold the shapes.

BOTTOM ROW:
- Glue the plaster shapes onto a wooden stick.
- Smooth the surface with a straightedge to level the starch mixture evenly.
- Firmly press the stamp into the powder and carefully pull it out.

Making the Alcohol Pralines

Any kind of hard liquor without sugar can be used in making alcohol pralines. Popular options include brandies, especially Kirschwasser and Poire Williams, and whiskey. The pralines can be enrobed in dark, milk, or white couverture, although 63% dark couverture is most commonly used.

Alcohol Syrup

INGREDIENTS	METRIC	US	VOLUME
Sugar	1000 g	35.3 oz	5 cups
Cold water	400 g	14.1 oz	1¾ cups
Alcohol (any kind of hard liquor)	200 g	7.1 oz	1 cup
Nonacidic liquid color (optional; see Note)	as needed	as needed	as needed
YIELD (SEE NOTE)	**1500 g**	**52.9 oz**	**7½ cups**

1   Slowly bring the sugar and cold water to a boil over medium heat. Brush the inner sides of the pot with water to remove any sugar crystals that may have formed, and remove any impurities from the surface with a sieve. Boil until the syrup reaches 226°F/107.8°C. (Using cold water slows the boiling process, allowing more time for the sugar crystals to dissolve.)

2   Once the syrup has reached 226°F/107.8°C, shock the pot in cold water to prevent the solution from cooking further from the heat of the pot. Cover the top of the pot with a damp towel and let sit until the syrup cools down to 140°F/60.0°C. This should take approximately 10 minutes. Check occasionally to make sure no crystals are forming on the surface of the syrup. If crystals form, spray a mist of water over the surface until they disappear.

3   Pour the alcohol into the cooled syrup and mix gently with a spoon. Stir only enough to just combine the alcohol and syrup; the act of pouring the mixture in the final use will aid in mixing the syrup and alcohol further. Too much agitation will cause crystallization. Be careful not to touch the bottom or sides of the pan while stirring, as that would also accelerate the formation of sugar crystals.

NOTE: If desired, liquid color without acidity can be added to the cold water before bringing to a boil. Colors with acidity should be avoided, as the acidity could prevent crystallization.

The total yield for the alcohol syrup will be less than the sum of the ingredients, because some water will evaporate while the syrup is boiling.

Slowly bring the sugar and water solution to a boil to remove impurities.

Sugar-Crusted
Alcohol Pralines

INGREDIENTS	METRIC	US	VOLUME
Alcohol syrup	1500 g	53.9 oz	7½ cups
Couverture, tempered, for dipping	240 g	8.5 oz	1 cup
YIELD: 120 PRALINES	**1740 g**	**62.4 oz**	

1 Warm a funnel dispenser by placing it upside down over the pot so that the heat rises up to warm it or by using a torch. Pour the alcohol syrup into the funnel to dispense into the molds.

2 Dispense the syrup into each imprinted cavity of the starch powder.

3 As soon as all the cavities are filled, sift additional starch powder over the tray to fully cover the base of each shape. Let the tray sit for 24 hours without turning.

4 After 24 hours, carefully remove the pralines from the starch. The starch can be reused after removal of the pralines, if desired, and should be kept dry if it will be used again.

5 Carefully brush off the excess powder. Make sure to do this away from the other pralines so that if one of the pralines breaks, it will not wet the other pieces.

6 Cover the pralines in the couverture by enrobing them or dipping them in couverture using a dipping fork.

7 Let set overnight at room temperature.

8 Store in an airtight container at 57° to 61°F/13.9° to 16.1°C in a dark, dry place.

FIRST ROW:
– Pour the alcohol into the cooled syrup and stir gently.
– Pour the alcohol syrup into a dispenser.

SECOND ROW:
– Dispense the syrup into each imprinted cavity of the starch powder.
– Sift starch powder over the pan to fully cover each shape.

THIRD ROW:
– Carefully remove the shapes from the powder.
– Using a soft brush, carefully brush off excess powder.

FOURTH ROW:
– Use an enrobing machine to cover the pralines in chocolate.
– If the syrup has been boiled correctly, the alcohol praline should have a thin sugar crystal crust beneath the chocolate.

Part 3: Creating Chocolate Showpieces

10

Chocolate Bases and Tubes

The base is an essential part of any showpiece, but it is often forgotten as we focus on the more decorative elements of a piece. The base must be in harmony with the rest of the piece, so its form, shape, and texture are very important. In addition to a functional and attractive base, showpieces need height. Chocolate tubes are an easy way to create this height. Depending on whether they are to be used for support or for decoration, tubes can be hollow or filled, and they can be colored as desired to complement the rest of the piece.

Chocolate Bases

Any simple cutout or molded chocolate shape can be used as the base for a showpiece, but there are a number of techniques that can also be used to create more interesting decorative bases. These include using ice to shape a distinctive-looking base and adding shapes or designs by casting a base using silicone or gelatin pieces.

Creating Bases on Ice

This unique technique is very fast and can be used for making sculpture supports without any molds.

1   Place ice cubes into a plastic bag to keep the ice from touching the chocolate directly. Place the bag into a bowl.

2   Pour tempered chocolate over the bag of ice cubes and immediately place into the refrigerator so the chocolate will set around the edges first. The middle portion of the chocolate should remain in its liquid form.

3   After 2 minutes in the refrigerator, tap on the top of the chocolate in the center of the bowl to check the consistency. It should feel softer in the center than on the edges where the chocolate has begun to set.

4   When the edges have begun to set and the center is still soft, carefully remove the chocolate mass from the bowl and separate from the plastic bag.

TOP ROW:
- Place ice cubes into a plastic bag and place in a bowl.
- Pour tempered chocolate over the bag of ice cubes.
- Check after 2 minutes; the chocolate should be set on the outside but still liquid on the inside.

BOTTOM ROW:
- Immediately cut the chocolate into pieces.
- Assemble the support right away, before the chocolate fully sets.
- Even a support can carry a line and look elegant, which enhances the finished piece.

5   Use a knife to cut the chocolate mass into pieces.

6   Using the liquid chocolate to adhere the pieces together, immediately begin to attach the pieces to one another to create a base. The chocolate will set very fast, so it is essential to work quickly and without second-guessing the placement of the pieces. If the chocolate begins to set up before all the pieces have been attached, use additional chocolate in a pastry bag to attach the remaining pieces together.

VARIATION

A different kind of support can be created by pouring chocolate directly on top of the ice in a bowl. The chocolate will not bloom and turn gray because, by running slowly over the ice, it will temper itself. The look of the support will depend on the size and form of the ice cubes and on the viscosity of the chocolate. With large, square ice cubes and thick chocolate, the base will look heavy and bulky, while small, round ice cubes and chocolate thinned with 30% cocoa butter will create a lighter, airier base. This technique works best if the chocolate is at a temperature of approximately 104°F/40.0°C. After the chocolate has set, remove the chocolate mass from the bowl and place on a rack to let the water drain. Finish the base with colored cocoa butter or a cocoa butter–chocolate mixture, as desired.

–   Pour the chocolate mixture directly over ice cubes.
–   Remove the chocolate from the bowl and let the water drain on a rack.

Casting a Base Using Silicone or Gelatin Pieces

The base is normally the most basic part of the showpiece. However, in an effort to make a piece more interesting, the base can be created using a variety of shapes and textures made out of gelatin or silicone. When this technique is used, the piece should always carry the same theme as the base.

1   Create molded gelatin or silicone pieces in the desired shapes or patterns using the techniques in Chapter 11 on page 245–247. If using silicone, the resulting chocolate will be shiny. If using gelatin, the chocolate will be matte or bloomed because the chocolate will absorb moisture from the gelatin.

2   Place the molded gelatin and/or silicone pieces within a framed area on a piece of parchment paper or a Silpat.

3   Pour tempered chocolate within the frame, over the molded pieces. Let the chocolate set at room temperature.

4   Once the chocolate has set, flip the base over and remove the parchment paper.

5   Remove the frame. Then gently remove the molded silicone or gelatin pieces to reveal the imprinted surface of the base.

BOTTOM ROW:
- Pour chocolate within the frame over the molded silicone or gelatin pieces.
- Remove the frame and gently remove the molded pieces.
- Because chocolate absorbs moisture from the gelatin, the chocolate will be dull where gelatin pieces were used. Chocolate will not absorb moisture from silicone, so the chocolate will be shiny where silicone pieces were used.

Chocolate Tubes

Tubes are used primarily to create height and dimension in showpieces. The tube itself can be hollow or filled and plain or decorated with color. Tubes can be made with a PVC or clear acrylic pipe, or they can be shaped with paper, acetate, or transfer sheets. Using a pipe is the easiest method. Using paper, acetate, or transfer sheets requires more hand skills but has the benefit of allowing the tube to be easily colored and adjusted to any desired diameter.

Creating Tubes Using a Pipe

You can use any kind of PVC pipe or clear acrylic pipe for this technique. It is important that the pipe is not bent and is smooth on the inside with no ridges so it will cleanly release the crystallized chocolate. Creating tubes using a narrower diameter pipe, approximately ½ to 1 in/12 to 25 mm inside diameter, is much easier than using wider pipes, as the chocolate will set much faster and will release more easily from the narrower pipes.

1   Pour tempered chocolate onto an acrylic base. Once the chocolate on the base starts to set, begin to pipe chocolate into the PVC or acrylic tube at an angle, making sure the chocolate does not pour out onto the table.

2   Fill the pipe as far as you can without spilling the chocolate out onto the table, then completely press one end of the pipe into the setting chocolate on the base, preventing the chocolate from spilling out of the pipe. If the pipe is not completely filled, top it off with tempered chocolate after it has been set into the base.

3   As soon as the chocolate in the pipe has set, break it off the base, clean the outside of the pipe, and place it in the refrigerator.

4   The chocolate should contract and release itself from the tube after about 5 minutes for very narrow tubes (½ to 1 in/12 to 25 mm) or 10 to 15 minutes for larger tubes. If using a clear acrylic pipe, you will be able to see when the chocolate is completely released from the pipe. Once the chocolate has contracted and fully released itself, remove the pipe from the refrigerator and remove the set chocolate from the tube.

–   Before fully filling the pipe, press the pipe onto the setting chocolate on the acrylic base.
–   Immediately after the chocolate sets, break it off the base and clean the end of the pipe.
–   Once the chocolate has contracted, remove it from the pipe.

Creating Tubes by Hand

In this method, a piece of parchment, newsprint, or copy paper is used to roll the chocolate into a tube shape. Note that chocolate sets more quickly on marble than on wood, so if the chocolate is setting too quickly when working on marble, try working on a wooden surface instead. If a shiny tube is desired, a sheet of acetate can be used in place of the paper.

1   Cut a long strip of paper the same width as the desired length of the tube, and place it flat on the table. Then cut an additional 2-in/50-mm strip of paper that is slightly longer than the desired length of the tube.

2   Determine the desired circumference of the tube and place the smaller strip of paper that distance from the edge of the larger piece. This will serve as a guide and provide a clean edge when spreading the chocolate.

3   Pipe tempered chocolate on the section of paper marked off with the strip and use an offset spatula to evenly spread the chocolate.

4   Immediately after spreading the chocolate, slide the sheet away from you slightly and lift the smaller strip of paper, leaving a clean rectangle of chocolate.

5   As soon as the strip has been removed, lift the ends of the chocolate-covered paper, roll toward the other side of the chocolate rectangle, and gently press the seams together, carefully shaping a circular tube.

TOP ROW:
- Pipe chocolate on the part of the paper closest to you, below the strip.
- Use an offset spatula to spread the chocolate.
- Immediately after spreading the chocolate, move the sheet up and lift the strip of paper.

BOTTOM ROW:
- Lift the ends of the chocolate-covered paper and gently press the seams together.
- Gently roll the tube all the way up the remaining paper.
- Remove the paper once the chocolate has completely set.

6   Gently roll the tube all the way up the remaining paper. Let it sit until the chocolate has completely crystallized, about 15 minutes at room temperature or 3 to 5 minutes in the refrigerator.

7   Once the chocolate has completely set, unroll and remove the paper.

VARIATIONS

PIPED TUBES: To create piped tubes, set up the paper per the directions above, but pipe the chocolate over the paper in diagonal lines instead of spreading with the spatula. Be sure to work very quickly since the tube needs to be formed before the chocolate sets. Immediately after piping, remove the paper strip and roll the chocolate-covered paper into a tube following the directions above. Let set completely before removing the paper.

COLORED TUBES: Set up a transfer sheet and a strip of acetate following the same directions used above for rolling tubes with paper. Drizzle colored cocoa butter onto the transfer sheet and spread with a spatula. Then drizzle a second color of cocoa butter over the first color, if desired, and spread with a spatula. Cover the colored cocoa butters with white chocolate so that the inside of the tube will appear white. Immediately after spreading the chocolate, remove the plastic strip and roll the chocolate-covered transfer sheet into a tube following the directions above. Let set completely before removing the acetate.

NOTE: *To achieve a great shine, it is best to slowly release the acetate right before using the tube.*

–   To create piped tubes, pipe the chocolate onto the paper instead of spreading it.
–   Immediately after piping, move the sheet up and lift the strip.
–   Gently press the seams together and roll the paper into a tube.

TOP ROW:
- Spread the first color with an offset spatula and repeat with the second color.
- Adding a little dark chocolate over the colored cocoa butter helps to achieve a darker red.
- Cover the colored cocoa butter with white chocolate.

BOTTOM ROW:
- As soon as the strip has been removed, lift the ends of the chocolate-covered acetate.
- Gently press the seams together and roll the tube all the way up.
- Once the chocolate has completely set, release the tube from the acetate.

Piped and colored tubes

Creating Triangle Tubes

Triangle tubes can be created simply by using poster board or acetate. These tubes can create volume and elegance on a showpiece.

1   Draw the desired triangle shape on poster board or acetate and cut out using an Exacto knife. It is much easier to work with triangle shapes that have a single curve, rather than two curves like an S.

2   Score the middle of the shape all the way down using an Exacto knife. This will allow the template to bend appropriately.

3   Begin to bend the template along the scored line, then unbend and place it flat with the scored part facing down toward the table.

4   Pipe tempered chocolate all the way down the surface of the template.

5   Use a spatula to smooth the chocolate evenly over the entire template.

6   As soon as the chocolate begins to set, remove the template from the table.

7   Bend the chocolate by refolding the template along the scored line, and let set at room temperature. Refrigeration is not advisable, as it will force the crystallization too quickly and may bend or curve the original shape too much.

8   Remove the chocolate from the template as soon as it has set completely in order to prevent additional curvature due to the shrinking of the chocolate.

9   Spread tempered chocolate onto a piece of parchment paper or newsprint. Before the chocolate sets, lay the curved chocolate piece directly on top to close the triangle. If the bottom edges of the curved piece are not flat, melt the edge of the open side on a food warmer or a hot sheet pan before placing the shape on top of the spread chocolate.

10   As soon as the chocolate is set, cut out the completed triangle shape along the edges, being sure to make a few release cuts along the sides as well.

11   After the crystallization is complete, remove the triangle piece from the paper.

FIRST ROW:
- Draw and cut out the desired shape on poster board.
- Once scored, begin to bend the template, then flatten it back.
- Pipe chocolate all the way down the surface of the template.

SECOND ROW:
- Using a spatula, smooth the chocolate evenly.
- As soon as the chocolate begins to set, remove it from the table.
- Bend the chocolate along the scored line.

THIRD ROW:
- Once the chocolate has set, remove the poster board.
- Apply chocolate on parchment paper, lay the curved chocolate directly on it, and cut along the edges.
- After the crystallization is complete, remove the triangle piece from the paper.

11

Chocolate Décor

This chapter details the techniques used to create unique shapes and accessories that can be used to decorate a showpiece or to add nuance to desserts, cakes, or entremets.

Molded Chocolate Shapes

The same techniques outlined in Chapter 7 can be used on larger scale molds to create three-dimensional shapes that give visual impact to showpieces. Larger molds to be used for decoration are not typically filled and capped; rather, they are cast and left hollow. The hollow halves can be glued together to create a whole sphere or egg.

Decorating Molded Shapes

Even with a simple form, color can be used to add a dramatic effect to molded chocolate. Molds can be decorated using the same techniques outlined in Chapter 7 for airbrushing, smearing, and splattering or by piping chocolate into the mold in the desired design before casting.

- Pipe tempered dark chocolate lines back and forth in one direction, then rotate the mold and repeat in the next direction. Cast with white chocolate.
- Pipe dots of tempered chocolate into the mold, starting with larger dots in the middle and gradually smaller dots as you work your way toward the outside of the egg. Cast with white chocolate.
- Swirl a thin layer of chocolate into the mold with your finger in a circular motion. The mold has to be covered before the chocolate starts to set, otherwise overcrystallization will be forced, taking away the shine.

SECOND ROW:
- Pipe dark and white chocolate into the mold. Swirl together with your finger to create a marble effect.
- Use a paintbrush to press colored cocoa butter into the mold, then dark chocolate, to create a sponged effect.
- Airbrush colored cocoa butter into the mold. Immediately after airbrushing, use a Colour Shaper to create a vertical swirl down the center of the mold.

THIRD ROW:
- Press gold leaf into the mold. Swirl red cocoa butter into the mold over the gold leaf using your finger. Repeat on one half of the mold using dark chocolate.
- Splatter the mold with dark chocolate. Spray with colored cocoa butter, then with white cocoa butter. Cast with dark chocolate.
- Thicken melted chocolate with a splash of Kirschwasser. Immediately pipe into the mold in a spiral. Do not cast.

Texturing Molded Shapes

Chocolate will reflect any texture it is exposed to—from paper to textured plastic to wallpaper. Texture can even be created by spraying frozen chocolate with cocoa butter. When molding chocolate, the interior of the mold is used to create the textured surface, since the chocolate contracts as it cools.

Creating Velvet Texture

Spraying a frozen chocolate shell with cocoa butter causes the chocolate to crystallize immediately, giving the shape a dull velvety texture.

1 Cast the molds with the desired type of chocolate.

2 Unmold, then freeze the unmolded chocolates for about 5 minutes for a smaller piece, or 10 minutes for a larger piece. Immediately after removing the chocolates from the freezer, spray colored cocoa butter onto the surface. This will create a velvet effect.

3 After spraying, let the chocolates sit for several hours without touching to avoid leaving a fingerprint.

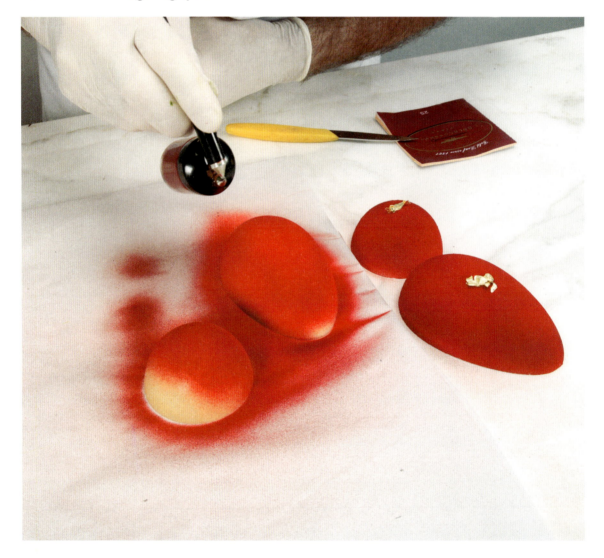

Gelatin Molds

Another way to give texture to chocolate is by using gelatin or silicone molds. Gelatin molds are easy to create using the technique outlined below. The same techniques can be accomplished using silicone; however, gelatin is much less expensive. Using silicone is a two-part process requiring both silicone and a hardener. If using silicone, be careful to follow the package directions regarding the ratio of hardener to silicone. Gelatin molds can be made from gelatin powder or leaves, using any chocolate mold or another non-conventional item such as wallpaper.

1   If using gelatin leaves, cut the leaves into small pieces. Using a ratio of 6 parts water to 1 part gelatin, combine the gelatin leaves or powder with the water and let bloom for 10 minutes.

2   If using textured wallpaper or another such item, use metal bars to create a frame directly on top of the wallpaper.

3   Warm the bloomed gelatin in the microwave. Pour into the molds or the prepared frame. Let it set completely at room temperature for about 30 minutes or in the refrigerator for about 5 minutes.

4   Once the gelatin has fully set, gently unmold, or if using a frame, remove the frame and peel the gelatin off the textured paper.

5   Place the molded gelatin into the chocolate mold.

6   Use a sharp knife to cut off excess from the molded gelatin strip.

7   Fill the mold with tempered chocolate.

8   Let sit for a few minutes before pouring the chocolate out of the mold. If a thick cast mold is necessary, cast the mold twice to create an even thickness. Letting the molds sit for a longer period of time will only create a thicker rim, but the bottom will not have the same thickness.

9   To pour out the chocolate from the mold, tilt the mold over the bowl and use the handle of a spatula to knock out the excess chocolate.

10   Scrape off the excess chocolate and place the mold face down on newsprint.

11   As soon as the chocolate has set, release the mold from the paper and clean off any excess chocolate from the edges. Place in the refrigerator for a few minutes to aid in releasing the chocolate from the mold.

12   Remove the molds from the refrigerator as soon as the chocolate has visibly released from the mold. Release the chocolates from the mold.

13   Remove the gelatin from the chocolate. Be careful not to touch the chocolate and damage the shine.

14   The shaped areas can be decorated with piped chocolate as desired.

THE ART OF THE CHOCOLATIER

- Let gelatin leaves bloom in water for 10 minutes, then warm in the microwave and pour into the molds.
- Use metal bars to create a frame over the wallpaper and pour in the gelatin.

SECOND ROW LEFT:
- Once the gelatin has fully set, gently peel it off the textured paper.
- After placing the gelatin strip into the mold, use a sharp knife to cut off the excess gelatin strip.

THIRD ROW LEFT:
- Fill the mold with tempered chocolate.
- After pouring out the chocolate, place the mold face down on the newsprint.

FOURTH ROW LEFT:
- Release the mold from the paper and clean off excess chocolate from the edges.
- Once the chocolate has visibly released from the mold, remove the egg from the mold.

FIFTH ROW LEFT:
- Carefully remove the gelatin from the molded egg.
- The shaped areas can be decorated with piped chocolate.

Cut-Out Chocolate Shapes

Disposable templates for all kinds of shapes can be made out of cardboard. If there is a template shape you plan to use frequently, however, such as a holiday-themed shape, you may prefer to have the template made in plastic so that it can be washed and reused. Plastic templates can be made by cutting the shapes out of a plastic sheet by hand, or they can be cut by a template company using a laser. Premade templates are also available for purchase, but these are used more for wedding cake decoration than for chocolate showpieces.

Any type of chocolate can be used to create chocolate shapes for showpieces. It is not necessary to use the most expensive couverture. Using newsprint to pour and flip the chocolate will absorb cocoa butter, giving a flat matte look to the finished shapes. For smaller chocolate pieces, newsprint is ideal. For bigger pieces, however, a stronger paper such as drawing paper or the paper from a flipchart is recommended. Parchment paper is often used, too, but because it doesn't absorb the cocoa butter, the chocolate may show little waves.

1   Place the desired type of paper onto either a wooden board or a marble slab, depending on the complexity of the template. If it is a complex design, wood is a better choice, since it is warmer than marble. This will allow more time to work with the chocolate before it crystallizes. Pour chocolate onto the paper and spread with an offset spatula. The chocolate should be spread approximately ¼ in/6 mm thick for smaller pieces and slightly thicker for larger pieces.

2   As soon as the chocolate has set, place the template on the chocolate. Be sure to place it right side up. It is possible that the bottom side of the chocolate will end up having a lip where the template is cut out. Therefore it is important to place the template on the chocolate with the bottom side down.

3   Using a nonserrated knife with a very thin blade, such as an Exacto knife, immediately cut around the template before the chocolate crystallizes.

4   After cutting around the template, make several release cuts in the excess chocolate to facilitate removing the shape intact.

5   Before the chocolate crystallizes, place a sheet of paper on top of the cut chocolate and template and flip the entire piece of chocolate over.

6   Immediately remove the paper from the top of the chocolate. If the paper stays on for too long, the chocolate will curl.

7   Once the chocolate has completely set, use the tip of the Exacto knife to remove the excess pieces.

8   Trim the edges of the released piece with an Exacto knife as needed.

FIRST ROW:
- As soon as the chocolate has set, place the template on top.
- Use a thin, nonserrated knife to cut out around template.
- Place a sheet of paper on top of the chocolate and flip it over before it fully crystallizes.

SECOND ROW:
- Quickly remove the paper to prevent the chocolate from curling.
- Once the chocolate has completely set, remove the excess pieces.
- Trim the edges with an Exacto knife.

Creating a Double Chocolate Layer

For shapes to be used as the base or supporting pieces on a bigger showpiece, a thicker layer of chocolate is needed. The easiest way to create a thicker layer is to pour chocolate into a frame with the desired thickness or to pour the chocolate between metal bars. Pour the chocolate into the frame and evenly spread with an offset spatula, then use a metal bar to even out the chocolate within the frame. Cut out the template following the directions above.

If there are no frames or bars available, a double layer of chocolate can be created to yield a thicker, sturdier chocolate shape. While the first layer of poured chocolate is still tacky, pour a second layer of chocolate over the top. Use an offset spatula to spread the second layer of chocolate on top of the first, and lightly shake the paper to level the chocolate. Cut out the template following the directions on page 248.

Creating Bent Shapes

For pieces that are to be bent, place the template on the chocolate and use an Exacto knife to cut deep enough through the chocolate so that the bottom paper is also cut. Before the chocolate fully sets, remove the cut piece along with the paper underneath and bend as desired. As soon the chocolate is set, remove the paper. Use a paring knife to smooth out the edges of the cut piece, and use a paper towel to smooth out the chocolate and remove any fingerprints or flaws.

- Before the chocolate sets, remove the cut-out pieces along with the paper underneath and bend as desired.
- Use a paring knife to clean the edges.
- Use a paper towel to smooth the piece and remove any flaws or fingerprints.

Adding Texture

Embossing

Cut a pattern for the embossed design out of wide clear packaging tape and place it on top of the cut-out chocolate shape. Roll chocolate on with a paint roller, covering the pattern and the chocolate piece. Be sure to cover the surface before the chocolate you are rolling on sets to avoid forced crystallization. Remove the pattern before the rolled-on chocolate sets.

LEFT: A range of techniques can be employed to create different textured surfaces on chocolate.
RIGHT: Remove the tape from the chocolate before the brushed on chocolate sets.

Using Transfer Sheets

Roll chocolate onto the cut-out shape with a paint roller. Before the rolled-on chocolate sets, press on a transfer sheet. Remove the transfer sheet before the chocolate sets to give a textured surface to the chocolate.

Adding Toppings

Use a paint roller to roll chocolate onto the cut-out chocolate shape. Before the rolled-on chocolate sets, sprinkle on cacao nibs, vermicelli, croquant, or any other desired topping. Be sure to cover the surface before the chocolate you are rolling on sets to avoid forced crystallization.

LEFT: Remove the transfer sheet before the chocolate sets to create texture.
RIGHT: Before the rolled-on chocolate sets, sprinkle on chocolate nibs.

Using Wallpaper

Cut a piece of textured wallpaper into the desired shape. If desired, sprinkle with gold dust. Brush colored cocoa butter onto the piece of wallpaper. Make sure not to force the crystallization by overbrushing it once the cocoa butter has set. If using dark chocolate, brush white cocoa butter over the colored cocoa butter to ensure that the bright color will show.

Pipe chocolate onto the brushed piece of wallpaper and spread with an offset spatula. Lift the piece of wallpaper up from the table before the chocolate sets.

To create a curved shape, lay the piece into the inside of half a PVC pipe before the chocolate sets. To create a flat shape, lay the piece flat and place an acrylic base on top to prevent the shape from curling while the chocolate sets.

As soon as the chocolate is set, remove the acrylic or remove the curved shape from the PVC pipe. To ensure a shine, wait a couple of hours before removing the wallpaper from the chocolate. If the chocolate is needed immediately, place it in the refrigerator for a few minutes, then carefully remove the wallpaper.

FIRST ROW:
- Brush colored cocoa butter onto a cut-out piece of wallpaper.
- Pipe white chocolate over the cocoa butter and spread with an offset spatula.
- Lift up the piece from the table before the chocolate sets.

SECOND ROW:
- Set the piece into a half PVC pipe.
- After the chocolate has completely crystallized, remove the wallpaper.
- Dark, white, or milk chocolate can be textured using this technique.

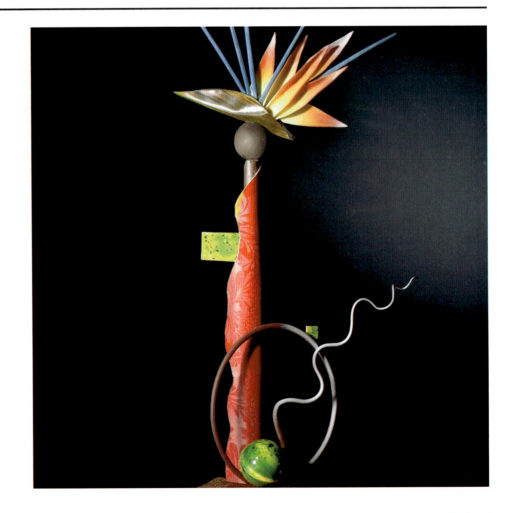

THE ART OF THE CHOCOLATIER

Using Textured Plastic

Chocolate will take on the design of any textured material. To create a flat textured shape using textured plastic, pour the chocolate onto the textured plastic, then tilt the plastic to spread the chocolate around. Once the chocolate has completely set, remove it from the plastic to reveal a mirrored texture. Flat textured pieces can be used as bases or supports for showpieces, or they can be cut into shapes and used for showpiece décor.

FIRST ROW:
- Pour chocolate onto a textured sheet of plastic.
- Tilt the plastic to spread the chocolate around.

SECOND ROW:
- Once the chocolate has completely set, remove it from the plastic to reveal a mirrored texture.

Creating Free-Form Textured Shapes

Instead of casting chocolate onto a flat, textured surface, another option is to use granulated substances to create a free-form textured chocolate shape. Chocolate can be cast in a variety of ingredients, such as sugar, grated chocolate, miniature chocolate curls, cocoa nibs, flours, truffle vermicelli, sprinkle décor, or anything else that will hold its form when chocolate is poured into it.

Place the desired ingredient in a bowl, create a well in the bowl, and pour tempered chocolate into the well. Let the chocolate sit for a moment, and sprinkle more of the desired ingredient over the top to coat the chocolate completely. Before the chocolate sets, move the coated chocolate around with your fingers to create a free-form solid. Once the chocolate has completely set, remove the chocolate from the bowl and brush off the excess coating.

ABOVE:
- Create a well in the bowl of vermicelli and pour tempered chocolate into the well.
- Before the chocolate sets, sprinkle with vermicelli and move the chocolate around to create a free-form shape.
- Remove the chocolate from the bowl once it has completely set.
- Chocolate can be cast in a variety of different granulated substances.

Using Chocolate Shapes: Creating a Chocolate Box

The technique for creating a chocolate box is shown on page 259 using a heart-shaped base, but any shape box can be created using these techniques. The heart shape is very popular as it can be filled with pralines, making the decoration practical as well as beautiful.

1   Using the techniques on page 248, cut out the desired shape for the base of the box. Cut out another piece of chocolate in the exact same shape and size for the top of the box. Then cut another piece in the exact same shape, but approximately ½ in/12 mm smaller on all sides, to form the inner piece.

2   Pipe tempered chocolate onto the bottom piece, then immediately center the inner piece on top before the piped chocolate sets, to "glue" the bottom and inner pieces together.

3   Place a strip of acetate on the table. The acetate must be longer than the perimeter of the inner piece for the box, and its width should be the desired height of the box. Pipe chocolate onto the strip of acetate, then use an offset spatula to evenly spread the chocolate.

4   As soon as the chocolate starts to set, lift the acetate strip from the table.

5   With the acetate facing out, use the inner chocolate piece as a guide to wind the chocolate-covered acetate around the perimeter of the box, securing it in place onto the edge of the inner piece.

6   Use scissors to cut off the excess acetate. If you are using supports, let the chocolate box sit with the acetate still attached to the sides while you make them.

7   Supports under the boxes make them look more elegant and make them easier to handle. To create supports, use a sphere mold to create half spheres of the desired size, or use purchased half spheres. Alternatively, you can cut out square or round pieces of chocolate to use for the supports.

8   Pipe tempered chocolate onto the half spheres.

9   Using the same template that was used to create the top and bottom box shapes, place the filled supports around the inside perimeter of the template in such a way that they will evenly support the box.

10   Once the chocolate inside the half spheres starts to set, place the bottom of the box onto the half spheres and allow it to sink into the piped chocolate and set in a level position. Continue to let sit at room temperature until the supports and side walls have completely set.

11   Once the side walls have set, peel off the acetate strip.

12   Spray the base and lid of the box with a mixture of 40 percent cocoa butter and 60 percent chocolate before decorating as desired. Use an airbrush if spraying only one piece, or a commercial spray gun if spraying multiple boxes at once. The box can be sprayed with any color as desired. Using some red in the cocoa butter–chocolate mixture is a good way to add a warmer, friendlier tone to the color.

FIRST ROW:

- Pipe chocolate onto the bottom piece.
- Before the piped chocolate hardens, center the inner piece on top.
- Pipe chocolate onto a strip of acetate and use an offset spatula to spread it evenly.

SECOND ROW:

- As soon as the chocolate starts to set, remove the acetate from the table.
- With the acetate side facing outward, use the inner chocolate piece as a guide around which to wind the strip of chocolate and acetate.
- Cut off the excess acetate.

THIRD ROW:

- Pipe chocolate onto half spheres and spread them along the traced outline of the box.
- Once the chocolate starts to set, place the bottom part of the box onto the piped half spheres.
- Once the side walls have completely set, peel off the acetate.

Chocolate Accessories

Chocolate Cigarettes

Chocolate cigarettes can be made in a variety of colors and patterns, using any type of chocolate desired.

1   Spread a thin layer of tempered chocolate directly onto a marble with an offset spatula. Clean the edges of the chocolate with a triangle spatula to make a nice rectangle.

2   As soon as the chocolate sets, rub your hand over the chocolate to rewarm it and increase the elasticity.

3   Press a knife onto the chocolate and pull the knife inward, shaving off the chocolate into a cigarette.

–   Spread a thin layer of chocolate on the marble and shave off cigarettes.
–   White and dark chocolate zebra cigarettes.

VARIATIONS

ZEBRA CIGARETTES: After spreading the thin layer of chocolate, immediately drag a fine-tooth comb across it. Depending on the desired effect, the comb can be dragged straight across or in a zigzag or wave motion. As soon as the first layer sets, use an offset spatula to spread a second layer of contrasting-colored chocolate over it. The chocolate should not be thicker than ⅛ in/3 mm. Shape the edges, hand warm, and shave into cigarettes as above.

–   Spread dark chocolate onto the marble and drag a fine comb across the chocolate.
–   Use an offset spatula to spread white chocolate over the combed dark chocolate.
–   Press down with a knife to shave off the chocolate.

THREE-COLOR CIGARETTES: Place two or three strips of tape onto the marble, spaced according to the desired design. Spread the first layer of chocolate. Immediately drag a fine-tooth comb across the chocolate, straight across or in a zigzag or wave motion. As soon as the chocolate sets, spoon a contrasting color of chocolate onto it and use an offset spatula to spread thin. Remove the strips of tape, then spread a third color of chocolate over the top. Shape the edges, hand warm, and shave into cigarettes per above.

NOTE: If the marble is cold, white chocolate should be used first since it sets more slowly than dark chocolate, allowing more time to work with it.

FIRST ROW:
- Drizzle red-colored chocolate onto the combed dark chocolate.
- Use an offset spatula to thinly spread the colored chocolate.
- Remove the strips of tape.

SECOND ROW:
- Cover with a thin layer of white chocolate and clean the edges.
- Once the chocolate has set, press down with a knife to shave off cigarettes.
- Three-color cigarettes with a reverse candy cane design.

Chocolate Shavings

Chocolate shavings can be used as a décor element for showpieces, and they are useful for hiding imperfections. They are often used to surround flowers instead of leaves. They can be made from any type or color of chocolate.

1   Spread a thin layer of tempered chocolate directly onto a marble with an offset spatula. Clean the edges with a triangle spatula to form a sharp rectangle.

2   Once the chocolate sets, rub your hand over it to warm it and to increase elasticity.

3   Use a triangle scraper to shave off the chocolate in a fast, curving outward motion.

NOTE: White chocolate sets more slowly than dark chocolate, allowing more time to shave it off as compared to the dark chocolate.

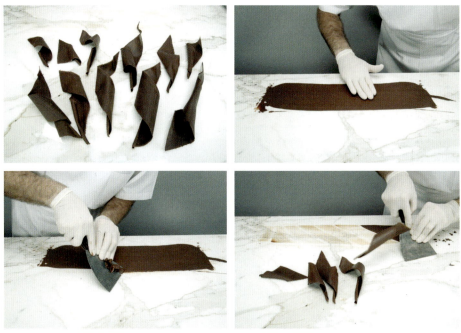

FIRST ROW:
- Simple one-color shavings.
- Warm the thinly spread chocolate with your hand to increase elasticity.

SECOND ROW:
- Immediately clean the edges to form a sharp rectangle.
- Use triangle scraper to shave off the chocolate using a fast, curving motion.

VARIATION

MARBLED CHOCOLATE SHAVINGS: Drizzle dark chocolate onto a marble tabletop, and before it sets, cover with white chocolate, slightly blending them together to create a marbled look. Use an offset spatula to spread the marbled chocolates into a thin layer. Shave off curls as described on page 262.

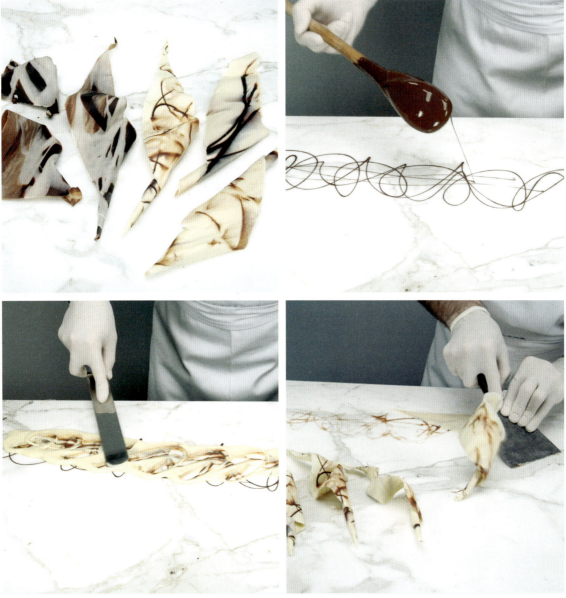

FIRST ROW:
- Different styles of marbled shavings can be created using contrasting colors.
- Drizzle dark chocolate onto the marble.

SECOND ROW:
- Before it sets, cover with white chocolate and blend to create a marbled look.
- Use a triangle scraper to shave off the chocolate using a fast, curving outward motion.

Chocolate Curls

Chocolate spiral and triangle curls can be used as decoration on cakes, tarts, or plated desserts or on chocolate showpieces.

1   Drizzle one or more colors of cocoa butter onto a piece of acetate. The cocoa butter should be on the warm side (88° to 90°F/31.1° to 32.2°C) since it will be smeared, forcing crystallization.

2   Use an offset spatula to smear the colored cocoa butter across the acetate. Stop smearing before the cocoa butter sets to avoid forcing crystallization and reducing the shine.

3   Drizzle tempered milk or dark chocolate over the smeared colored cocoa butter.

4   Cover the drizzled chocolate with tempered white chocolate, and use an offset spatula to evenly spread the white chocolate to cover the sheet. If using dark chocolate instead of white for this step, the cocoa butter and drizzled chocolate should be sprayed with white cocoa butter first so that the colored cocoa butter shows through.

5   Right after the chocolate has set, use an Exacto knife to cut it into triangles 4 in/100 mm long by 1½ in/38 mm wide, making sure not to cut through the acetate (see template, page 351).

6   While the chocolate is still pliable, place a sheet of parchment paper over the chocolate and curl the "sandwich" at an angle. Refrigerate for a few minutes to force the crystallization.

7   Release the acetate right before using to protect the shiny surface from dust and daylight. If the curls are needed immediately, remove the plastic slowly to retain the shine.

FIRST ROW:
- Drizzle red and orange tempered cocoa butter onto the acetate.
- Drizzle tempered dark chocolate over the smeared colored cocoa butter.

SECOND ROW:
- Cover with thin layer of tempered white chocolate.
- Carefully cut the triangle shapes, being careful not to cut through the acetate.

THIRD ROW:
- Place a sheet of parchment paper over the chocolate and curl it at an angle.
- Release the curls from the acetate.

VARIATIONS

STRAIGHT TRIANGLE CURLS: Use a paring knife to cut the chocolate into narrow elongated isosceles triangles 5 in/127 mm long by ¾ in/20 mm wide, being careful not to cut through the acetate (see template, page 351). Cover with parchment paper and curl straight around a rolling pin. Refrigerate and release as described on page 265.

– Cut narrow, elongated isosceles triangles, being careful not to cut through the acetate.
– Cover with parchment paper and curl straight around a rolling pin.
– Release the finished curls from the acetate.

SPIRAL CURLS: Cut the chocolate into triangles 7 in/178 mm long by ¾ in/20 mm wide (see template, page 351). Cover with parchment paper and roll at an angle, then refrigerate and release as above.

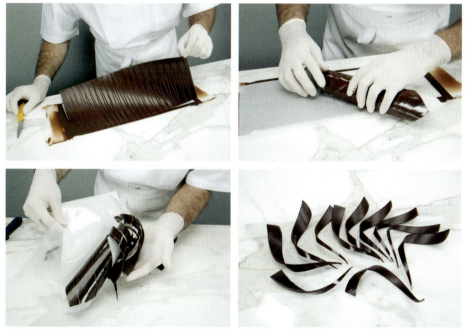

FIRST ROW:
– Cut the acetate into long, narrow triangle strips.
– Cover the chocolate with parchment paper and roll at an angle.

SECOND ROW:
– Release the curls from the parchment paper and acetate.
– The finished curls can be used for decoration.

Spiral Cones

Spiral cones are just another way to curl chocolate. These curls are used mostly for decorating cakes and desserts, but they can also be used as another element for chocolate showpieces.

Spread a thin layer of chocolate onto the marble. Before it fully sets, place a triangle spatula at the edge of the chocolate. Hold down one side of the spatula and push and turn the other side 90 degrees to one side, forming a spiraled cone.

LEFT: Spiral cones
RIGHT: Hold down one side of the spatula and push and turn the other side at a 90-degree angle to form a spiral cone.

Fettuccini Curls

Like the spiral cones above, these curls are an effective way to decorate any showpiece, cake, or dessert. These curls are finer in size and give a delicate look.

1   Using an offset spatula, spread a thin layer of chocolate onto a strip of acetate 6 to 8 in/150 to 200 mm long by 3 in/76 mm wide.

2   Immediately draw a fine-tooth comb across the chocolate.

3   Before the chocolate sets, lift up the piece of acetate and twist, chocolate side in, into the desired curl shape.

4   Place the curled acetate into a piece of PVC or cardboard pipe and let set at room temperature. If needed immediately, place in the refrigerator for a few minutes. Leave the acetate on the chocolate until the curl is needed, as it will protect the chocolate from dust and will keep it shiny for a longer time.

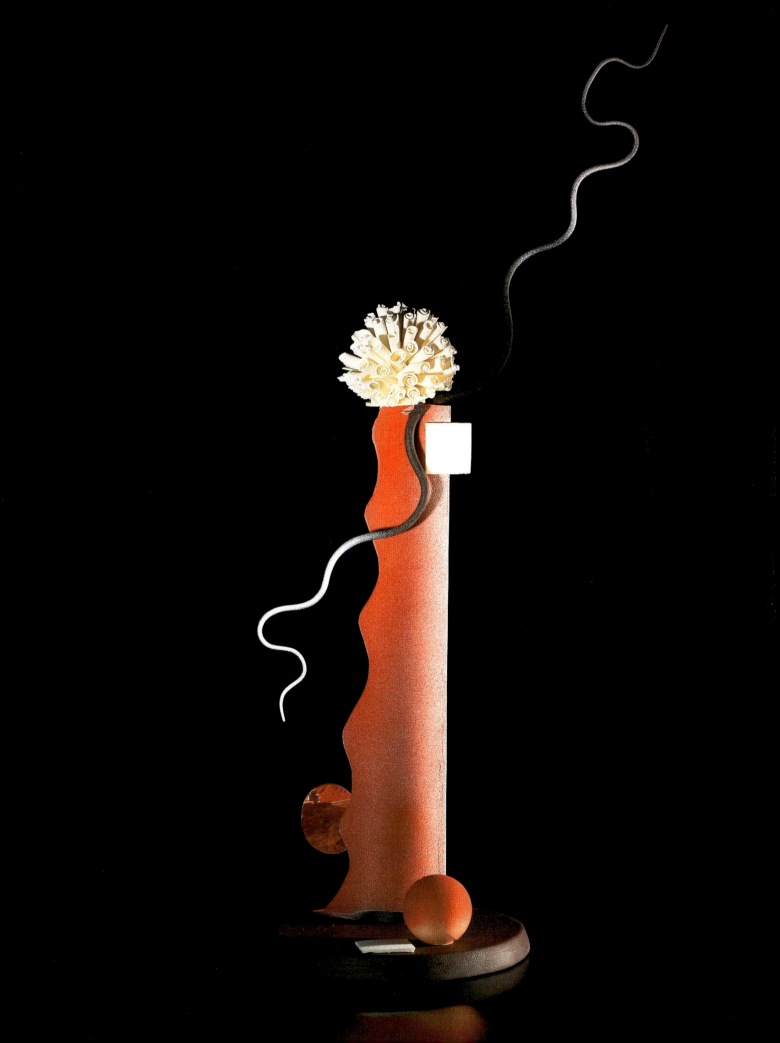

VARIATIONS

TRANSFER SHEET CURLS: Instead of a plain piece of acetate, the chocolate may be spread onto a decorated or printed transfer sheet.

FIRST ROW:
- Cover the acetate or transfer sheet with a thin layer of chocolate.
- After spreading, immediately comb the chocolate.
- Release the chocolate from the marble.

SECOND ROW:
- Curl or twist the strip.
- Let the curled strip rest in a half tube in order to hold its shape.
- Release the finished curls from the transfer sheet strip.

PIPED-TOGETHER CURLS: To hold the curls together pipe chocolate at the end of the acetate strip before curling. The curls will not fall apart when the acetate is released.

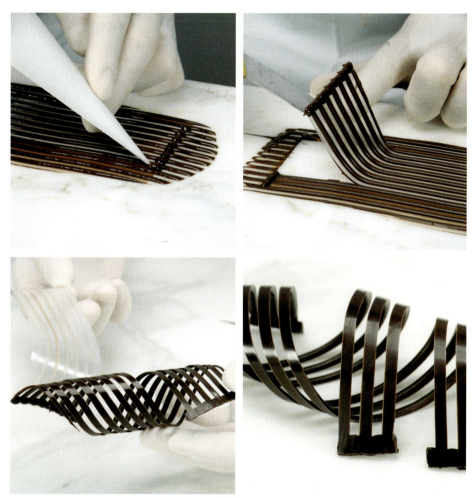

FIRST ROW:
- To hold the curls together pipe chocolate at the ends of the acetate strip.
- Release the strip off the table immediately, before the chocolate sets.

SECOND ROW:
- Release the finished curl off the acetate.
- Piped-together Fettuccini Curls.

Nest

This technique has many potential uses depending on the desired look. It can be used to create a bird's nest, as shown here, or the chocolate can be used to look like straw.

1   Pipe tempered chocolate onto frozen marble in a back-and-forth motion. The chocolate will crystallize almost immediately.

2   Cut off the ends of the piped chocolate with a knife to create the desired length strands.

3   Use a triangle spatula to immediately remove the chocolate strands from the marble. The chocolate will become brittle if it stays on the frozen marble for too long, so it is important to cut the chocolate and remove it from the marble immediately.

4   Immediately after removing the strands from the marble, bend them into a circle to shape the bird's nest or arrange into any other desired shape.

5   Let the chocolate rest at room temperature. Condensation will form on the chocolate as it rests. It is important to let the chocolate rest after shaping because it will be sensitive to temperature, and it can melt easily in your hands if moved around.

–   Pipe tempered chocolate onto frozen marble in a back-and-forth motion.
–   Use a triangle spatula to remove the chocolate strands.
–   Immediately after removing from the marble, bend the strands to shape the bird's nest.

VARIATION

Piped chocolate strands created using the method above can be bent in any way to create a variety of shapes, or just kept straight.

12

Modeling
Chocolate

Modeling chocolate is not widely used any more in confectionery work. However, it is very pliable and easy to use, and it is an ideal way to create natural-looking, hand-molded items, such as roses and other flowers, for use in decorating showpieces.

Creating Modeling Chocolate

Modeling chocolate can be made from dark, milk, or white chocolate. If using milk or white chocolate, extra cocoa butter must be added to bring more stability to the modeling chocolate.

Dark Modeling Chocolate

INGREDIENTS	METRIC	US	VOLUME
Water	80 g	2.8 oz	⅓ cup
Sugar	120 g	4.2 oz	½ cup
Glucose	300 g	10.6 oz	1 cup
Dark couverture, 63%, melted	1000 g	35.3 oz	7 cups
YIELD	1500 g	52.9 oz	8¾ cups

Milk or White Modeling Chocolate

Water	80 g	2.8 oz	⅓ cup
Sugar	120 g	4.2 oz	½ cup
Glucose	300 g	10.6 oz	1 cup
Cocoa butter tablets	100 g	3.5 oz	1 cup
Milk, 37%, or white couverture, melted	1000 g	35.3 oz	7 cups
YIELD	1600 g	56.4 oz	9¾ cups

1   Combine the water and sugar in a saucepan and bring to a boil over medium heat. Continue to boil, stirring, until the sugar is fully dissolved. Add the glucose and stir to combine, but do not allow the mixture to return to a boil. Remove the saucepan from the heat.

2   If making milk or white modeling chocolate, add the cocoa butter and stir to combine. The syrup should be warm enough to completely dissolve both the glucose and the cocoa butter. Stir until all the ingredients are completely combined. This will bring the

temperature down slightly so the mixture can be incorporated into the chocolate more quickly in the next step.

3   Make sure the melted chocolate is as cool as possible. Place the chocolate in a bowl and add the syrup mixture. Stir to combine and create the modeling paste. The lower the temperature of the chocolate when the syrup mixture is added, the easier it will be to emulsify the mixture to create the modeling paste. If the chocolate is too warm, the cocoa butter will melt and rise to the surface of the mass, creating a crust around the modeling paste.

4   Table the mixture on marble until it becomes pasty and pliable. This will ensure that the finished modeling paste is smooth and does not have any cocoa butter lumps. If the syrup was too hot when mixed into the chocolate, the cocoa butter may have melted and will appear clear instead of opaque. Tempering the mass by tabling will aid in crystal formation and will return the cocoa butter to the desired opacity.

5   The finished modeling chocolate should be pliable after tabling as a result of crystallization. Modeling chocolate should be stored at room temperature for 2 hours before use to allow final crystallization to occur. If the mixture is needed immediately, roll it out flat and refrigerate for a few minutes to speed the crystallization process.

–   Add the syrup mixture to the dissolved chocolate.
–   Table the modeling chocolate mass to mix thoroughly.
–   The chain reaction of crystallization will cause the modeling chocolate to turn into a pliable paste.

Using Modeling Chocolate

Creating Cut-Out Flowers

A variety of simple flowers can be created from modeling paste by using different sized cutters to achieve the desired shapes.

1   Roll out the modeling chocolate to ⅛-in/3-mm thickness or less, and use flower cutters to cut out shapes.

2   Swirl a ballpoint tool gently into the center of each cut-out shape to create the body of the flower.

3   Use an airbrush and water-based airbrush color to color the flowers as desired.

4   Pipe white chocolate inside each flower to create the stamen.

5   Sprinkle granulated sugar over the flowers before the chocolate fully sets.

6   If desired, use a different shape cutter to create additional cut-outs for the base of the flowers. Attach the flowers to the bases using a dot of melted chocolate. It is best to use untempered chocolate here because it will set more slowly than tempered chocolate, giving you time to pipe dots onto a whole tray of flowers and set the pieces together before the piped chocolate sets.

FIRST ROW:
– Use a flower cutter to create simple flower shapes.
– Using a ballpoint tool, swirl gently into the paste to create the body of the flower.
– Regular water-based color can be airbrushed on to the flower.

SECOND ROW:
– Sprinkle sugar over the freshly piped chocolate inside the flower before it sets.
– Different shapes can be used to create bases for the flowers.
– Finished modeling chocolate flowers.

Creating a Rose

You can never go wrong with roses. Roses are probably the most commonly made type of modeling paste flower, and they are ideal for Valentine's Day, Mother's Day, and any other festive event. Most people like roses and they are requested often, so it is very important to master this technique.

When forming a rose from modeling chocolate, if the petals become too soft from handling, simply let them rest on the marble for a minute and then resume working.

1   Sprinkle a small amount of cornstarch onto your work surface to prevent sticking. Roll out the modeling chocolate to ⅛ in/3 mm thick, cut out about 10 circles of the same size, and place on a marble slab.

2   Use the back side of a teaspoon to flatten the edges of each circle.

3   Roll your palm in a circular motion over each chocolate circle. This will warm the cocoa butter in the chocolate, creating a nice shine.

4   Remove one of the circles from the marble with a paring knife and roll it up tightly on one side, keeping the other side open, to create a rosebud. Pinch the bottom quarter of the bud together so that it will stand on your working surface.

5   Remove another circle with a paring knife. Use your fingers to gently fold the bottom sides of the circle inward, leaving the top portion open to create a hollow, open effect. Then gently bend the very top right and left edges of the circle outward away from you to create a curled petal.

6   Immediately attach the completed petal to one side of the rose bud.

7   Repeat step 5 to create additional petals with the remaining circles of modeling chocolate. Attach each petal to the rosebud, overlapping one petal over the next, to create the full rose.

8   Freeze the completed roses for about 10 minutes. Remove from the freezer and immediately airbrush with the desired color of cocoa butter to create a velvet effect.

9   If desired, gold or luster dust can be used over the airbrushed chocolate to achieve a shimmery effect. Place some of the luster dust on the tip of a paring knife and gently blow it over the finished roses. The dust should settle easily onto the roses' velvety surface.

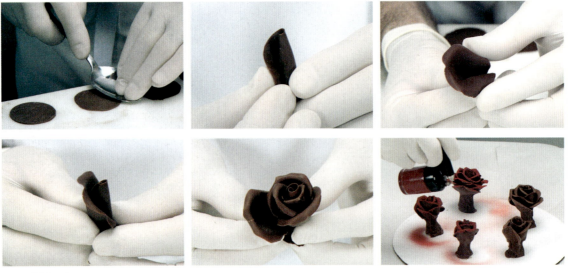

FIRST ROW:
–   Using the back side of a teaspoon, flatten the edges of the circles to form petals.
–   Remove one circle with a paring knife and roll into a rosebud shape, keeping one side open.
–   Create a shaped petal by pushing the lower part of petal together and folding both upper sides of the petal backward.

SECOND ROW:
–   Immediately attach the petal to the rosebud shape.
–   Attach one petal after the other until the desired shape is achieved.
–   Airbrush the finished roses with colored cocoa butter.

NEXT PAGE:
–   Modeling chocolate roses can be created in a variety of sizes.

Creating a Woven Basket

The woven basket, like the chocolate box on page 258, is a nice decoration that can be sold on its own or filled with chocolates. Because the basket is not a very tall decoration, it is easier to pack and transport than any other type of showpiece. The woven part of the basket is made from modeling chocolate, while the base and chocolate sticks are made from regular couverture.

1   Using the techniques on page 248, cut out the desired shape for the base of the box.

2   On the same template used to cut out the base, mark small circles in an evenly spaced pattern around the border of the template. Place the template over the cut-out base, and using the dots on the template as a guide, make impressions in the chocolate with a knife.

3   To create the chocolate sticks, fill a drinking straw completely with melted chocolate, then refrigerate for 5 minutes. Unmold the sticks by pushing the chocolate out of the straw using a skewer. Cut each piece into sticks 1½ to 2 in/38 to 50 mm long. You will need the same number of sticks as there are dots on the chocolate base.

4   Warm a metal stick slightly smaller than the chocolate sticks over a flame. Press the warm end of the metal stick gently into the impressions in the chocolate base to melt

holes into the chocolate. Immediately place one chocolate stick into each of the holes. Let sit until the melted chocolate has completely crystallized.

5 Use your hands to roll a small piece of modeling chocolate into a long rope about ¼ in/6 mm thick. The longer you can make the rope, the better. If the modeling chocolate is breaking easily, the marble may be too cold. Rolling the chocolate out on a wooden surface like a cutting board will prevent the chocolate from breaking.

6 Carefully weave the rope of modeling chocolate around the sticks, creating one layer on top of the next. When you reach the end of the rope, fold the end inside the basket. Roll out another long rope and place one end right next to the folded-in end of the first rope, so that the break between the two is nearly invisible. Continue weaving layers around the sticks with the second rope.

7 Continue rolling out ropes of modeling chocolate and weaving additional layers around the sticks until you reach the top of the sticks to complete the basket. Different colors of modeling chocolate can be alternated from one layer to the next to achieve a more dramatic effect.

8 To finish the basket, roll out two long ropes of modeling chocolate, lay them next to one another, and twist at both ends to create a long twisted rope. Cut the twisted rope to fit the perimeter of the basket, and place it on top of the woven section to create a finished edge.

- Using a warm metal stick, gently melt holes into the base and immediately place the chocolate sticks in the holes.
- Carefully weave modeling chocolate around the sticks.
- Finish the basket with a twisted double string to close the entire shape.

Food Processor Modeling Chocolate

A simple form of modeling chocolate can be created easily using a food processor. This technique results in a malleable, quick-setting form of chocolate that is ideal for creating simple shapes and forms.

1 Place coins of dark, milk, or white couverture in a food processor and process for approximately 3 minutes. The chocolate will be cut down into very small pieces, and the friction of the blending will cause the pieces to warm up and form a modeling paste.

2   As soon as the chocolate paste starts to come together and tumble in the food processor, stop processing, remove the modeling paste, and immediately begin to roll or model it by hand as desired. If the chocolate is processed for too long after forming a paste, it will become too warm and the cocoa butter in the chocolate will come out of temper, causing the finished modeled pieces to become gray and dull.

Process chocolate coins in the food processer for approximately 3 minutes to form a modeling paste.

Creating Rolled Shapes

Chocolate modeling paste created in the food processor will set quickly and can hold hand-rolled shapes better than ordinary modeling chocolate.

1   Roll the modeling chocolate out into a long rope by hand.

2   Continue to roll the chocolate rope using an acrylic or cardboard sheet to ensure a nice, even surface. If the chocolate is setting up and becoming brittle, the marble may be too cold or you may be rolling out the chocolate too slowly. To avoid this, a wooden surface or plastic cutting board can be used in place of the marble, although this will not replace a lack of hand skill.

3   Immediately after rolling out, use your hands to bend the chocolate into the desired shapes and let set. The chocolate should set within a few minutes.

–   Roll the chocolate with a cardboard sheet to ensure a nice even surface.
–   Immediately after rolling, bend the chocolate into the desired shape.
–   Simple shapes and forms can be achieved using chocolate prepared in the food processor.

13

Chocolate Flowers

Chocolate flowers are a beautiful way to add color and dimension to a showpiece. There are a variety of techniques that can be used to make chocolate flowers. They can be made with white, milk, or dark chocolate and can be sprayed with any color of cocoa butter. Dark chocolate is generally preferred for chocolate flowers, because it is stronger and holds up better than other type of chocolate. However, working with dark chocolate requires better hand skills, as it sets faster and is less forgiving than white chocolate.

Shaved Flowers

Shaved flowers get their name from the shaving technique used to create the petals. This technique gives a different shape and look to the finished flower.

1. Thinly spread tempered chocolate onto the marble using an offset spatula. Spread the chocolate thin enough so that the marble shows through ever so slightly, but no thinner. If it is spread too thin, the petals will be too fragile to assemble into a flower. Let the chocolate set. This will take about 1 minute for dark chocolate or up to 2 minutes for milk or white chocolate, depending on the temperature of the room and marble.

2. As soon as the chocolate is set, rewarm it by gently rubbing the top surface of the chocolate with the palm of your hand. This will enhance the flexibility of the chocolate.

3. Immediately after warming the chocolate, place a round cutter about 4 in/100 mm in diameter at one edge of the chocolate. Holding the cutter at approximately a 45-degree angle, pull it toward you in a quick, steady motion to produce a chocolate curl. While the chocolate is still on the warm side, pulling the cutter through it will cause it to roll up and form a rosebud.

4. As the chocolate becomes cooler, continue using the same technique to form petals. Holding the cutter at an angle of less than 45 degrees will create wider petals, and holding it at an angle greater than 45 degrees will result in narrower petals. Timing is essential for this technique. If the chocolate is too warm when you begin curling the chocolate, it will stick to the cutter and will not curl up correctly. If the chocolate is too cold, it will break and will not curl at all. You will need anywhere from 12 to 20 petals, depending on the desired size of the flower.

5. To assemble the flower, set two Styrofoam squares on the marble and cover each piece of Styrofoam with parchment paper. This will help keep the temperature of the chocolate steady, since the marble may be too cold.

Continued on page 290.

THE ART OF THE CHOCOLATIER

6　Pipe a small circle of tempered chocolate at least 1 in/25 mm in diameter onto each piece of Styrofoam. One will be used as a base for the assembling of the flower, and the other to adhere the petals. It is very important to pipe the base circle to 1 in/25 mm or more in diameter to keep the flower from falling apart when it is sprayed or touched during the assembly process.

7　Place the rosebud into the piped chocolate on one of the Styrofoam squares. One by one, dip the base of each petal into the other pool of chocolate and then place the petals around the rosebud, overlapping each petal slightly over the previous one.

8　When all the petals have been added, use an airbrush to spray water-based color over the entire flower. Then airbrush just the tips of the petals with a contrasting water color, if desired. It is not necessary to use colored cocoa butter because the shaved chocolate's unique texture can absorb the water color. Note that if the flower is made of white chocolate and will be stored or displayed in a room with high humidity, the color may turn darker or more intense due to the high sugar content of the chocolate.

FIRST ROW:
-　Spread the chocolate thin enough so that you can see the marble through the chocolate.
-　Use a cutter to pull the chocolate toward you, producing a curl.
-　While rosebuds can be created by shaving off warmer chocolate, petals are formed from colder chocolate.

SECOND ROW:
-　Pipe small circles of chocolate onto paper that is resting on Styrofoam and place the rosebud on one circle.
-　Use the second circle to dip the petals when assembling the flower.
-　Use water color to airbrush the finished flower.

Rolled Flowers

The rolled technique creates a more complicated, "busy" flower. These flowers look best on simpler, quiet showpieces that do not have a lot of other movement or color.

1 Dampen the marble with a little bit of water and place an acetate sheet on the marble. Spread a thin layer of tempered chocolate, no thicker than 1⁄16 inch/1.5 mm, onto the acetate sheet in a rectangle at least 16½ × 11½ in/406 × 293 mm. Let the chocolate set for about a minute.

2 As soon as the chocolate begins to set, use a paring knife to cut elongated curved diamond shapes through the chocolate, being careful not to cut through the acetate (see template, page 352). A paring knife works best for this, because an Exacto knife is too sharp to cut the chocolate without cutting through the acetate as well. Use up the entire rectangle of chocolate to create enough petals for the flower.

3 Place a sheet of parchment paper on the top of the cut chocolate and loosely roll the acetate sheet up diagonally to form a tube approximately 2½ in/64 mm in diameter. This entire technique of cutting and rolling must be completed before the chocolate is completely set.

4 Let the rolled up acetate sheet and chocolate set for at least 30 minutes at room temperature or 5 minutes in the refrigerator.

5 Once the chocolate is completely set, unroll the acetate sheet. The curls should naturally fall off the sheet onto your work surface.

6 To assemble the flower, set two Styrofoam squares on the marble and cover each piece of Styrofoam with parchment paper. This will help keep the temperature of the chocolate steady, since the marble may be too cold.

7 Pipe a small circle of tempered chocolate at least 1 in/25 mm in diameter onto each piece of Styrofoam. One will be used as a base for assembling the flower, and the other to adhere the petals. It is very important to pipe the base circle to 1 in/25 mm or more in diameter to keep the flower from falling apart when it is sprayed or touched during the assembly process.

8 Starting with the longer petals first, dip the center of each petal into one of the circles of chocolate, then place the petals onto the other piped circle. Begin by placing the first two petals in an X formation, one on top of the other, then continue laying additional petals over the first two, working around in a circular formation and overlapping the center of each petal over the others until you have made one complete circle. Then add half-petals in between the larger ones, dipping each into the piped chocolate before placing it down on the flower, to achieve a realistic effect. If necessary, break some of the curled petals to get the size and shape needed to complete the design of the flower. *Continued on page 292.*

9 To complete the flower, create a small chocolate sphere using a sphere mold and use tempered chocolate to attach it in the center of the petals. Place the completed flower in the freezer for 5 to 10 minutes.

10 Remove the flower from the freezer and, if using dark or milk chocolate, immediately use an airbrush to spray it with white cocoa butter. Priming the chocolate by spraying it with white cocoa butter before spraying on a color will help to intensify whatever color is used next.

11 Use an airbrush to spray the desired color cocoa butter over the white primer. If the flower is sprayed immediately after removal from the freezer, it will create a velvet sheen because the cocoa butter will set immediately upon contact with the flower. If the color is not applied fast enough, the tips of the petals can defrost and the chocolate will become shiny instead of maintaining a velvet texture. You may want to keep a cold spray on hand to keep the chocolate cold throughout the spraying process.

12 If desired, attach gold leaf flakes in the middle of the flower using a brush or a pencil eraser. This looks especially good on a darker colored flower.

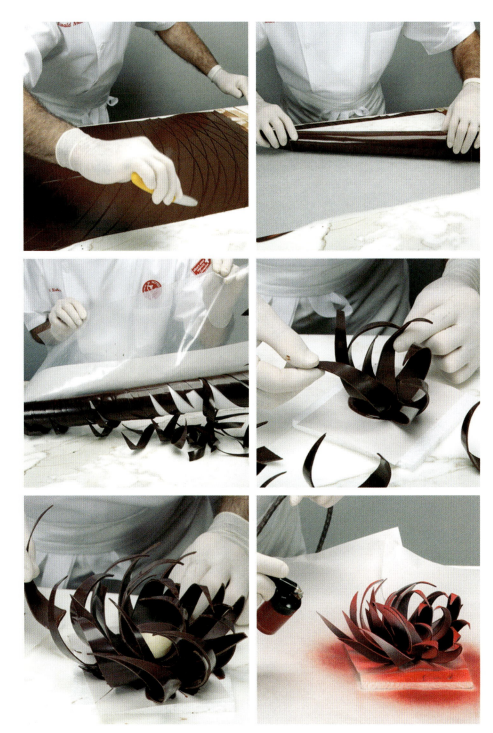

FIRST ROW:
- Use a paring knife to cut elongated diamond shapes through the chocolate.
- Place a sheet of parchment paper on top of the chocolate and roll diagonally.

SECOND ROW:
- Unroll the acetate sheet and the curls will naturally release.
- Assemble the flower on one piece of Styrofoam, and use the other for dipping the petals in chocolate.

THIRD ROW:
- Break some of the petals as needed to achieve the desired shape.
- Spray the frozen flower first with white and then with red cocoa butter.

Straight Knife-Dipped Flowers

You can use any type of knife to achieve this technique, depending on your personal preference, as long as it is at least 3 in/80 mm long.

The difference between the straight knife-dipped technique and the curled knife-dipped technique on page 297 is in how the chocolate is allowed to set. To create the straight petals for this flower, the petals are left flat on the table to set.

1   Dampen the marble with a little bit of water and place an acetate sheet on the marble. Set a large bowl of tempered chocolate next to the acetate sheet.

2   Dip a knife into the chocolate, about 3 to 4 in/80 to 100 mm deep. How deep you submerge the blade will determine the length of the finished petals. Using a fluid motion, place the chocolate-covered knife blade flat down on the acetate sheet, then pull up, toward yourself, and away to create a petal. It is important to raise the knife up as you pull it toward yourself, because if you place the knife down and pull without raising it up, there will not be enough chocolate on the transfer sheet to create strong petals, and it will be much more difficult to assemble the flower.

3   Continue using the same technique to create enough petals for the flower, varying the size of the petals as desired by dipping the knife into the chocolate deeper for longer petals and less deep for shorter ones. You will need anywhere from 30 to 45 petals to create a medium-size flower. Let the finished petals set on the acetate sheet for about 30 minutes at room temperature or 5 minutes in the refrigerator. Once set, curl the acetate away from the chocolate and gently remove the petals from the sheet.

4   Using an offset spatula, spread tempered chocolate onto a marble to approximately ⅛ in/3 mm thick. Use a metal cutter to cut out a circle 2 in/50 mm in diameter. Let the circle sit for about 5 minutes.

5   Using the chocolate circle as a base, pipe a ring of tempered chocolate around the inside perimeter of the circle, and attach the larger petals to the circle one by one, laying each petal flat onto the base with at least ½ in/13 mm of the petal overlapping the base. Or, alternatively, pipe chocolate directly onto the petals or dip each petal in the melted chocolate, then attach to the circle in a ring.

6   Continue to pipe on melted chocolate and place the petals in rings to build the flower, placing each new ring inside and on top of the previous ring until you reach the center of the circle. If desired, use slightly smaller petals as you get closer to the center of the flower. Attach the petals in a symmetrical pattern to create a fully bloomed flower.

7   Place the completed flower in the freezer for 5 to 10 minutes.
Continued on page 296.

8   Remove the flower from the freezer and, if using dark or milk chocolate, immediately use an airbrush to spray it with white cocoa butter. Priming the chocolate by spraying it with white cocoa butter before spraying on a color will help to intensify whatever color is used next.

9   Use an airbrush to spray the desired color cocoa butter over the white primer. If the flower is sprayed immediately after removal from the freezer, it will create a velvet sheen because the cocoa butter will set immediately upon contact with the flower. If the color is not applied fast enough, the tips of the petals can defrost and the chocolate will become shiny instead of maintaining a velvet texture. You may want to keep an cold spray on hand to keep the chocolate cold throughout the spraying process.

ABOVE:
- Any type of knife can be used in this technique. Press the chocolate-dipped knife onto the acetate, then pull up and away from the acetate.
- Using a chocolate circle as a base, attach the larger petals first in a circle.
- Attach the petals symmetrically until a full bloom effect is achieved.

BELOW:
- A completed knife-dipped flower.

VARIATIONS

CURLED KNIFE-DIPPED FLOWERS: Use a knife to create petals using the technique outlined on page 295, but before the chocolate sets, place the acetate sheet in a half-tube to create curled petals. Once the chocolate has set, remove the curls from the acetate sheet and assemble the flower as described above. If desired, use a sphere mold to create a chocolate sphere and place it in the center of the flower after the first ring of petals has been set, then add additional petals as desired around the sphere. To create a bigger flower, add additional petals underneath the outside row by pushing them into the circular chocolate base before it has completely set.

ABOVE:
- Dip a paring knife into white chocolate and press down, then up and away from the acetate, to create petals.
- Place the first layer of petals around the outside of the piped circle.
- Place a chocolate sphere in the middle and continue to build the flower around the sphere.

BELOW:
- A completed knife-dipped curled flower.

FULL-BLOOM KNIFE-DIPPED FLOWERS: Create curled knife-dipped petals as described on page 297. For the base, create a chocolate sphere using a sphere mold. Using tempered chocolate, attach chocolate circles to the top and bottom of the sphere. Attach the first row of petals to the top circle, facing downward so that they cover the sphere. Then add rows of petals to the top of the base, facing upward, to complete the flower as described below.

ABOVE:
– Place a sphere between two chocolate circles, and attach the first row of petals pointing downward.
– Place the second row of petals facing upward on the circle.
– Continue to build the flower by placing petals facing upward, working inward toward the sphere.

BELOW:
– A completed full-bloom knife-dipped flower.

Paper Flowers

This technique involves using paper cutouts to shape the chocolate petals. This is a very easy technique that can be used to create large flowers.

1 Cut out the desired shape and size petals from a sheet of copy paper and place the cutouts flat on the marble. Pipe tempered chocolate onto the paper petals. You will need to pipe approximately 40 petals to create the flower, with a mixture of small and large petals.

2 Use an offset spatula to spread the chocolate evenly over the paper cutouts to a thickness of less than $1/16$ in/1.5 mm.

3 As soon as the chocolate begins to set, use a paring knife to lift the chocolate-covered paper petals from the marble. The excess chocolate should come away easily as you lift up the paper cutouts.

4 Immediately shape each petal by holding the paper-covered side and gently bending the outer edges.

5 Let the chocolate set completely, for about 5 minutes, then remove the paper from each chocolate petal.

6 Set a Styrofoam square on the marble and cover it with a piece of parchment paper. This will help keep the temperature of the chocolate steady, since the marble may be too cold. Place a metal ring around the Styrofoam square to serve as a support for the flower petals.

Continued on page 302.

7   Using an offset spatula, spread tempered chocolate onto the marble to approximately ⅛ in/3 mm thick. Use a metal cutter to cut out a circle about 3 in/76 mm in diameter, and let set for about 5 minutes. Place the chocolate disc on the Styrofoam. On another Styrofoam square covered with parchment paper, pipe another circle of tempered chocolate to use for dipping the petals.

8   Dip each petal into the melted chocolate and place onto the chocolate disc, starting at the outside with the largest petals and working your way in, to build the flower. Place the petals flat on the circle, overlapping each one slightly over the last. If desired, spray the flower with cold spray after attaching each petal to freeze them in place immediately and keep them from moving around as you add the subsequent petals. Use the smallest petals in the center to finish the flower.

9   Place the completed flower in the freezer for five to ten minutes.

10   Remove the flower from the freezer and, if using dark or milk chocolate, immediately use an airbrush to spray it with white cocoa butter. Priming the chocolate by spraying it with white cocoa butter before spraying on a color will help to intensify whatever color is used next.

11   Use an airbrush to spray the desired color cocoa butter over the white primer. If the flower is sprayed immediately after removal from the freezer, it will create a velvet sheen because the cocoa butter will set immediately upon contact with the flower. If the color is not applied fast enough, the tips of the petals can defrost and the chocolate will become shiny instead of maintaining a velvet texture. You may want to keep a cold spray on hand to keep the chocolate cold throughout the spraying process. Spray with the desired color of cocoa butter.

FIRST ROW:
- Spread chocolate onto the paper petals and remove the petals from the table once the chocolate starts to set.
- Shape the petal by gently bending the outside in.
- Once the chocolate has completely crystallized, remove the paper.

SECOND ROW:
- Start to attach the petals to the base from the outside in, supporting the first row with a ring.
- To increase efficiency, cold spray may be used after attaching each petal.
- Finish the flower with smaller petals.

VARIATIONS

DIPPED AND PAPER FLOWERS Prepare an assortment of petals using both the Curved Knife-Dipped and the Paper techniques. If desired, use a different type of chocolate with each technique for contrast. Begin assembling the flower using the paper petals around the outside, then finish with the knife-dipped petals on the inside. Finish with the desired colors of cocoa butter.

PIPED PISTILS: Create a paper flower, but do not fill the center with smaller petals. Instead, pipe short lines of tempered chocolate onto an acetate sheet, placing the lines in groups of three attached at one end. Before the chocolate sets, release the acetate from the table and place it in a half-pipe to create a curve. To force the crystallization, place the tube in the refrigerator for a few minutes, then remove and release the pistils from the acetate. Dip the pistils in tempered chocolate and attach to the center of the flower, then finish with the desired colors of cocoa butter.

ABOVE:
- Pipe small rows of three on the acetate sheet.
- Place the pistils in a half-pipe.
- Attach the pistils inside the flower.

BELOW:
- A completed paper flower with piped pistils.

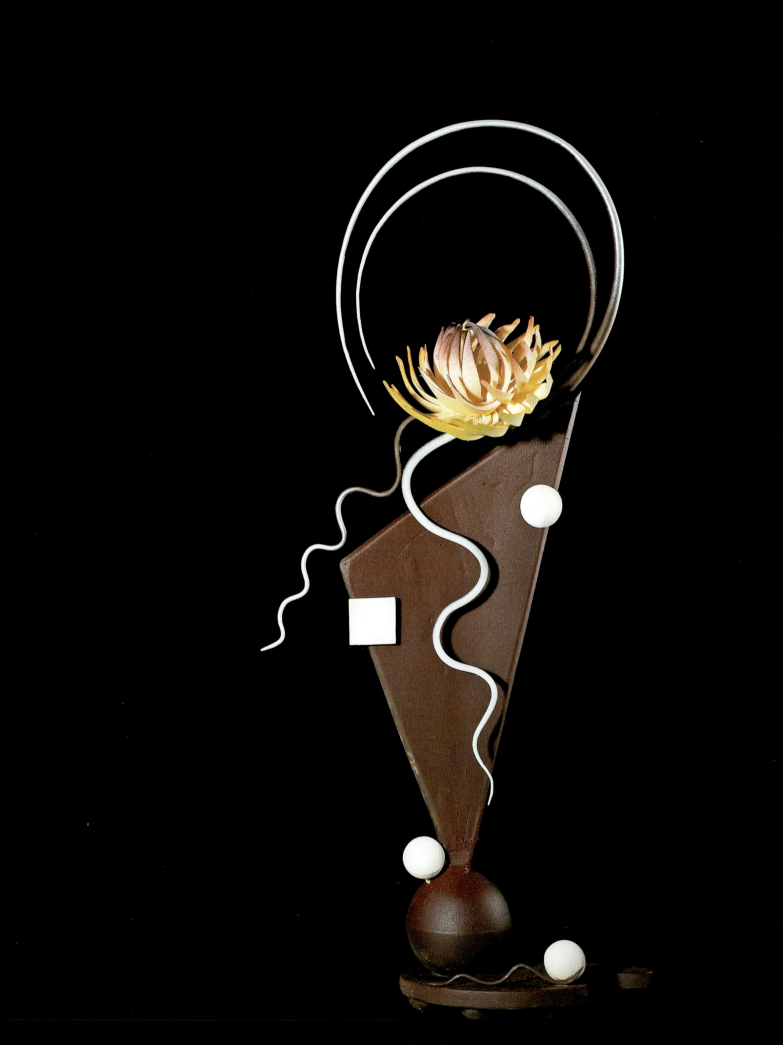

Birds of Paradise

These tropical flowers are created using both acetate and paper cutouts to achieve a contrast between shiny and dull pieces of chocolate. They are an ideal decoration for an exotic showpiece.

1 To create the base, cut out a piece of acetate in a leaf shape 6 in/150 mm long. Dampen the marble with a little bit of water and place the acetate cutout on the marble. Brush the acetate with yellow cocoa butter and let it set. Then brush with red cocoa butter and let it set. Finish with a coat of green cocoa butter and let the colored cocoa butters set completely.

2 If using dark chocolate, brush a layer of white cocoa butter over the colored cocoa butters. This will help the colors to show up much better.

3 Pipe tempered dark chocolate onto the acetate cutout, then spread with a spatula to about 1/16 in/1.5 mm thick. Dark chocolate should always be used for the base of this flower, as the base must be able to hold the weight of the other components and dark chocolate is stronger than white or milk chocolate.

4 As the chocolate begins to set, use a paring knife to release the acetate from the table. Fold it in half to form it into an oblong shape with the acetate on the outside. Leave an opening approximately 1 in/25 mm wide at the open end.

5 To form the petals, cut out petals at least 5 in/127 mm long from a piece of copy paper and place on the marble. Pipe tempered white chocolate onto the petals and spread with a spatula.
Continued on page 308.

THE ART OF THE CHOCOLATIER

6 As soon as the chocolate begins to set, use a paring knife to release the paper petals from the table. Immediately fold each petal in half lengthwise with the paper on the outside, being careful not to make a crease.

7 Once the white chocolate is completely set, remove the paper from the petals. Dip one end of each petal into tempered dark chocolate and insert the dipped end into the base. Repeat with the rest of the petals, attaching them right next to one another with the open ends facing in the same direction, until they fill the full length of the base.

8 Use an airbrush to spray water color onto the petals. If desired, use more water color on the tips of the petals to create a shaded effect from top to bottom. Because the petals were made with paper, they will absorb water color easily and do not require the use of colored cocoa butter.

9 Wrap the base in a layer of aluminum foil to help keep it cold and shiny. Using the technique on page 260, create chocolate cigarettes slightly longer than the height of the petals. Dip each chocolate cigarette in tempered chocolate and insert into the base of the flower in between the petals.

10 Use an airbrush to spray the cigarettes with white cocoa butter and let set.

11 Leave the acetate and foil on the base of the flower until it is ready to use, and store at room temperature. The acetate will protect the base from fingerprints, spray color, and dust. When the flower is ready to be attached to a showpiece, remove the foil and the acetate, then attach the flower as desired.

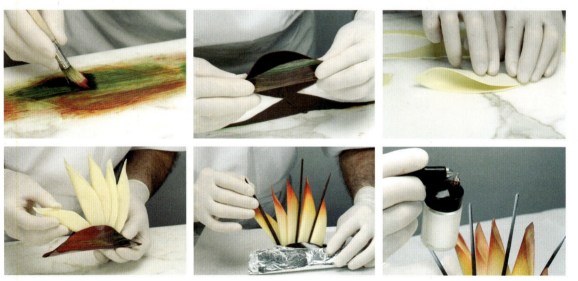

FIRST ROW:
- Brush yellow cocoa butter onto the acetate, followed by red, green, and white.
- Release the petal from the table and form into an oblong shape.
- Release the white chocolate petal from the table and bend in half, paper-side out.

SECOND ROW:
- Dip each petal in dark chocolate and attach inside the base.
- Place the chocolate cigarettes in between the petals.
- Spray the cigarettes with white-colored cocoa butter.

14

Painting, Piping, and Assembling Three-Dimensional Figures

Painting is a great way to add two-dimensional decoration to a showpiece, while piping makes it possible to build up more dimension. This chapter will illustrate how to create three-dimensional shapes and figures by building up chocolate using the piping and spot-tempering techniques, as well as how to use molds to create larger figures. There are several different techniques that can be used to bond molded chocolate pieces together to create an animal or other type of figure.

Painting

Cocoa painting is widely documented in books and dates back to the early 1900s, though it became more popular after World War II. However, it is very time consuming and requires expert hand skills, and today transfer sheets and silk screening are more widely used for decorating confections. Nonetheless, colored cocoa painting is still a valuable skill for chocolatiers to learn.

In past years, it was popular to use a mixture of cocoa powder, oil, and a little cocoa butter for painting. Today, regular water-soluble food coloring is generally used instead to make the process easier. The disadvantage of using food coloring is that once it is painted on, it becomes permanent, whereas the older method was more forgiving, as mistakes could be corrected by simply adding warm oil to thin the "paint" and absorb the color. White paint can be created by mixing cocoa butter and titanium dioxide, which is available in any store that sells wedding cake supplies. The food color can be painted onto marzipan or pastillage, though the white color of pastillage causes more contrast and can make the finished painting look harsh. Because chocolate contains a lot of fat, it will not absorb water color well and should not be used as a surface for cocoa painting. After the painting is completed, food lacquer may be used to seal the painting and give an extra shine to the design.

1   Select a picture you would like to replicate. The complexity of the picture should depend on your hand skills; if you do not have a great deal of experience in cocoa painting, it is best to start with a simple image.

2   Place your picture flat on the work surface and cover with a layer of transfer or parchment paper. Using a soft-lead pencil, trace the image onto the transfer or parchment paper. Lift the paper with the traced design off the original picture and flip it over, then retrace the image on the opposite side of the parchment or transfer paper.

3   Roll out a piece of marzipan or pastillage to the desired thickness. Immediately place the parchment or transfer paper with the penciled design on top of the marzipan, and use your hand or a ballpoint tool to press down gently over the lines and transfer the image onto the marzipan. The design will adhere better if freshly rolled marzipan is used because of the higher moisture content of the marzipan.

4   Remove the transfer sheet from the marzipan to reveal the traced design.

5   Using a paintbrush thick enough to hold a good amount of paint, begin to color in the design by outlining the outside first with the desired colors of food coloring. Then continue to fill in the image with the desired colors, working inward toward the center of the design.

6　Let set until the painting is completely dry. This will happen almost immediately if no titanic dioxide was used in the paint, but it can take up to an hour if a large amount of titanic dioxide was used.

7　If desired, spray the painting with food lacquer to seal it. Store at room temperature until ready to use.

ABOVE:
- Transfer your design from parchment paper onto freshly rolled out marzipan using a ballpoint tool.
- Remove the parchment paper to reveal your design on the marzipan.
- Using water-soluble food color outline the design first, then shade it.

BELOW:
- A finished painting on marzipan

Spraying Chocolate

Another way to add color and a nice finish to a showpiece is by spraying the piece with a mixture of cocoa butter and chocolate. While the technique is similar to airbrushing, it utilizes a larger spray gun, available at any hardware store. The cocoa butter–chocolate mixture can be made from dark, white, or milk chocolate, and any color cocoa butter can be used. While 40 percent cocoa butter to 60 percent chocolate is the standard ratio, a higher percentage of cocoa butter should be used if the chocolate has a low viscosity. When combined, the mixture should have the same viscosity and appearance as oil.

1   Combine chocolate and cocoa butter to thin the chocolate using a ratio of 40 percent cocoa butter to 60 percent chocolate. Table the mixture of cocoa butter and chocolate to temper.

2   Warm the chocolate spray gun slightly in a low oven before using. The gun should be "hand warm," approximately 98°F/36.7°C. Otherwise, the cold metal of the gun may cause the chocolate–cocoa butter mixture to firm up and block the nozzle of the spray gun.

3   Shield the piece you will be spraying with acrylic or cardboard to protect the surrounding area. If you spray a great deal of showpieces on a regular basis, you may even want to build a spraying booth for this purpose.

4   Fill the spray gun with the tempered chocolate–cocoa butter mixture. Test the gun by spraying onto a piece of paper first, and adjust the spray gun to achieve the desired flow. Once the gun has been adjusted as desired, spray the chocolate over the showpiece. It is very important to spray evenly over the entire piece, so that there is a consistent amount of spray covering every part of the showpiece.

VARIATIONS

PATTERNS: Create a template in any desired shape out of cardboard or acrylic, and hold the template over the surface being sprayed to create a silhouetted shape or design. By moving the template slightly each time you spray the piece, it is possible to create a gradated look with varying shades of the same color.

VELVET TEXTURE: Freeze the chocolate prior to spraying to create a velvet texture. The sprayed chocolate will set immediately on contact with the frozen surface and will develop a dull, velvety look. Dimension can be added by protecting part of the piece with acrylic or cardboard while spraying, resulting in a shiny section that contrasts with the velvet spray.

-    Use a cardboard or acrylic circle to create shades when spraying chocolate.
-    Very simple effects can be created using this technique.
-    To create this velvet look, the heart was frozen, then sprayed with a template placed over the top.

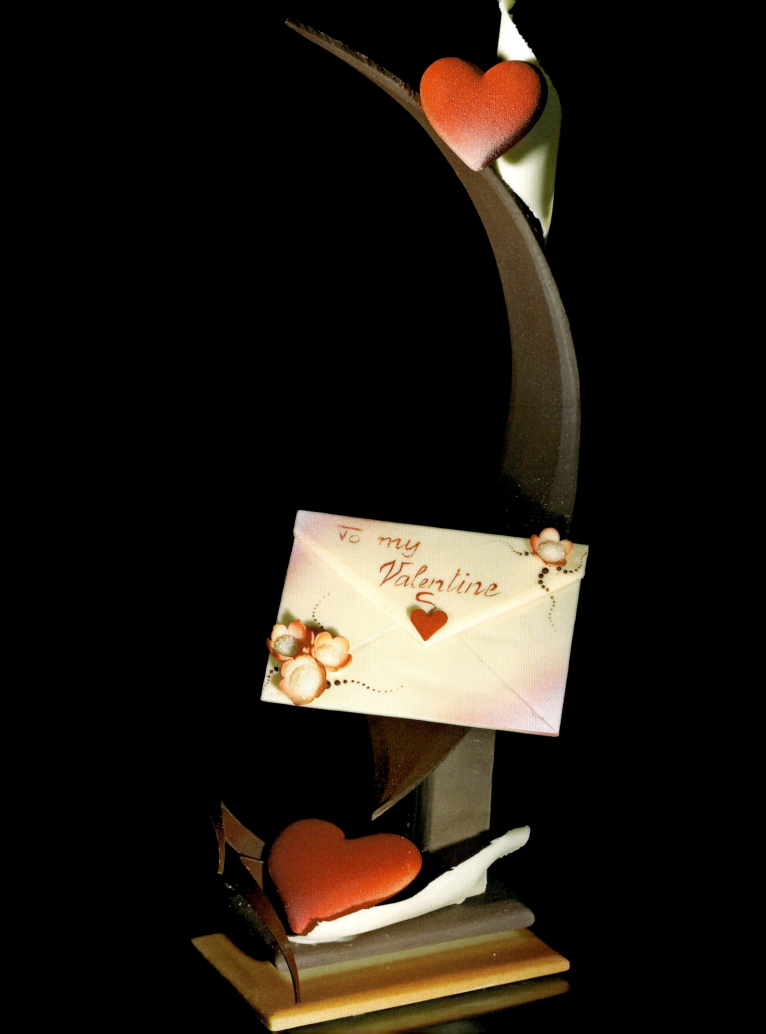

Chocolate Piping

Piping is a skill that allows the chocolatier to create shapes or even an entire scene with depth and dimension, rather than using flat cutouts. In order to create dimension, the chocolate must be tempered to the correct consistency. It should be on the cooler side, and the consistency should be thin enough to flow through a pastry bag, but thick enough that it will adhere to the surface it is piped on and hold its shape without running. While chocolate for piping can be thickened with a few drops of alcohol or syrup if absolutely necessary, it is better to achieve the correct consistency by tempering the chocolate, then letting it rest at room temperature for 10 to 15 minutes so crystallization thickens the chocolate to the correct viscosity.

Creative techniques can be used to add additional effects to a piped shape or scene that cannot be achieved using cut-out shapes. For example, because piping creates a three-dimensional surface, confectioners' sugar dusted over a piped figure will rest on the contours of the chocolate to create an illusion of depth that would not be possible on a simple cut-out piece.

Contour Piping

1   Sketch the design to be piped onto a piece of paper, and place the paper underneath a clear acetate sheet.

2   Table the chocolate to be used for piping to temper it, then let rest for 10 to 15 minutes to cool and thicken. Fill a piping bag with the tempered chocolate, and begin to pipe the chocolate onto the acetate sheet to fill in the design. If the chocolate is the right consistency, it should not be necessary to outline the design first.

3   Continue piping until the entire design has been filled in. For any areas of the piece that should appear thicker than the rest, pipe over the design a second time to create more volume.

4   To add small, simple accents to the design with a different type of chocolate, dip the point of a paring knife into the tempered chocolate and dot it onto the surface of the piped design before the piped chocolate sets. This is much faster than preparing another piping bag. If more complex accents are desired, however, fill a separate piping bag with the tempered chocolate and pipe directly onto the surface of the piped design before it sets.

5   Let the chocolate set until it begins to curl up a bit and release itself from the acetate. As soon as it is set, remove the piece from the acetate and store at room temperature until ready to use.

-   If the chocolate is the right consistency, no outlining is needed to fill in the design.
-   The eye can be added by dipping a knife into white chocolate.
-   Let the chocolate sit until it curls up and releases itself from the acetate.

Three-Dimensional Piping

Three-dimensional figures can be created using a number of different techniques, including carving and molding. However, piping three-dimensional figures, though time consuming, is the best way to create figures with delicate, fragile components, such as the thin legs of an animal figure. The basic technique is the same as the technique for contour piping outlined above, but two symmetrical piped figures are built up and attached together to create one three-dimensional piece.

1   Sketch the design to be piped onto a piece of paper, then sketch or trace a mirror image of the same design on a separate piece of paper. Place each piece of paper underneath a clear acetate sheet. For an animal figure like the deer shown here, it is easier to create the head separately and attach it later so that the head can be turned to one side or the other.

2   Table the chocolate to be used for piping to temper it, then let rest for 10 to 15 minutes to cool and thicken. Fill a pastry bag with the tempered chocolate. Pipe the chocolate onto the first acetate sheet to outline the entire shape first. Then immediately fill in the shape before the piped outline sets.

3   To build up the mass of the piece and create a more three-dimensional shape, pipe additional layers of chocolate over the first piped layer before it has completely set. Continue piping over the design until the desired thickness has been achieved. Repeat with the second acetate sheet to create the other half of the figure.

4   Let sit until the chocolate is completely set, about 10 minutes, then release both halves from the acetate sheets. Flip the shapes over and place them onto the marble. Fill the pastry bag with additional tempered chocolate, and pipe onto the other side of each shape to build dimension. As with the first side, it is best to outline the shape with piped chocolate first and then fill in the center before the outline sets. Pipe over both halves until they have reached the desired thickness.

5   When the piped chocolate has begun to set but still feels tacky, lift both pieces off the marble and connect them together. The still-tacky chocolate should help the pieces to naturally adhere together.

6   To fill in any gaps between the pieces, pipe a small amount of tempered chocolate onto the marble. Use a paring knife to move the chocolate back and forth until it begins to thicken, then scoop up some of the thickened chocolate on the knife and spread it onto the piece to fill in the gaps. Immediately smooth out the chocolate using the paring knife, and let the piece set for about 10 minutes. During the assembly process, the warmth of your hands can cause the surface of the chocolate to begin to melt. If this occurs, the chocolate may bloom once the piece is finished. To prevent this, paper can be used to hold the piece while adhering the halves together and filling in the gaps.

7   If creating the head for an animal figure separately, sketch and pipe over the two mirror-image halves using the same technique used to create the body. Let both piped halves set completely.

8   To build up the head, pipe about 2 tablespoons of tempered chocolate onto the marble. Use a paring knife to spot-temper the chocolate by moving it back and forth on the marble until it thickens, becomes pasty, and just begins to set. Scoop up a small amount of the thickened chocolate on the paring knife and, working quickly, spread it onto one of the piped halves. Use the paring knife to build up and shape one half of the head. Repeat with the rest of the spot-tempered chocolate and the other piped half.

9   Warm a spatula with a torch. Carefully touch the flat, piped sides of both pieces of chocolate to the spatula to warm them slightly, then attach the two pieces together and let set for about 10 minutes, or spray with cold spray to set immediately.

10   Once the chocolate is set, immediately use a paring knife to shave off any excess chocolate and shape the piece as desired.

11   To attach any part of the figure that was created separately, such as the head, use spot-tempered chocolate. Pipe a small amount of tempered chocolate onto the marble

and use a paring knife to move it back and forth on the marble until the chocolate begins to thicken. Scoop up a small amount of the spot-tempered chocolate and spread it onto one of the pieces to be attached, then immediately bring the two pieces together and let set for about 10 minutes. Once the chocolate has set, use the paring knife to shave off any excess chocolate where the two pieces were joined together.

12   Use modeling chocolate (see Chapter 12) to create any final touches needed to complete the figure. To create ears for the deer figure shown here, model a teardrop shape with your hands and press it flat on the marble, then fold it into the desired shape. Use tempered chocolate to attach the ear to the figure before the modeling chocolate hardens. To create a tail, shape another teardrop shape, flatten, and make cuts as desired to achieve a hair effect. Pick up the tail and roll it into a folded shape, then attach to the figure using tempered chocolate.

13   Store the completed figure at room temperature until ready to use.

FIRST ROW:
–   Pipe the outline first, then immediately fill in the rest of the shape so the chocolate melds into one piece.
–   Outline and fill in another layer of chocolate to add dimension.
–   Connect the pieces together, fill in the gaps, and immediately smooth out the chocolate.

SECOND ROW:
–   Pipe the outline for the head and fill in with piped chocolate.
–   Spot-temper the chocolate to create a paste.
–   Immediately use the paste to build up the head.

THIRD ROW:
–   Glue the two pieces together by warming both halves on a torched spatula.
–   Once the chocolate has set, shave off the excess with a paring knife.
–   Attach the head using spot-tempered chocolate.

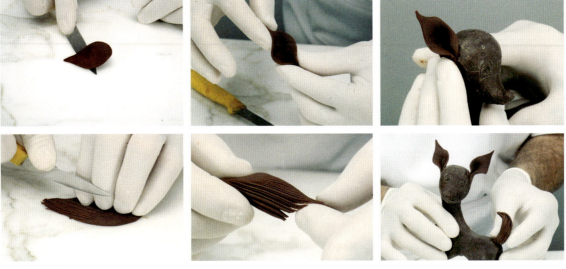

FIRST ROW:
- Modeling chocolate can be used to create the ears. Start by flattening a drop shape.
- Bend the drop shape to mold it into an ear.
- Use tempered chocolate to attach the ears before the modeling chocolate hardens.

SECOND ROW:
- For the tail, flatten a drop shape and cut finely to achieve a hair effect.
- Pick up the piece and roll a bit to give the tail some volume.
- Use tempered chocolate to attach the tail to the body.

Creating Three-Dimensional Figures from Molded Shapes

Another way to create three-dimensional chocolate figures is by creating and assembling molded shapes. Using molded shells, it is possible to create pieces with the same level of detail as a carved piece but that can be completed much more quickly while using a great deal less chocolate. Molded spheres, eggshells, and other shapes can be combined to create the volume needed for three-dimensional animals and other figures.

1 To begin, sketch a very simple drawing of the figure using basic shapes such as circles, ovals, and rectangles. Animation books are a great reference for inspiration. Then gather shell molds that match the shapes and proportions used in your drawing.

2 Cast all the shell molds with the desired types of chocolate (see Casting, page 138–139). Let set until the chocolate is completely crystallized. All the pieces must be cast before you begin assembling the figure.

3 To assemble the base shapes for the figure, unmold both halves of each shape. Melt the edges of both halves slightly using a food warmer, warm oven, or a spatula warmed with a torch, then attach the halves together. Let set about 10 minutes until the chocolate is completely crystallized.

4   To create a "hollowed-out" sphere shape like the ones used to create the eyes of the owl on page 325, unmold one half-sphere and place it flat on the marble. Warm a round cutter with a torch and place it down on the sphere to melt off the top of the shell.

5   Flip over the hollowed-out sphere half and pipe tempered chocolate onto the inside edge. Attach it to the other, nonhollowed-out sphere half to create a complete sphere with an indentation on one side.

6   To attach two completed shapes together to begin assembling a figure, scratch the surface of the first shape with a knife or melt slightly using a food warmer or a spatula warmed with a torch. This will create a rough area where the second piece will be attached.

7   Melt the second shape slightly in the spot where it will be attached to the first piece, then gently press the two pieces together to join them. Melting the shape itself before attaching it will create a much stronger bond than using tempered chocolate as glue. Because the chocolate is out of temper, the pieces will need to set for a long time—up to 20 minutes—before the piece is completely set.

8   To join two pieces that do not fit together cleanly, use spot-tempered chocolate to bond the two pieces and fill in any gaps between them. Pipe a small circle of tempered chocolate onto the marble surface and use the edge of a paring knife to table the chocolate. As soon as it begins to set, scoop the chocolate up on the paring knife and spread it onto one of the two pieces to be joined together.

9   Attach the second piece and immediately use the paring knife to smooth out any excess chocolate. This must be done quickly, because the spot-tempered chocolate will set almost immediately, and cleaning and smoothing out the surface will be much more difficult after the chocolate has set.

10   Continue to attach molded shapes to the body of the piece as needed to create the desired figure. To fill in any gaps or ridges or to create additional features, such as the ears shown here, use the spot-tempering technique described above to table-tempered chocolate. Apply the spot-tempered chocolate to the piece with the paring knife and shape and smooth it as needed.

11   To add detail to the surface of the figure, cut a template out of a piece of tracing, parchment, or copy paper. Place the template flat on the marble and use a spatula to spread tempered chocolate over the top.

12   As soon as the chocolate has begun to set, remove the template from the marble. The excess chocolate should come away easily as you lift up the template; the chocolate should be a bit tacky at this point.

13   Quickly place the template chocolate side down on the body of the piece. It should adhere nicely if the chocolate is still tacky. Let set 5 to 10 minutes until the chocolate is completely crystallized, then remove the paper.

14   Once the figure is complete, paint or spray as desired and let set completely. Store the completed figure at room temperature in a dark place until ready to use.

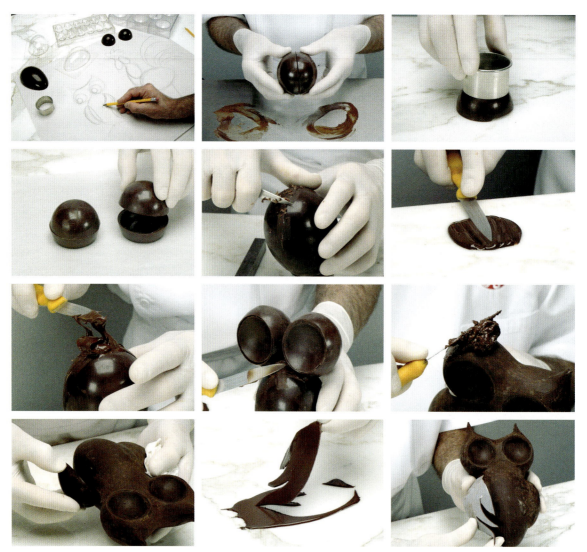

FIRST ROW:
— Begin with a simple drawing and try to find shell molds to achieve the desired shapes.
— To assemble shells, warm the edges a little and then join.
— To create "eyes," use a warm cutter to melt the top off of the shell.

SECOND ROW:
— Place the cut-off top of the shell down flat. Attach the remaining part of the cut half-shell with the narrow end down, then attach a full half-sphere on top.
— Scratch off the shiny surface to make a rough patch, so the pieces to be attached will adhere better.
— The spot-tempering technique will force fast crystallization.

THIRD ROW:
— As soon the chocolate begins to set, scoop the chocolate up and use it to attach the pieces.
— After attaching, smooth out the chocolate immediately.
— Spot-tempering is best for filling gaps or creating mass like the ears shown here.

FOURTH ROW:
— If additional volume is needed, use the desired shapes to continue building the piece.
— Cover a paper template with chocolate and remove it from the marble as soon the chocolate starts to set.
— Quickly place the template chocolate side down onto the piece to adhere.

15

Creating a Competition Piece

Competing and creating a showpiece can be one of the most exhilarating experiences in your career. However, to achieve success, it is essential not only to practice a great deal but also to mentally prepare for the competition. Creating a support network of friends, family, and coworkers is also very important and can be a critical factor in achieving success.

Preparing to Compete

Competing is fun, but it is also hard work and requires many hours of physical and mental preparation. There are many things to consider when making the decision to compete. Some of the key steps in preparing for the big event include:

1 SELECTING THE RIGHT COMPETITION: It is a good idea to attend one or more competitions as a spectator to see firsthand how they are run. Then you must determine what type of competition to train for. In some, competitors bring finished pieces to display for judging, while in others, the competitors create their pieces in front of the judges. Whichever type you choose, as a beginner you will probably want to start with one or more local competitions.

2 GAINING EXPERIENCE: Volunteering to assist a competition team is an optimal way to get valuable experience and to gain an understanding of what happens during the event. You may be able to find opportunities to volunteer by talking to the organizers of the event or by checking the Internet. It may also be helpful to find a mentor who has trained and competed before to pass on the knowledge he or she has gained through these experiences.

3 RESEARCHING THE EVENT: Learning about the event beforehand is critical. Some essential things to research include the details of the venue, such as what the temperature and humidity of the space will be like, and what supplies you should plan to pack and bring to the event. It is also important to learn about how you can organize your work space at the event and how you will be able to present the finished showpiece.

4 GETTING TO KNOW THE JUDGES: Educate yourself beforehand about the judges—who they are, their tastes in showpieces, and what they would like to see. Try to find out what has made previous winners stand out among the rest in order to figure out any trends and determine how to best impress the judges. All of this is very important and should not be taken lightly or overlooked when preparing for a competition.

5 UNDERSTANDING THE RULES: Read the rules carefully and make sure there are no misunderstandings. Most mistakes happen because competitors don't understand the rules or don't follow them correctly. Understanding what kinds of ingredients, molds, and tools are allowed is very important. The rules will also dictate the theme and purpose of the showpiece, and the theme will be the anchor for the piece and the driving force behind your design.

Understanding the Theory of Design

In preparing to compete, it is also essential to understand the basic elements of the theory of design. The proper use of color, geometric shapes and designs, and size and proportion are the keys to successfully designing your own original showpiece.

Color

Color is a very important element in showpieces. Used wisely, it can enhance the look of a showpiece and also indicate the piece's meaning. The theme will help determine which colors to choose. Color can evoke a feeling such as cold or warmth, a season, such as summer or winter, or even a place like the tropics. It can also be used to express emotional states like happiness, sadness, hope, aggression, anger, innocence, and love.

Colors in the red, orange, and yellow family, including yellowish greens, are considered warm colors, while purples, blues, and darker greens are considered cold. In general, it is best to use warmer colors in the foreground and colder colors in the background of a showpiece to help achieve an impression of depth and space. Darker colors generally work well for smaller elements in a showpiece, as they attract attention and help to draw the eye to these smaller components. Lighter colors work better for larger elements that would appear too heavy or intense if they were in a darker shade.

The colors can broken down into several different categories—primary, secondary, tertiary, and complementary—that are all related to one another through the color wheel.

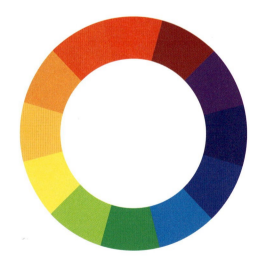

The basic color wheel will give you an understanding of how to choose complementary colors for a showpiece.

Primary Colors

The three primary colors, which are placed opposite one another in a triangle on the color wheel, are red, yellow, and blue. All other colors are made from these three.

Primary colors are the three basic colors from which other colors are derived.

Secondary Colors

Mixing any two of the primary colors together results in one of the secondary colors: orange, green, and purple. The secondary colors are found between the primary colors on the color wheel. Orange is made by mixing red and yellow, green is made by mixing blue and yellow, and purple is made by mixing red and blue. Mixing all three primary colors together results in black, gray, or brown, because they absorb all the colors that they cover.

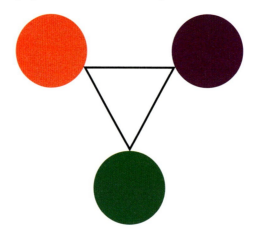

Secondary colors can be produced by combining primary colors.

Tertiary colors

Tertiary colors fall in between the primary and secondary colors on the color wheel. Each tertiary color is formed by mixing a primary color with an adjacent secondary color. For example, blue and green can be combined to form the tertiary color blue-green.

Tertiary colors can be produced by mixing primary and secondary colors.

Complementary Colors

Complementary colors are those colors found opposite one another on the color wheel. When used in equal proportions in a showpiece, they can help bring a perfect balance to the piece. Examples of complementary colors include:

– Yellow and Purple
– Blue and Orange
– Red and Green

White and black, while not technically colors, are also opposites that can be used together to provide balance in a piece.

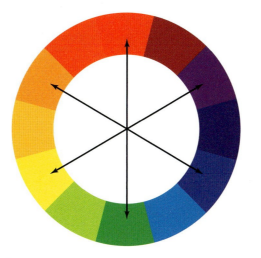

Complementary colors appear on opposite sides of the color wheel.

Triadic Colors

Traidic colors are found at the three opposite corners of the color wheel. Green, orange, and violet, for example, are three triadic colors. As with complementary colors, a set of triadic colors can be used together to create balance in a showpiece.

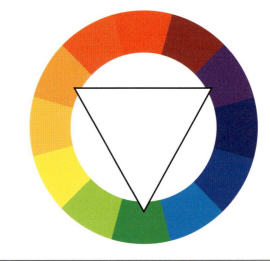

Triadic colors are equally spaced around the color wheel.

Color and Meaning

The following are a range of colors and their traditional meanings:

WHITE Purity, virginity, truth, innocence, faithfulness, life, peace, original light

BLACK Sadness, mourning, the end of things, chaos, silence

RED Aggression, stimulation, fire, blood, impulsiveness, anger, power, strength, love

GREEN Hope, renewal, harmony, balance, loyalty, vegetative life, youth, calm

BLUE Responsibility, spirituality, faithfulness, loyalty, purity, research, rest, quietness, faith, justice

ORANGE Sociability, sympathy, intelligence, wisdom, idealism, inspiration, enthusiasm

YELLOW Cleverness, intelligence, openness, creativity, wildness, happiness

PURPLE Comprehension, generosity, tactfulness, spirituality, modesty, melancholy, truth, suffering, mysticism, royalty

PINK Regeneration, baptism, birth, softness, prudence, tenderness, modesty, sensual pleasure, love, graciousness

GRAY Neutrality, warmth, balance, monotony, boredom, mourning

BROWN Decomposition, dead leaves, treason, mourning

Geometric Shapes

Shapes are a basic element of design. They are made up of closed contours and can be two dimensional, as in the case of a flat square, or three dimensional, as in the case of a cube. Like colors, geometric shapes can be used to convey meaning, and opposite shapes, like opposite colors, can be used to bring balance and creativity to a piece. Three-dimensional shapes such as cubes and spheres are an ideal way to gain volume and height in a showpiece and can be used alongside solid, plane bases to provide contrast.

The basic types of shapes that can be used in showpieces include flat squares and rectangles, circles and ovals, triangles, and diamonds, as well as their three-dimensional counterparts, such as cubes, spheres, cylinders, and pyramids.

Shapes and Meaning

Like colors, geometric shapes often have traditional meanings:

SQUARES are symbols of equality, perfection, and the shaping of ideas.

CIRCLES symbolize unity and wholeness.

TRIANGLES are associated with the number three. Pointing upward, triangles can symbolize fire, manpower, and trinity. Pointing downward, they can symbolize water or femininity.

DIAMONDS are symbols of high value or brilliance.

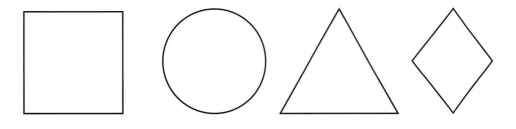

Natural Shapes

In designing a showpiece, it may also be useful to consider a variety of natural shapes, such as leaves, hearts, stars, puddles, and so on. These kinds of shapes or designs often have their own meanings as well, such as:

LEAVES	Renewal, life, spring, changing
SUN	Heat, warmth, happiness
MOON	Darkness, romance
STAR	Celebration, space
DOVE	Peace, harmony, love
CLOVER LEAVES	Good luck
OWL	Knowledge, wisdom
HEART	Love, harmony

Size and Proportion

Composing a showpiece is an act of artistic expression, and like any other work of art, a showpiece should have power, harmony, and elegance. An aesthetically correct showpiece must have a focus point that draws the viewer's eyes into the creative composition.

The Golden Ratio

For hundreds of years, visual artists have been studying the best ways to frame their subjects, and have discovered a mathematical phenomenon that can be used to determine the best place to set the focus point for any composition.

The "Golden Ratio" is the ratio between two segments such that the smaller segment (a) is to the larger segment (b) as the largest segment (b) is to the sum of two segments (a+b). Artists and architects have used the concept of the golden ratio for years to determine the proportions of their work, and the same ratio can be used to approximate the ideal height or width of a showpiece and determine the focus point.

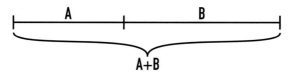

The Golden Ratio can be used to determine a showpiece's height.

The golden ratio is represented mathematically by phi (1.618033). To use this geometric relationship to determine the ideal proportions for a showpiece where the base length is known, the length must be divided by 2, then multiplied by 1.618033. For example, if the base of a showpiece is 30 cm long, the golden ratio can be used to figure out the ideal height and width for the piece:

Length: 30 cm
Width: W
(L /2) x 1.618033 =W
30 cm / 2=15 cm
15 cm x 1.618033 = 24.27 cm
Width = 24.27 cm

The ideal width for the showpiece, based on the Golden Ratio.

Once you have determined the width of the showpiece, you can use the golden ratio to determine the height based on the length and width. The sum of the length and width, divided by 2 and then multiplied by phi, will give the ideal height for the piece.

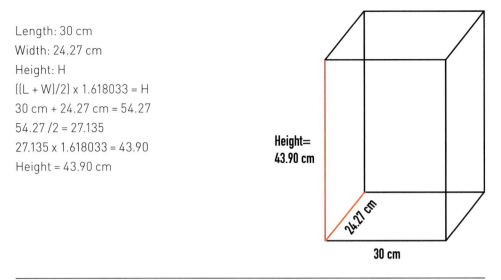

Length: 30 cm
Width: 24.27 cm
Height: H
((L + W)/2) x 1.618033 = H
30 cm + 24.27 cm = 54.27
54.27 /2 = 27.135
27.135 x 1.618033 = 43.90
Height = 43.90 cm

Height=
43.90 cm

24.27 cm

30 cm

The ideal height for the showpiece, based on the Golden Ratio.

Thus, a pleasant size for the showpiece, based on the 30 cm long base, would be 30 cm long by 24.27 cm wide by 43.90 cm high.

Showpieces intended for competition are often created to be much higher than the Golden Ratio might indicate. However, the Golden Ratio is a foolproof way to achieve perfect balance and symmetry in a piece. If the piece described above were created with a 30 cm x 24.27 cm base, but the height was less than 43.90 cm, it would look imbalanced because the base would appear too heavy for the height.

Finding the Focus Point

When glancing at a showpiece, the viewer's eyes will automatically try to extract meaning from the image. There is usually a focus point or "sweet spot" that stands out and draws the eyes to it, and this focus point should indicate what the showpiece is all about. It is very important to consider the placement of the focus point for a showpiece. Although every showpiece is different, and the creator must determine the best design for each, there are basic mathematical rules that can be used to help approximate the best focus point for a piece.

To find the focus point of a showpiece using the Golden Ratio, divide the height of the piece by 1.618033. The result is the ideal height for the focus point. So using the example above of a showpiece whose height is 43.90 cm, the focus point can be determined as follows: 43.90/1.618033 = 27.13. Thus, the focus point should be placed 27.13 cm above the base of the showpiece.

If more than one showpiece is being presented on the same table, the size of the table should be used as the "base" and the height and focus points for the showpieces should be determined based on that table size. This means the pieces should be taller when being presented in a group on a large table than if they were being presented individually on a smaller base.

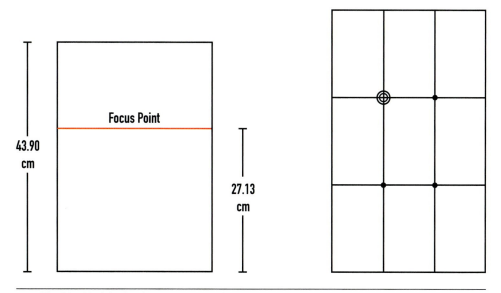

LEFT: The ideal height for the focus point of the showpiece. RIGHT: Using the Rule of Thirds, a sculpture can be divided into thirds to find the ideal focus points.

The Rule of Thirds

The Rule of Thirds is an even simpler way to identify the ideal focus point for a showpiece. Using both the Rule of Thirds and the Golden Ratio will result in approximately the same focus point, but the Rule of Thirds is much easier to understand. The rule states that if an image is divided into equal thirds both vertically and horizontally, the dividing lines can be used as guides for the focus points of the image.

There is no need to have a degree in mathematics to use the Rule of Thirds. Simply divide your frame into nine compartments, using two equally spaced vertical lines and two equally spaced horizontal lines. Those lines will intersect in four places, and those intersections represent the ideal focus points for the showpiece.

Using the Rule of Thirds will help prevent the showpiece from appearing too crowded or "busy," as it allows the subject room to breathe. Of course there are exceptions to any rule, and the same goes for using the Rule of Thirds. In some cases, the designer may want to ignore these compositional guidelines in order to convey a feeling of tension in the showpiece.

Creating the Showpiece

Once you have studied the basic principles of design and have mentally prepared for competition, it is time to begin the process of actually creating the design for your showpiece. It is important to start with careful research, brainstorming, and sketching to create a plan for the piece before you begin to work with actual equipment and ingredients.

Researching the Theme

Search on the Internet or visit a library to learn more about the theme and its corresponding elements. It can be helpful to jot down a list of key words, colors, and so on that pertain to the theme, to help identify the primary elements for your showpiece. For example, if the theme you are working with is "Fall," you might compile a list of key words such as turning leaves, pumpkins, football, harvest, Halloween, Thanksgiving, and turkey, and you might note orange and brown as key colors. Meanwhile, an "Ocean" theme might inspire a list including water, ships, anchors, shells, coral reefs, fish, waves, sunset, sand, treasure chests, and the color blue. You may even want to write a short essay incorporating the key words to bring the theme to life. Then you can use your text to inspire a drawing that incorporates the primary elements of the theme, which will form the basis for your showpiece.

The elements you choose to include in your sketches and in your finished piece should reflect your own personal taste but should also be balanced and should respect established design concepts. You may choose to work with more realistic elements based on nature, which are easily recognizable to the viewer but can be difficult to copy well, or with more abstract elements, which may be easier to create but can be difficult for the viewer to identify. Keep in mind that in your final design, all the elements must be balanced and in harmony with one another, and it should be easy for the viewer to understand.

Designing the Piece

Once you have gained an understanding of the theme and have decided which key elements to include, the design process can begin.

Start the design of the piece by drawing a smooth curve or straight line, and use the Rule of Thirds to help set the focal points. Then begin to arrange the elements you want to include on this main line, beginning with the primary elements first, at the main focus points. If there are a lot of small elements you want to include, you may want to group them close together so that they are related, rather than spaced out throughout the piece.

Keep in mind that every showpiece should have a beginning and an end—the placement of the main elements should help to lead the eye from the top to the bottom or from the bottom to the top. Also remember that when it comes to texture, form, and color, opposites attract. You may want to consider using a mix of opposite textures, shapes, and colors, such as rough and smooth textures, dull and shiny surfaces, and round and rectangular shapes.

- Use the Rule of Thirds to identify a focus point along the support line.
- As the sketch progresses, add elements along the support line and around the focus point.
- A cardboard model can help you to visualize the piece before creating it in chocolate.

As you fill in your sketch, empty space will begin to appear. Empty space is important in order to make the piece look light and elegant and to avoid overcrowding. Remember that more is not always better, and try not to use more elements than necessary to express the theme. The showpiece must show a sense of movement, look light, and be pleasing to the eye.

Once you have completed a sketch of the piece, create a model made out of cardboard and paper to help visualize how the finished piece will appear. To go a step further, you may even want to airbrush the pieces to get a sense of how the colors will work. This will give you a good idea of what the final showpiece will look like before you begin working with any real ingredients, which can be costly.

Choosing the Color Balance

The shapes and colors can be the most important elements of a showpiece. Once the theme has been established, choosing the color becomes almost second nature. A main color is generally selected to complement the theme, and this main color is usually a primary color. To make sure that the piece does not become too colorful or too busy, use only one main color. Based on that main color, choose a secondary color to use more sparingly in the piece. Complementary colors work without fail, so it is always a good idea to choose colors that are opposite one another on the color wheel. Black and white are not technically colors, and they can both be used as desired throughout the piece.

Some examples of strong color combinations include:

THEME Christmas
MAIN COLOR Red
OPPOSITE COLOR Green

In this case, the piece would be mainly red, but there must be a little bit of green included as well to provide balance. If equal amounts of red and green were used, the color scheme would be too confusing to the eye.

THEME Marine Life
MAIN COLOR Blue
OPPOSITE COLOR Orange

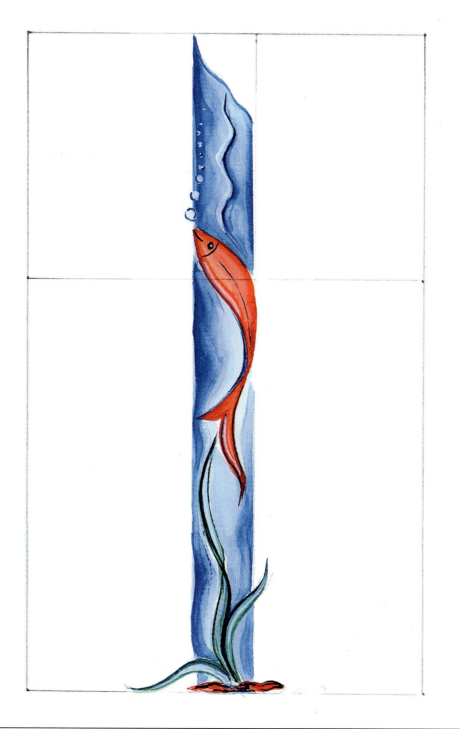

The combination of orange and blue in this design is an example of good color balance.

Assembling the Showpiece

Before you begin to work with chocolate, decide carefully which techniques will work best for each of the elements you plan to create. The same showpiece can look different depending on whether the elements are cut out from flat pieces of chocolate, piped, carved, or molded. Sometimes a piece will look best if its components are flat, giving a quieter look, while other pieces may look best with piped sections that have many contours.

Creating the showpiece will be a lot easier and less stressful if you take the time up front to plan out the sequence of steps and practice all the needed techniques. When working with chocolate, be very clean and precise and take the time to perfect each of the techniques you are using. Once you have perfected the techniques, work on improving the time it takes you to create each element of the showpiece. For example, you may be able to consolidate steps by spreading and cutting, coloring and airbrushing, and casting and unmolding all of the various elements at the same time in order to shave time off of the total process.

Once you are confident in each of the techniques needed to create the showpiece elements, consider the organization of your working tools and ingredients. You should always start by creating the base for your showpiece first, followed by any main supporting elements, and then add in the finer details and smaller decorative elements last. While practicing, try to work in a controlled area, keeping the space small, and make sure to place all your needed tools and ingredients in the order in which they will be needed. Keep unnecessary tools off of the table, and ensure that your working space is clean at all times. Be mindful of the waste you are producing at every step, and make an effort to minimize this waste at all times.

Practicing the components of a showpiece can help you to refine your design and improve your work time.

The best way to practice the techniques and *mise en place* for creating a showpiece is to actually do mini demonstrations or timed trials, either for small groups or by yourself. Doing timed trials will help you get used to the pressure of the real competition and will prepare you for what to do when something goes wrong (and it will!). During the practice sessions, never be tempted to throw away your mistakes and start over. By forcing yourself to learn how to "fix" things on the spot, you will gain the confidence needed to be a strong competitor.

Remember, being creative is only a small part of designing a successful showpiece. It is also necessary to have an understanding of the techniques needed to turn your creativity into something you can use. It can be frustrating to develop a creative idea for a showpiece without having the technical knowledge and experience needed to express that idea. That is why it is essential to master the fundamental techniques outlined in chapters 3, 7, and 10–14 before you begin the process of creating full showpieces. With thorough preparation, a strong understanding of the principles of design, and a mastery of the fundamentals of working with chocolate, you will be well on your way to defining your own personal style and creating stunning, award-winning showpieces.

Appendix: Templates

The templates on the following pages can be used to reproduce the showpieces seen throughout this book. All templates can be enlarged or reduced as needed to fit your own designs.

Template components shaded in tan indicate pieces that are meant to be molded rather than cut out or piped using a template. These molded components have been included in the appendix to show the correct sizing and proportions for each piece.

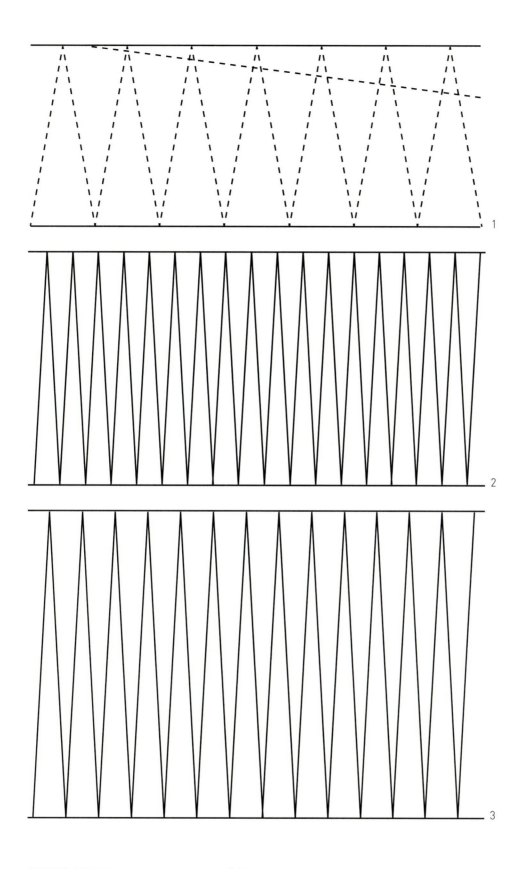

CUTS FOR CHOCOLATE CURLS, page 265 (1). The dotted line shows the angle at which the paper should be rolled.
CUTS FOR STRAIGHT TRIANGLE CURLS, page 267 (2).
CUTS FOR SPIRAL CURLS, page 267 (3).

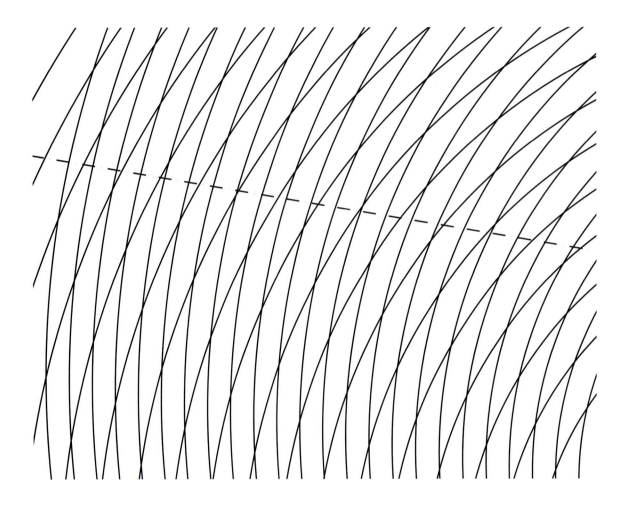

CUTS FOR ROLLED FLOWERS, page 292. The dotted line shows the angle at which the paper should be rolled.

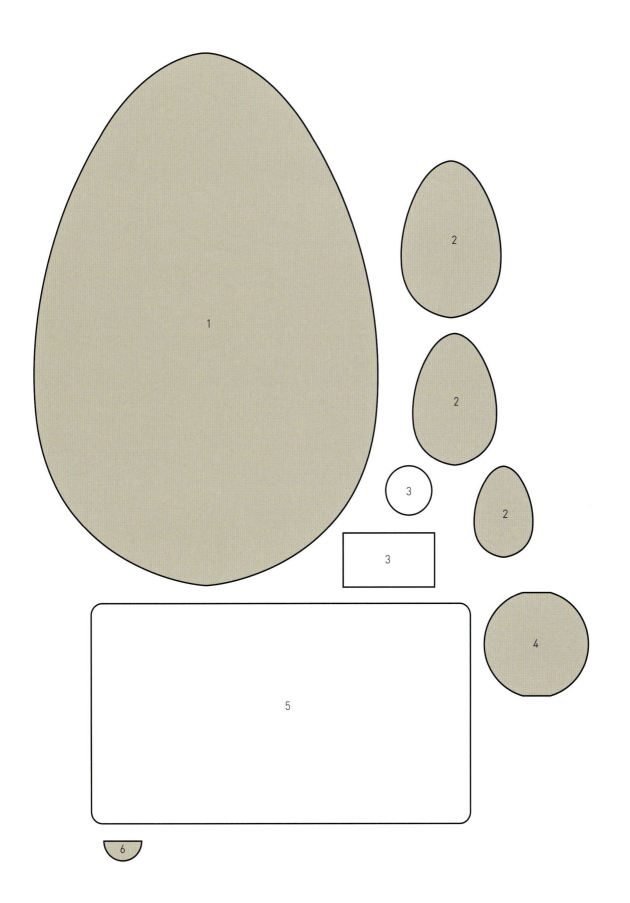

EASTER SHOWPIECE, page VIII. Large egg (1), small eggs (2), décor elements (3), sphere for egg support (4), base (5) and feet (6).

UNDERSEA SHOWPIECE, page 231. Anchor and fish.

THE ART OF THE CHOCOLATIER

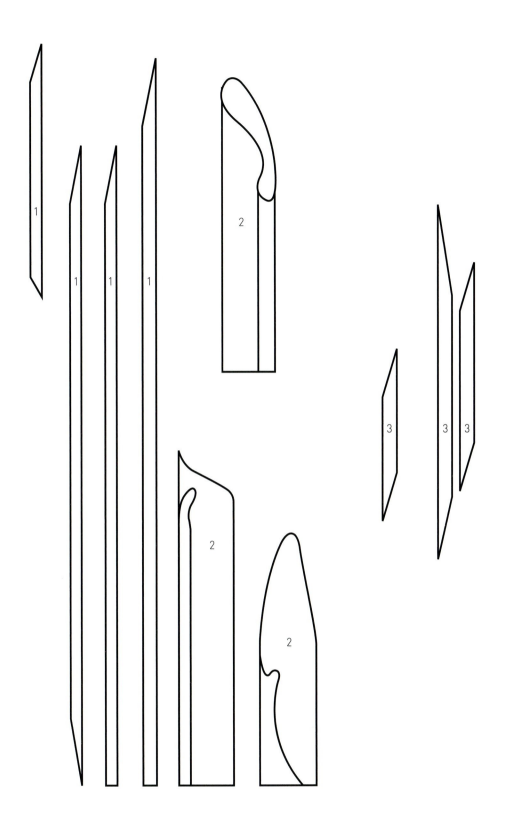

ROSES SHOWPIECE, page 232. Long filled tubes (1), hollow tubes (2), and short filled tubes (3).
(Continued on next page.)

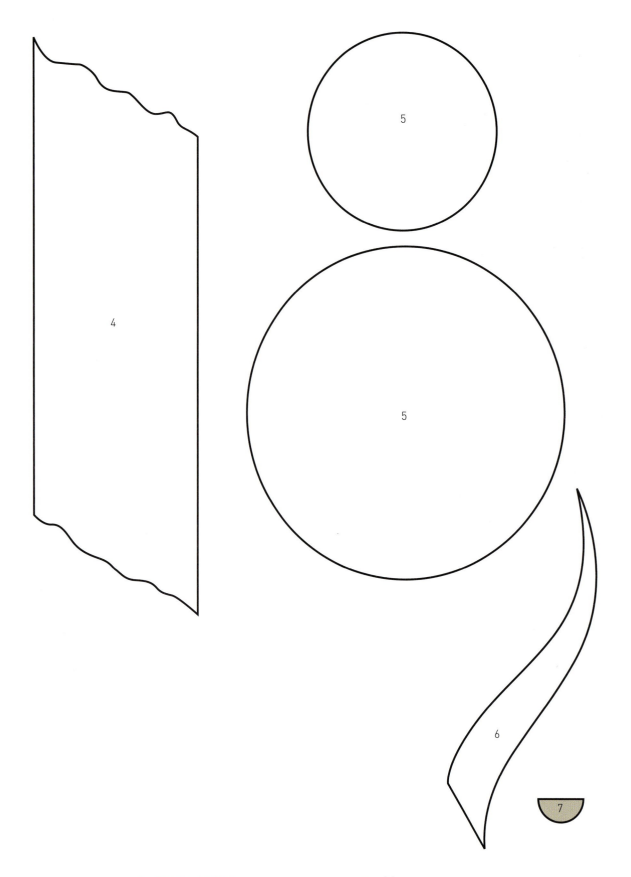

ROSES SHOWPIECE, *continued from page 355.* Base (4), rings for food processor modeling chocolate (5), second base (6), and feet (7).

MASQUERADE SHOWPIECE, page 239. Masks and fan blade.

ROOSTER SHOWPIECE, page 251. Base and rooster.

THE ART OF THE CHOCOLATIER

GUITAR SHOWPIECE, page 249. Guitar and stars.

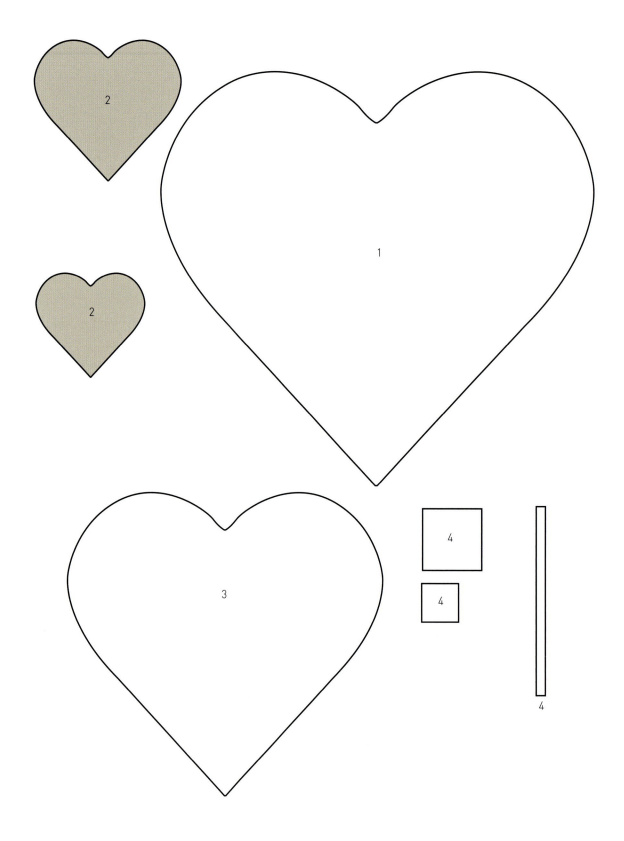

HEART BOX, page 258. Base/lid (1), small hearts (2), guide for rim (3), and other décor elements for lid (4).

THE ART OF THE CHOCOLATIER

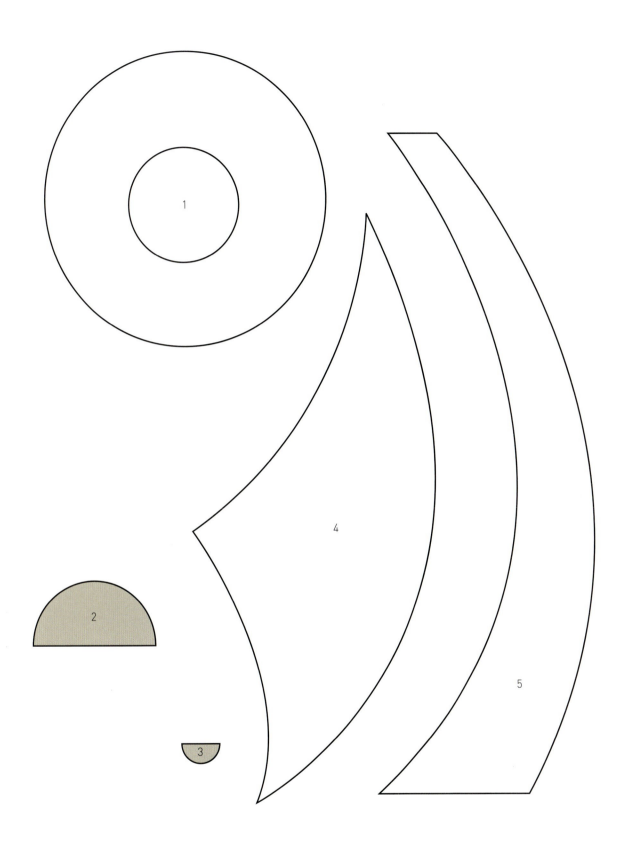

FLOWER HAT SHOWPIECE, page 263. Disc with cutout (1), half-sphere (2), feet (3), base (4), and support (5).

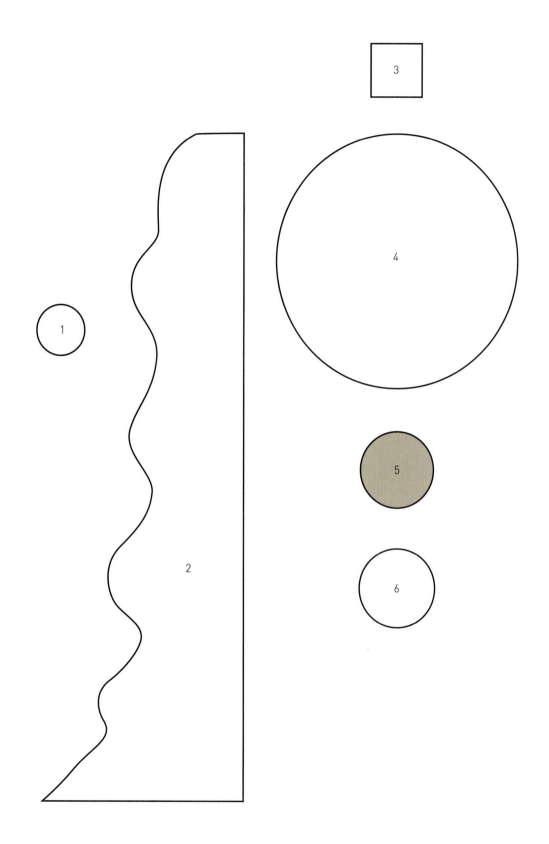

SPIRAL CONE FLOWER SHOWPIECE, page 269. Base for flower (1), support (2), square décor (3), base (4), sphere (5), flat circle décor (6).

WOVEN HEART BOX, page 283. Heart base with hole pattern.

YELLOW FLOWER SHOWPIECE, page 285. Butterfly.

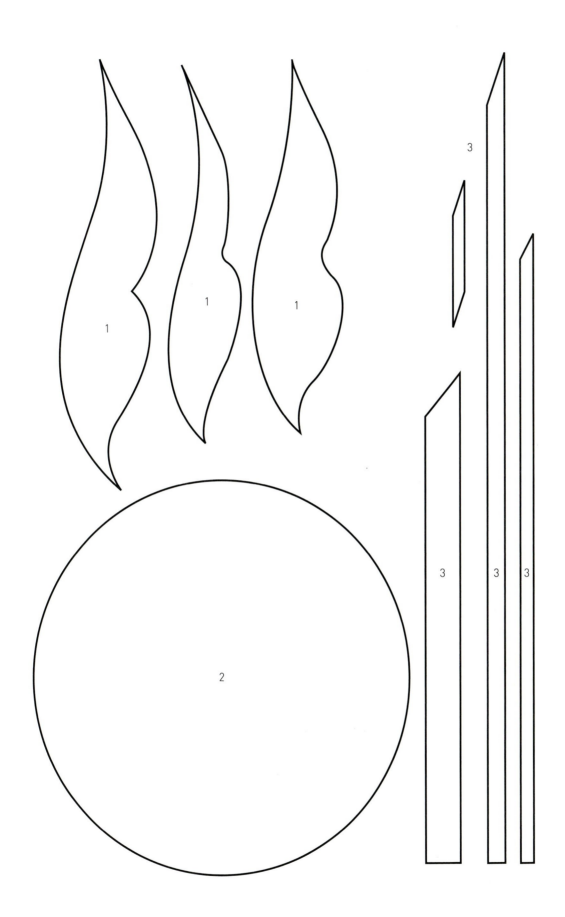

ORANGE ROSE SHOWPIECE, page 289. Leaves (1), ring for food processor modeling chocolate (2), and tubes (3). *(Continued on next page.)*

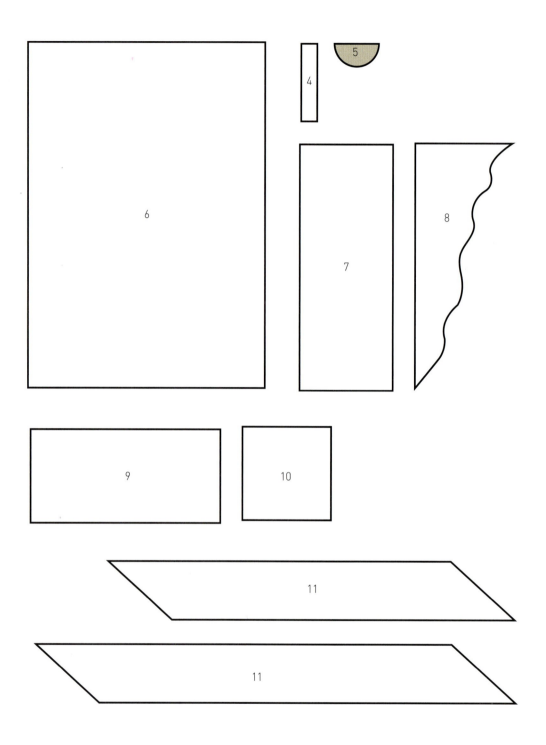

ORANGE ROSE SHOWPIECE, *continued from page 365.* Rectangle décor (4), feet (5), base (6), support (7), shape for textured cutout (8), upper base (9), square décor (10), and supports for chocolates (11).

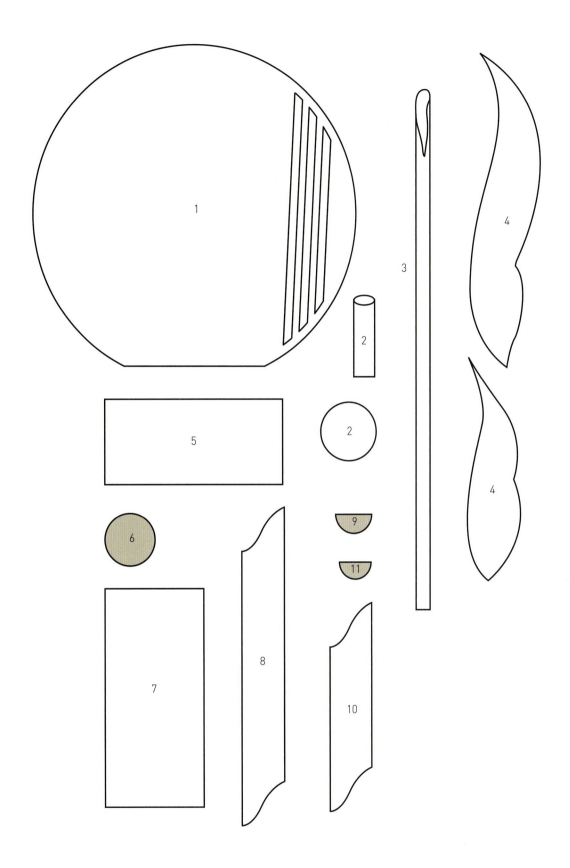

SUNSET SHOWPIECE, page 294. Background (1), supports for flower (2), tube (3), leaves (4), base for background (5), sphere (6), base for spheres (7), upper praline base (8) and feet (9), lower praline base (10), and feet (11).

BUTTERFLY SHOWPIECE, page 301. Butterfly (1), base (2), and heart (3).

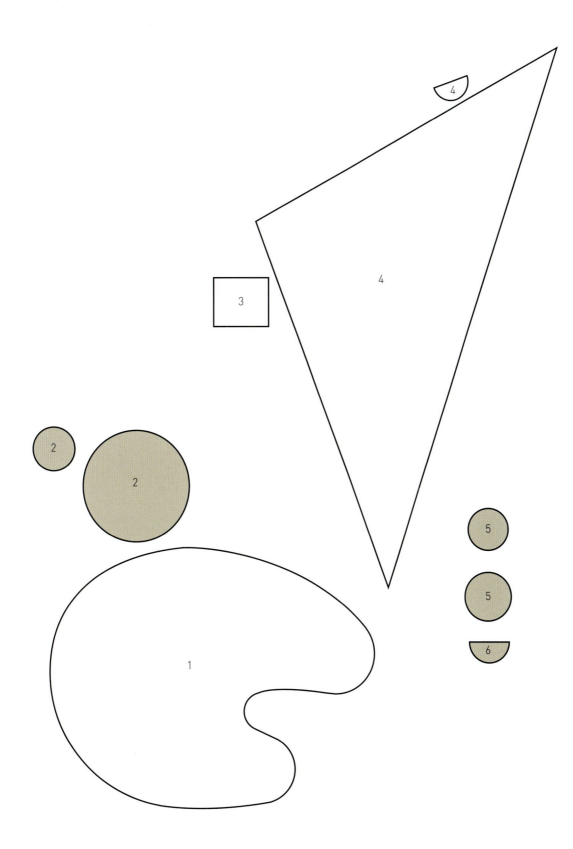

FLOWER SHOWPIECE ON TRIANGLE SUPPORT, page 305. Base (1), large and small spheres (2), square décor (3), triangle support and flower support (4), small spheres (5), and feet (6).

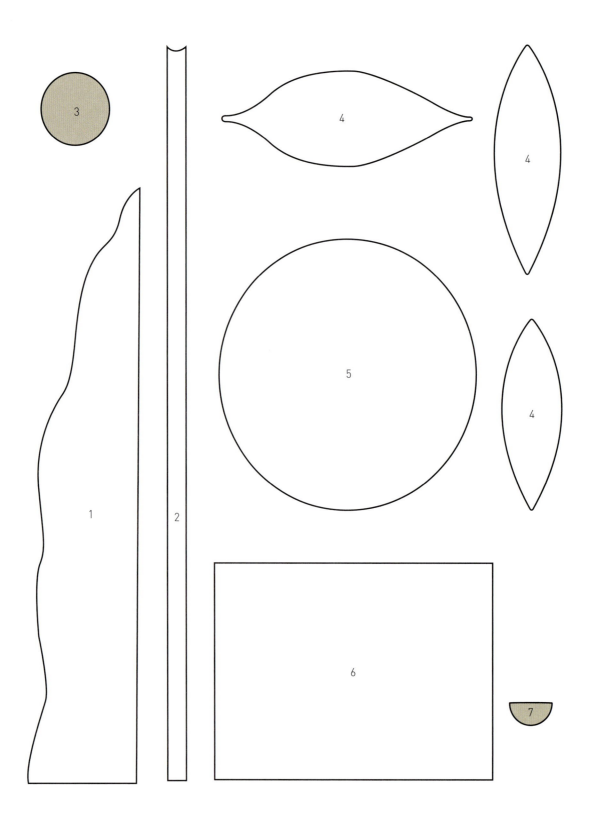

BIRD OF PARADISE SHOWPIECE ON RED SUPPORT, page 306. Shape for red wallpaper-textured support (1), tube (2), sphere for flower support (3), leaves (4), ring for food processor modeling chocolate (5), base (6), and feet (7).

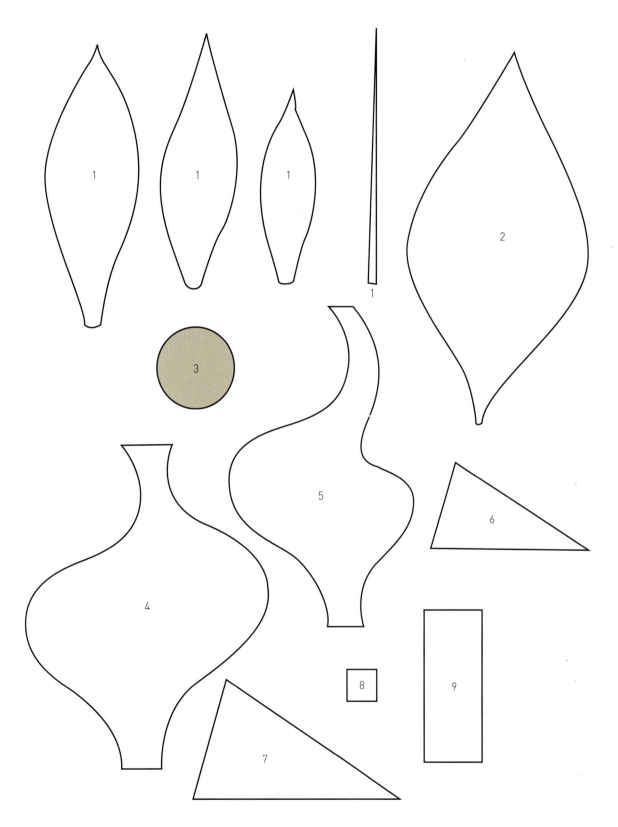

MODERN BIRD OF PARADISE SHOWPIECE, page 307. Petals (1), base of flower (2), sphere for flower support (3), back "vase" support (4), front "vase" support (5), small triangle base (6), large triangle base (7), square décor (8), and support (9).

SOUTHWESTERN BIRD OF PARADISE SHOWPIECE, page 309. Petals (1), base for flower (2), leaves (3), curved support (4), upper base (5), lower base (6), lower support (7), and sphere for flower support (8).

THE ART OF THE CHOCOLATIER

VALENTINE'S DAY SHOWPIECE, page 315. Lower base (1), upper base (2), support (3), envelope base (4), envelope flap (5), cutout for bent support shape (6), small heart and large heart (7).

WINTER SHOWPIECE, page 316. Evergreen tree, deer, and large tree.

THE ART OF THE CHOCOLATIER

HERON SHOWPIECE, page 317. Heron.

HUMMINGBIRD SHOWPIECE, page 318. Hummingbird.

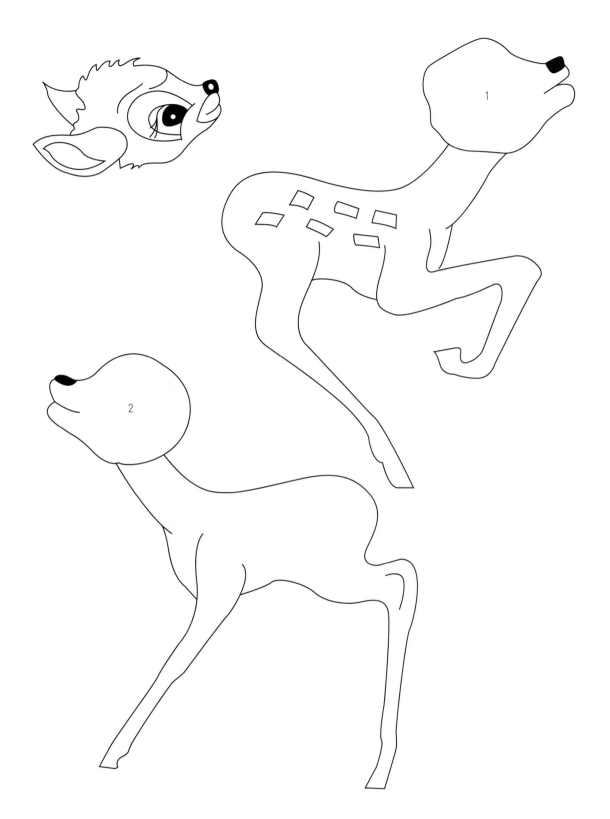

DEER SHOWPIECE, page 319. Deer, side 1 (1), side 2 (2).

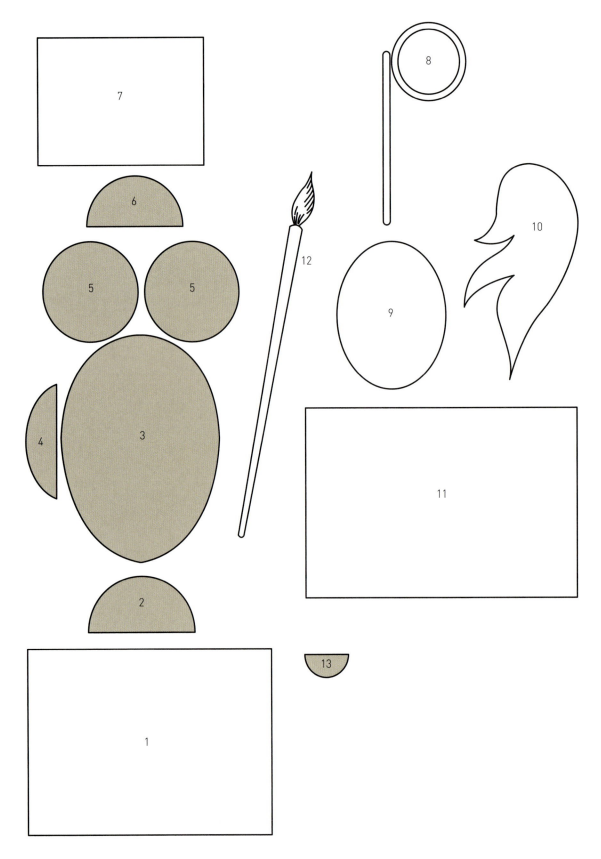

OWL GRADUATION SHOWPIECE, page 325. Book shape (1), support (2), body (3), egg shape for side (4), eyes (5), hat support (6), hat (7), eyeglass (8), cutout for center of body (9), wings (10), book shape (11), paintbrush (12), and feet (13).

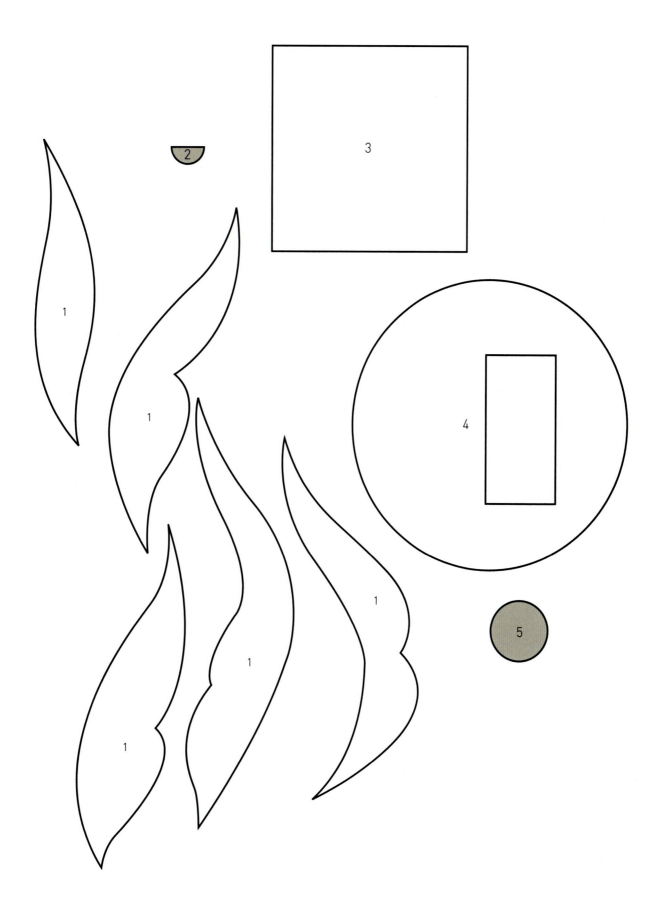

RED FLOWER SHOWPIECE, page 329. Leaves (1), feet (2), base (3), large circle support with cutout (4), sphere for center praline base (5). *(Continued on next page.)*

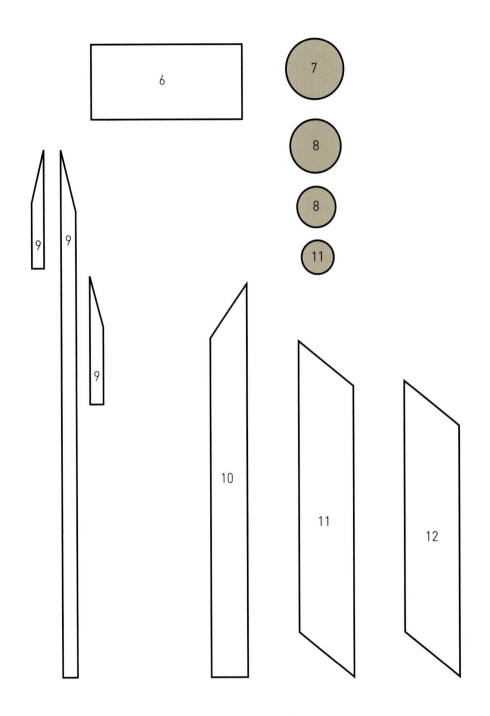

RED FLOWER SHOWPIECE, *continued from page 379.* Base for flower (6), sphere for flower support (7), spheres for décor (8), tubes (9), tube support (10), sphere to support praline base (11), and base for pralines (12).

CHRISTMAS SHOWPIECE, page 331. Tree ornament (1), half tree for back support (2), large tree (3), sled (4), stars (5), and base (6).

NEW YEAR'S EVE SHOWPIECE, page 336. Stars (1), base (2), champagne bottle with spray (3), glass (4), and bottle (5).

THE ART OF THE CHOCOLATIER

2

1

WHITE CORAL FLOWER SHOWPIECE, page 339. Base support (1), circle support (2).

HALLOWEEN SHOWPIECE, page 340. Witch (1), bats (2), moon (3), eaves (4), center of house (5), lower eaves (6), right side of house (7).

HALLOWEEN SHOWPIECE, page 340. Full haunted house (1), roof peaks (2), left side of house (3), center support (4), and tree (5).

OUTER SPACE SHOWPIECE, page 343. Components for large spaceship (1), components for smaller spaceship (2), components for tail of large spaceship (3), and base of large spaceship (4).

THE ART OF THE CHOCOLATIER

SWAN SHOWPIECE, page 347. Swans and support with heart cutouts.

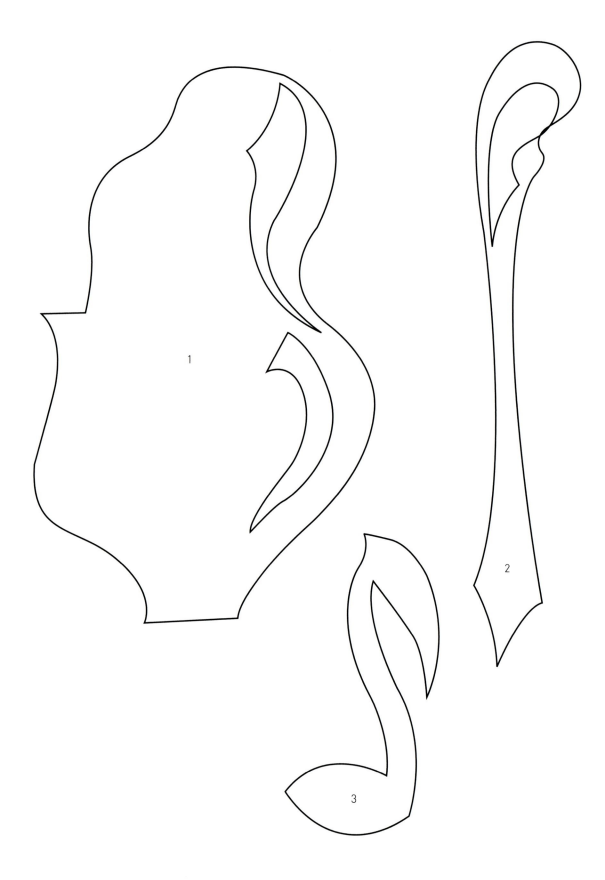

VIOLIN SHOWPIECE, page 349. Violin body (1), violin neck (2), and music note (3).

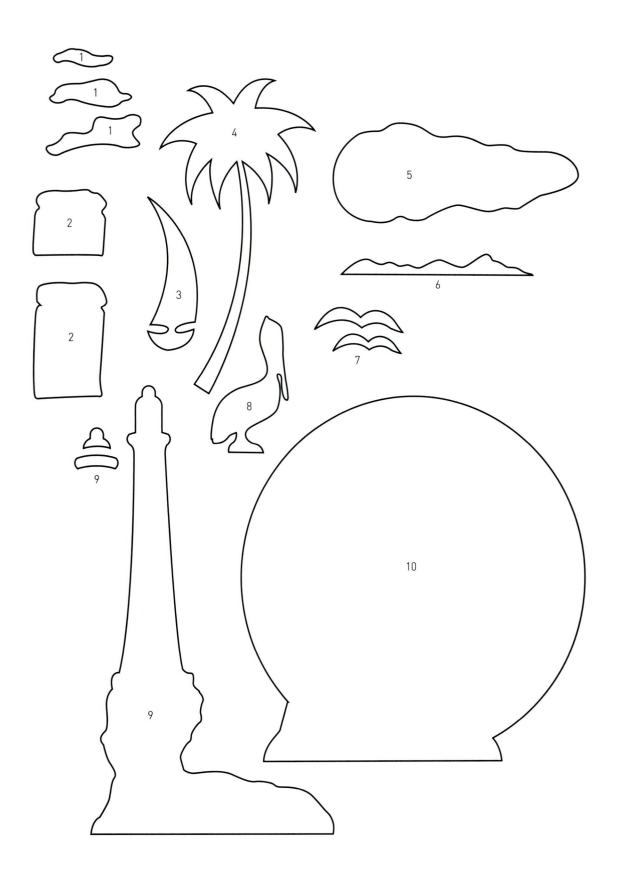

BEACH SHOWPIECE, page 408. Clouds (1), pilings (2), sailboat (3), palm tree (4), base (5), island (6), birds (7), pelican (8), lighthouse (9), and background (10).

Index

milk, 15

milk, 14

sour cream, 15

yogurt, 15

Dark chocolate. *See also* Dark couverture

about, 11

adding texture to, 253, *254*

for Birds of Paradise showpiece, 306

health effects from, 7

ideal working temperatures for

tempering, 43

shelf life of, 14, 52

using for chocolate flowers, 288–292

Dark Chocolate Discs, recipes using, 212,

213, 214, 215

Dark Chocolate Truffles, 157

Dark couverture. *See also* Couverture

in ganache formulas, 111, 112

recipes with, 70, 73, 74, 77, 78, 80, 85,

93, 96, 98, 146, 147, 148, 150, 154,

156, 160, 164, 166, 173, 176, 186, 188,

189, 190, 193, 195, 197, 200, 202, 204,

207, 208, 210, 212, 213, 215, 222

Dark Modeling Chocolate, 276

Dark rum, 23

Décor, chocolate, 241–248

Decorated molds

capping and unmolding, 140, *141*

casting, 138–139, *139*

filling, 140

preventing a lip, 139

using, 138–141, *139, 140, 141*

Decorating molded shapes, 242–243

Decorating techniques, 125–141

colored shell-molded chocolates,

134–141

transfer sheets, 126–*133*

Deer showpiece, 319

templates for, *377*

Design

colors in, 330–334

elements, meanings for

circle, 335

clover leaves, 335

colors, different, 334

diamond, 335

dove, 335

heart, 335

leaves, 335

moon, 335

owl, 335

square, 335

star, 335

sun, 335

triangle, 335

focus point of, 338

geometric shapes in, 335

Golden Ratio and, 337–338, *337, 338*

theory of, understanding, 330

Designing showpiece, 342, 344

Dextrin, 9

Dextrose. *See* Glucose

Diabetics, almond flour as good choice

for, 18

Diamonds, meaning of, 335

Digital instant-read thermometer, as basic

kitchen tool, 32, *30*

Dipped and paper flowers, 303, *303*

Dipping chocolates, 49–50, *49, 50*

troubleshooting, 50

Dipping forks, as basic candy-making tool,

33, *32*

Discs, chocolate, 62, *62*

Double chocolate layer, creating, 250

Dove, design meanings of, 335

Dried fruit, recipes with, 70, 73, 76, 77, 78,

80–82, 85

Drupe, 18

Dry conching, 11

Drying cocoa beans, 9

Duchess, 147–148, *148, 149*

E

Easter showpiece, *VIII*

templates for, *353*

Egg(s), molded, *242, 243, 246, 247. See

also* Molded chocolate shapes

Egg ganache, 113

Egg yolks, in fruit ganaches, 113

Embossing, 252, *252*

Empty space in showpiece, importance

of, 344

Emulsion(s), 108

for ganache, restoring, 122–123

separation as problem, 122

Endocarp, 18

Endosperm, 18

Enrobed confections

applying transfer sheets to, 131, *131*

ganache, 121, *121*

machine for, 36, *37*

Equipment, essential, 27–38

candy tools, 32–35

kitchen tools, 28–32

Escher, Heinrich, 7

Europe

chocolates in, 217

history of chocolate in, 6–7

Evaporated milk, 15

Exacto knife, as basic kitchen tool, 29, *30*

Exotic Curry Pralines, *179*, 189

F

Fat bloom, 51, 52
Fat content
    of couverture, 12
    as factor to separation, 122
    of good-quality cocoa powder, 11
    of milk chocolate, 11
    of nuts, 18–19
    of white chocolate, 12
Feet
    definition of, 49
    preventing, 50
Fermentation, 9
Fermented cocoa beans, *12*
Fettuccini curls, 268, *271*
Filled chocolates, origin of, 7
Filling trays, as basic candy-making tool, 33
Fils, Séchaud, 7
Finger-painting technique for mold
    decorating, 136, *136*
Finishing powder
    for Lemongrass Truffles, 163
    for Raspberry Truffles, 167
    for Strawberry-Mint Truffles, 169
Firm ball, as a stage of sugar boiling, 54
Flat shapes, adding texture for, 253
Flavonoids, 7
Flavor compounds and oils, 114
Flavored rum, 23
Flavorings
    for ganache, 113–114
    infusing cream or other liquids with
        agents, 113
Flaxseed, in Granola Mix, 85
Flower(s)
    chocolate, 289–*309*
    cut-out, 277–278, *278, 279*
    dipped and paper, 303, *303, 304*
    ganache and, 113
    knife-dipped, 295–299, *298*
    paper, 300–302, *302, 303, 304*
    rolled, 291–293, *292, 293*
    shaved, 288–290, *289, 290*
Flower, spiral cone, showpiece, *269*
    templates for, *362*
Flower hat showpiece, *263*
    templates for, *361*
Flower showpiece on triangle support, *305*
    templates for, *369*
Focus point of showpiece
    adding elements in sketches, *344*
    finding the, 338, 342
    Golden Ratio and, 338

    ideal height for, 338, *341*
    Rule of Thirds and, 341, *341*
Fondant
    about, 111
    in Quick Marzipan, 105
Food coloring in cocoa painting, 312, *313*
Food lacquer in cocoa painting, 312
Food processor, as basic kitchen tool, 28,
    28
Food processor modeling chocolate, 282,
    284, *284*
Forastero beans, 8, *8*, 9, 12
Forks, dipping, as basic candy-making
    tool, 33, *32*
Formulas
    butter ganache, 112
    cream ganache, 111
Frames, as basic candy-making tool, 33
French Marzipan, 99, 101, *102*
    recipe using, 154
Fresh whole milk, 14
Fructose, 16
Fruit(s). *See also specific types*
    candied, recipes using, 78, 80, 147
    Chocolate Fruit and Nut Blocks, 78, *79*
    Chocolate Fruit Bark, Chocolate, 77
    Chocolate Fruit Blocks, 77
    dried, recipes with, 70, 73, 76, 77, 78,
        80–82, 85
    Fruit and Nut Bark, 78
    Fruit and Nut Clusters, 76
    Fruit and vegetable purees, 114
    Pâte de Fruit, 86–88, 89, *86, 87, 88*
Fruit brandies, 24
Fruit peels
    ganache and, 113
    recipes with, 78, 80, 147
Fruit purees. *See also* Pâte de Fruit
    chart showing ratio of ingredients
        needed to create flavors, 89
    recipes with, 166, 168, 173, 181, 188,
        189, 190, 195, 200
Full-bloom knife-dipped flowers, 299, *299*
Funnel, as basic candy-making tool, 33, *32*

G

Ganache
    about, 15, 16, 22, 107
    additional ingredients used in making,
        113–114
    basic techniques for using, 116–121
        hand-rolled truffles, 116
        truffles with shells, 117–118
    for decorated molds, 140
    formulas, 111, 112

THE ART OF THE CHOCOLATIER

recipes using, 73, 184–185. *See also* Nuts

Peels, fruit
    ganache and, 113
    recipes with, 78, 80, 147

Pectin, recipe using, 168, 170, 178, 190

Pennsylvania, chocolate in, 7

Peppermint oil, 114

Percentages
    assigned to a couverture, 13
    of cocoa butter versus chocolate mixture, when spraying chocolate, 314

Peruvian walnut, 19

Petals. *See* Chocolate flowers; Paper flowers; Rose

Peter, Daniel, 7

Petit fours. *See* Small chocolate curls

Pink, meaning of, 334

Pipe, creating tubes with a, 233, *233*

Piped chocolate strands, 272, *272, 273*

Piped pistils, 304, *304*

Piped shapes, storing ganache for, 109

Piped-together curls, 271, *271*

Piped tubes, chocolate, 235, *235, 236*

Piping, chocolate, 317–321
    contour, 318
    ganache, for hand-rolled truffles, 116
    three-dimensional, 318, 320–321

Piping bags, as basic kitchen tool, 30, *30*

Piping tubes, as basic kitchen tool, 30, *30*

Pistachio(s)
    about, 19
    recipes with, 66, 70, 73, 77, 78, 80–82, 85, 94, 147, 164

Pistachios, Sandy, 66

Pistachio Truffles, 164, *165*

Pistils, piped, 304, *304*

Pizza cutter, as basic kitchen tool, 29

Plaques, using transfer sheets to decorate, 130–131

Plastic(s)
    about, 35
    acetate sheet(s), 35, 318, 320, *30, 321*
    acrylic base, 35
    acrylic tubes, 35, *30*
    spatula, 31, *30*
    textured, using, 255, *255*

Plasticizing, 11

Pods, cacao, about, 8–9

Pollination, 8

Polycarbonate magnetic molds, applying transfer sheets to, 132, *133*

Pool of chocolate around base, avoiding, 49

Port Wine, 215

Potassium Sorbate, 115

Powder, chocolate. *See* Chocolate powder

Powder, finishing. *See* Finishing powder

Powdered sugar. *See* Confectioners' sugar

Praline(s). *See also* Nuts, caramelizing
    Baileys Irish Cream as enhancer of flavor, 23
    butter ganache formulas for, 112
    cream ganache formulas for, 111
    molded, storing ganache for, 109
    slabbed, storing ganache for, 109
    sugar-crusted alcohol, 217–223

Praline Base, Gianduja, 103–104

Praline recipes
    Almond Rosette Pralines, 144, *144, 145*
    Apricot Pralines, 170–171
    Branches, 150, *150, 151*
    Cinnamon Pralines, 198–199
    Coconut Rum Pralines, 173–174, *175*
    Coffee Pralines, 176–177
    Cognac, 212
    Cointreau, 213
    Duchess, 147–148, *148, 149*
    Exotic Curry Pralines, *179,* 189
    Hidden Hazelnut Pralines, 146, *145, 146*
    Honey Nougat, *152,* 153
    Key Lime Pralines, 178–180, *179*
    Kirsch Points, 214
    Kumquat–Passion Fruit Pralines, 200–201
    Lemon Pralines, 181
    Lemon-Thyme Pralines, 204–206, *205*
    Macadamia Pralines, 182, *183*
    Maple Pecan Pralines, 184–185
    Marzipan Pralines, 154, *155*
    Mint Pralines, 186–187
    Opulent Duchess, 148, *149*
    Palet d'Or, 207
    Passion Fruit Pralines, 188
    Port Wine, 215
    Raspberry Orange Pralines, 190, 192, *191*
    Salted Caramel Pralines, 193–194
    Spearmint Pralines, 208–209
    Sugar-Crusted Alcohol Pralines, 222–223, *222, 223*
    Sweet and Silky Duchess, 148, *149*
    Tea Pralines, 202–203
    Tropical Chocolate Pralines, 195–196
    Vanilla Pralines, 210, *211*
    Yuzu Ginger Pralines, 197

Premium couverture
    about, 12, *12*
    understanding percentages, 13, *13*

melting with prewarmed sugar, 56
varieties of, 16–17
Sugar alcohol. *See* Sorbitol
Sugar bloom, 45, 52, *52*
Sugar-Crusted Alcohol Pralines
about, 217
Alcohol Syrup for, 220, *221*
making the molds, 218–219, *219*
recipe for, 222–223, *222, 223*
Sun, design meanings of, 335
Sunflower seeds, in Granola Mix, 85
Sunset showpiece, *294*
templates for, *367*
Supports
adding elegance to boxes, 257
using textured plastic for showpieces, 255
Swan showpiece, *347*
templates for, *387*
Sweet and Silky Duchess, 148, *149*
Sweetened cocoa powder
about, 11
shelf life of, 14
Sweetened condensed milk, 15
Sweeteners, 114
formula with cream, 114
Sweet spot, 338
Swirling technique to decorating transfer sheets, 130, *131*
Switzerland
chocolate glace in, 12
chocolate in, 7
Symbolism. *See* Meaning, for design elements
Syrup
Alcohol Syrup, 220, *221*
corn, 16
maple, 17

T

Tablespoons, as basic kitchen tool, 31, *30*
Tabling method for tempering chocolate, 47–48, *47*
Tartaric acid, 24, 86
Tea(s), ganache and, 113
Tea Pralines, 202–203
Temperature(s)
boiling, for marzipan, 99
fluctuation, 51
ideal, for mixing ganache, 109, 122
ideal, for storing chocolate, 14, 51
ideal, for tempering chocolate, 43, 46
ideal, when working with chocolate, 51
melting, for cocoa butter crystals, 40
oven, for tempering chocolate, 44

sugar boiling, 54
washing acrylic molds, 134
Tempering chocolate
about, 11, 39, 42–48
basic process, 42–43
direct method of, 43–44, *45*
machine for, 36, *37*
microwave procedure, 44, *45*
seeding method, 45–47, *46*
tabling method, 47–48, *47*
troubleshooting, 48
when piping, 317
Templates for showpieces, *350–389*
beach showpiece, *389*
birds of paradise showpiece on red support, *359*
butterfly showpiece, *368*
chocolate curls, *351*
Christmas showpiece, *381*
deer showpiece, *377*
Easter showpiece, *353*
flower hat showpiece, *361*
flower showpiece on triangle support, *369*
guitar showpiece, *357*
Halloween showpiece, *384–385*
heart box, *360*
heron showpiece, *375*
hummingbird, *376*
masquerade showpiece, *357*
modern bird of paradise showpiece, *371*
New Year's Eve showpiece, *382*
orange rose showpiece, *365–366*
outer space showpiece, *386*
owl graduation showpiece, *378*
red flower showpiece, *379–380*
rolled flowers, *352*
rooster showpiece, *358*
roses showpiece, *355–356*
Southwestern bird of paradise showpiece, *372*
spiral cone flower showpiece, *362*
spiral curls, *351*
straight triangle curls, *351*
sunset showpiece, *367*
swan showpiece, *387*
undersea showpiece, *354*
Valentine's Day showpiece, *373*
violin showpiece, *388*
white coral flower showpiece, *383*
winter showpiece, *374*
woven heart box, *363*
yellow flower showpiece, *364*

creating when spraying chocolate, 292, 314, *314*
Venezuela, 7
Vin aigre, 25
Vinegar, 25
Violin showpiece, *349*
    templates for, *388*

W

Wallpaper, using, 253, *254*
Walnuts, 19
    recipe with, 94. *See also* Nuts
Warmer, chocolate, as basic candy-making tool, 33, *32*
Water, as number one enemy of tempered chocolate, 45
Water activity measurements, 115
Water bath procedure for tempering chocolate, 45
Wave technique to decorating transfer sheets
    chocolate, 127, *127*
    spatula, 128, *128*
West Africa, 8
Wheat germ, in Granola Mix, 85
Wheel, color. *See* Color wheel
Wheel cutters, as basic kitchen tool
    caramel cutter, 29, *32*
    multiwheel, 29
    single wheel, 29
Whiskey. *See* Alcohol Syrup
Whisks, as basic kitchen tool, 32, *30*
White, meaning of, 334
White chocolate. *See also* White couverture
    about, 12
    adding texture to, *254*
    for Birds of Paradise, 306, 308
    ideal working temperatures for tempering, 43
    origin of, 7
    shaving time for, 262
    shelf life of, 14
    susceptible to oxidation, 52
    using for chocolate flowers, 289
White Chocolate Truffles, 158, *159*
White coral flower showpiece, *339*
    templates for, *383*
White couverture. *See also* Couverture
    in ganache formulas, 111, 112
    recipes with, 70, 73, 74, 77, 78, 83, 94, 158, 162, 164, 168, 172, 173, 178, 186, 188, 197, 210, 222
White Modeling Chocolate, 276–277
Wild crystallization, 41, *42*

Williams pear, 24, 99. *See also* Alcohol Syrup
Winnowing cocoa beans, 9–10
Winter showpiece, *316*
    templates for, *374*
Wood grain technique to decorating transfer sheets, 127, *127*
Working and storage conditions
    air, 52
    fluctuation in storage, 51
    fluctuation in working temperature, 51, *51*
    humidity, 51–52, *52*
    light, 52
    odors, 52
    poor hygiene, 53
    shelf life, 53
Woven basket, 281, 282, *282, 283*
Woven heart box, *283*
    templates for, *363*

Y

Yellow, meaning of, 334
Yellow flower showpiece, *285*
    templates for, *364*
Yogurt, 14, 15
Yuzu Ginger Pralines, 197

Z

Zebra cigarettes, 260, *260*